PENTAGON PRESS

COMMITTED TO SERVE THE ARMED FORCES

THE IMPROBABLE WAR

China, The United States and the Continuing Logic of Great Power Conflict

THE IMPROBABLE WAR

China, The United States and the Continuing Logic of Great Power Conflict

CHRISTOPHER COKER

PENTAGON PRESS

The Improbable War: China, The United States and the Continuing Logic of Great Power Conflict

First Indian Edition 2015

ISBN 978-81-8274-828-1

First published in the United Kingdom by C. Hurst & Co. (Publishers) Ltd., 41 Great Russell Street, London, WC1B 3PL. This edition published in arrangement

Published in India by

PENTAGON PRESS
206, Peacock Lane, Shahpur Jat
New Delhi-110049
Phones: 011-64706243, 26491568
Telefax: 011-26490600
email: rajan@pentagonpress.in
website: www.pentagonpress.in

Branch
Flat No.213, Athena-2,
Clover Acropolis,
Viman Nagar,
Pune-411014
Email: pentagonpresspune@gmail.com

Printed at Avantika Printers Private Limited.

'For the Gods perceive things in the future, ordinary people things in the present but the wise perceive things about to happen.'

(Philostratus, *c.*AD 172–250)

'That which we do not bring into consciousness appears in our lives as fate.'

(Carl Jung)

'If trouble comes when you least expect it, then maybe the thing is to always expect it.'

(Cormac McCarthy)

NOTE

All Chinese spellings are in the Pinyin version

CONTENTS

INTRODUCTION

Spoiler Alert: this book does not predict an impending war between China and the United States. Even if it sought to do so, such an exercise in speculation could hardly be relied upon given the dismal record of political scientists in predicting the future. The simple fact is that humans are not very good at making predictions with regard to those areas that are closest to our own intuition and experience. Human beings are most successful when looking at areas far removed from everyday life such as the interaction of elementary particles or the motion of distant astronomical objects (Barrow, 2011: 219). Science seeks to identify the regularities and commonalities behind appearances, the 'laws' and 'invariances', the 'constants' and 'principles': the patterns that allow reliable predictions to be made. To the extent that there are such laws in the social sciences they have rarely proven to be reliable. Human society is too complex.

It is particularly difficult to make accurate predictions in political science due to the ways in which political phenomena evolve and diverge over time. Although it is possibly to identify revolutionary and warlike situations, revolutionary situations, as Charles Tilly once argued, do not always lead to revolutionary outcomes and warlike situations do not always result in war (McLynn, 2012: 519). Politicians come and go; economic cycles reverse political fortunes; nationalist emotions erupt at unexpected moments; and, perhaps most significantly of all, human beings are capricious, they act on a whim.

This is not to say that politics is inherently unpredictable. It is possible to model state behaviour and even the behaviour of politicians. People act predictably some of the time, which is why it is possible to engage in behavioural profiling. But people do not behave predictably all of the time. Unlike historians who have the advantage of knowing how the story ends, the only available guide to political scientists is the logical rules of the game, the patterns or regularities that can be discerned in human behaviour over time. It is these which political scientists use to help politicians anticipate specific events. The most important trends of all involve the possibility of war, however 'improbable' such a prospect might appear at a given point in time.

The possibility of another great power war would strike many people as utterly improbable, and this belief is also held by senior political and military figures in China and the United States. In March 2013, for instance, General Yuan Liu, a major figure in the Chinese military, responded to a series of articles regarding heightened tension between China and its neighbours by declaring that 'War is just not on' (*Sunday Times*, 23 March 2013). I frequently encountered the same response when I told my colleagues that I was writing this book. Almost all of us are inclined to this view, particularly so in the West, perhaps, but also in Asia, a region with a series of unresolved territorial disputes. In questioning the received idea of the improbability of war, I have come to realise that this idea is rooted both in the meta-narrative that I and my colleagues have told each other for some time and in the prevailing paradigm of international relations, according to which peace promotes wealth. It is deeply entrenched in liberal thinking.

Yet despite asserting that great power war is unthinkable, China and the United States are still preparing for it, particularly now the global war on terror seems to be have lost its status as the defining struggle of the twenty-first century. While Paul Wolfowitz, the then deputy secretary for defence, told the Senate Armed Services Committee that the events of 9/11 had opened 'a window into our future' (Wolfowitz, 2001: 4), tomorrow's historians are more likely to conclude that 9/11 was simply a coda to the twentieth century rather than the opening fanfare of the twenty-first. Some political analysts already argue that 1979 was the real turning point—the year of the Iranian Revolution and the rise of Islamism. It was also the year that China opened its markets to the world, thereby beginning its inexorable rise, with the country soon to overtake the United States as the largest economy in the world (a position the latter has held since 1880).

If the world's two leading military and economic powers were to confront each other, would there be another world war? Mark Twain wrote that history never repeats itself, it only rhymes, and that is the entire point of this book. It aims to identify a recurrent logic in great power relations and periods of confrontation. The claim that great powers no longer go to war against each other may have become something of a truism, yet wars have a certain logic that is timeless even if that logic only persists as a general 'rule of thumb'. The sanguine claims of those who argue that great power war is obsolete should always be treated with caution. Indeed, as the historian Donald Kagan points out: 'Over the past two centuries, the only thing more common than predictions about the end of war has been war itself' (Kagan, 1995: 1).

It is the duty of scholars to challenge traditional thinking, to ask different kinds of questions and to provide new answers. The history of great power confrontation and conflict is of clear value in this regard because it allows us to understand the options available to the leaders of great powers during periods of tension (Gellner, 1988: 12). The possibility of a conflict between China and the United States is not an insight into the future but a possibility inherent in the present, and as a possibility it is not yet an inescapable fact.

A word about Logic

Let me offer an example of the logic of great power conflict, or in this specific case the logic of strategy. 'The paradoxical logic of strategy contradicts the logic of everyday life, it goes against all normal definitions of intelligence ... It only makes sense if you understand the dialectic. If you want peace, prepare for war. If you actively want war, disarm yourself, and then you'll get war' (Samuels, 2011). Edward Luttwak's premise is a case of Occam's celebrated razor: the simplest explanation is the most convincing. It is hardly new: Luttwak was quoting an old Roman maxim, *si vis pacem para bellum* (if you want peace prepare for war). Although this dictum has historically been borne out by events, this does not make it a scientific law. Parsimony tells us only what line of enquiry to exhaust first; it does not tell us what explanations are necessarily true. Often the logical explanation is simple and elegant. But sometimes it is not. Societies that do not prepare for war do not always invite attack. If the logic of events allows a certain consistency in human affairs to be identified this does not demand that humans will be consistent all the time

In order to be valid, an argument based on the underlying logic of war requires a conclusion that follows logically from its premises. This book explores a number of premises with regard to great power competition from which war should logically follow, all things being equal. To grasp the logic of a situation requires deduction—deciding which conclusions can be extracted from the premises—and it demands induction—determining which conclusions go beyond the premises. Both depend on our deductive and inductive abilities, which may be far less robust than we imagine (Goldstein et al., 2010: 20).

In addition, we are not naturally logical creatures. Even when people arrive at the right conclusion, they do not always act upon it and in not acting historians often say they did the right thing. Good reasoning may help us to deduce the logical consequences of our actions. However, it does not always follow that a country will take up a challenge posed by another or that it will be unwilling to accept that it has been outmanoeuvred. In certain circumstances a defeat can even be viewed as a victory. As Wittgenstein argued, our grasp of logic is exhibited both in accepting and rejecting the conclusions to be drawn from it (ibid.: 55).

Wittgenstein also insisted that the limits of logic are the limits of the world. In other words, the limits of logic determine what is possible. Yet the patterns of behaviour we identify are not really rules. They are regularities, and knowing these regularities will not necessarily help you succeed in life. Not recognising them, nevertheless, nearly always proves fatal, and if you are aware of the logic of events, at least the world looks different to you. You will accept that you do not live in a contingent universe where everything is explicable only in terms of chance or human caprice. There is a lot to understand about the world, and that understanding can be empowering. It can save you from being exploited by those who understand it better than you do.

In this book I will be identifying what I consider to be the main reasons why great powers go to war and why they often find themselves in a spiral of conflict from which they can't escape. I will be looking at the way in which they often misinterpret history and the main lessons it has to impart; recourse to war is very rarely irrational but it may be unreasonable, and the difference between the two is crucial to grasp. I will be looking at the logic of great power competition, especially when a rising power challenges the dominant one which may be less capable than in the past in defending the rules of the system. I will be looking at the logic of strategy; the need to forge a compelling strategic narrative and to be intelligent enough to craft an intelligent strategy. And I will be discussing how war too has a logic of its own; it has a positively protean ability to change, thus offering new options. Just when you think war has reached an evolutionary dead-end it springs its surprises—it finds a new evolutionary niche.

This book should not be filed away with fictional and non-fictional predictions of war such as H.G. Wells's *War in the Air* (1908), which imagined a Confederation of Eastern Asia (China/Japan) battling it out against the United States, or George Friedman's *The Coming War with Japan* (1990), which was published just as Japan entered its two lost decades. If a Sino-American war were to break out, I would estimate that it would do so within the next ten years. But it is also entirely possible that such an event will be avoided. Everything may well depend upon whether the great powers recognise the underlying logic of great power conflict.

A warning to the curious

It is important to add a disclaimer here. I am a political scientist, not a Sinologist. Any expertise I may claim has been acquired by the usual scholarly method. I have borrowed ideas from the most important scholarly works and built them into my own argument. Nor am I a historian. If I use historical analogies correctly it is due to what has been revealed by the vision and thoughts of others.

This book examines the prevailing discourse about a possible US–China conflict from the perspective of a phenomenologist of war. It aims to identify a logic to great power conflicts and examine whether such a logic applies in the case of US-Chinese relations. George Soros once stated that: 'My financial success stands in stark contrast with my ability to forecast events ... [E]ven in predicting financial markets my record is less than impressive: the best that can be said for it is that my theoretical framework enables me to understand the significance of events as they unfold' (Kay, 2011: 132). And this is about all that can be said with regard to any set of propositions used to anticipate forthcoming events—it is probably the best we can hope for.

Bias is inescapable in a work such as this, and my sympathies are largely with the United States. I have tried to be fair to China and to China's criticisms of the United States where I believe these are justified. I am critical of the poverty of much US strategic thinking and the United States' often blinkered pursuit of liberal internationalism (or interventionism) to the detriment of its own national interests.

However, given the logic of competition, I am convinced that China poses a greater threat to world peace than the United States because democratic societies are more accountable than non-democratic societies. The United States is a status quo power whose instincts, though they may often lead to war and conflict, are not necessarily belligerent. The same does not apply in the case of China. Nationalism is already proving to be a dangerous force in Chinese politics, and the military's relationship with the Chinese Communist Party (CCP) gives cause for concern. Perhaps the most disturbing aspect of China's rise, remarks the dissident Liu Xiaobo, is its almost 'pathological need' to overtake the West. Yet wars are not always the product of ambition or malice, but often result from miscalculation. They occur because plans backfire or because schemes are foiled by chance. When the (un)usual outliers—the events and personalities that cannot be factored into any account—are also considered, then it is impossible to avoid the conclusion that politics and war are often very illogical.

This book asks a series of questions about the nature of great power conflict and the prospect of a future war between China and the United States. What lessons, for example, can be learned from the most plausible historical analogy upon which we can draw, the First World War? What are the pitfalls of learning the wrong lessons? What importance should be attached to concepts such as the Thucydidean trap? Is national exceptionalism a driver of conflict? Do honour and reputation still spur people to contest each other's claims? If grand strategy involves social intelligence, then how intelligent are China and the United States? In drawing up their respective national strategies, are the two powers following any particular logic at all? Are they positioning themselves to avoid war, or to be better placed to prevail in the event that war breaks out?

The final question the book seeks to address concerns the form that such a war would be likely to take. In his post-apocalyptic novel, *Towards the End of Time*, John Updike depicted a war between the two countries in 2020:

> Looking back at the city's profile from the dizzying cloverleaf above the Charles, we saw the blue-glass, post-modern downtown buildings darkened in their post-war desolation, and rusty stumps of projected construction that had been abruptly abandoned, as too expensive for our dwindled, senile world.

The novel's chief protagonist, a white, angst-ridden, middle-class male, thinks of the early twenty-first century as a 'maimed and vindictive age'. The war had mostly been inspired by 'highly-trained young men and women in sealed chambers of safety reading 3-D computer graphics' (Updike, 1997: 286). Everyone had imagined that the conflict, if it was ever fought, would be conducted by teams of operators sitting in sealed cubicles, typing codes and commands into computers whose screens would display people as stylised icons, colour bars and pulsing network flows. It is precisely these highly trained young men and women, locked behind their screens, who are likely to be the principal characters in history's next great power war.

As will be explored in a later chapter, the prospect of two thermonuclear powers at war with one another defies belief. Or does it? A conflict fought in cyberspace would be non-kinetic when compared with a conventional conflict. But it would still be war. Indeed, Noah Feldman proposes the concept of a 'cool war', which 'is a little warmer than cold because it seems likely to involve almost constant offensive measures that, while falling short of actual warfare, regularly seek to damage or weaken rivals or gain an edge through violations of sovereignty and penetration of defences' (Feldman, 2013). It is surely germane to ask how long a cool war could maintain its thermal equilibrium.

Leveraging history

Future gazing is an ambiguous activity. The past can be seen but not influenced, whereas the future can be influenced but not foreseen. The human race is a forward-looking species with a bias towards the future. But this bias does not allow the future to be imagined without reference to the past. As the White Queen remarks in *Alice Through the Looking Glass*, it is a poor sort of memory which only works backwards. The study of history is impossible without understanding this truth. The people of the past were not able to see the future, and hindsight allows things to be seen which were invisible to them at the time. The occurrence of certain events often seems to have been so obvious that we are forced to question how they could have been so blind (Wilson, 2012: 86). The ability to think forwards, Lewis Carroll was telling us, helps to avoid the bias of hindsight. We think we know more than our ancestors. We see events from our own historical vantage point (through a looking glass). We interpret events not with the preceding events in mind but with those that came afterwards. This is important given the regrettable tendency of those who think they are good at assessing the past to think they are also good at predicting the future (Taleb, 2001: 56).

When contemplating the improbable—a conflict between the United States and China—the analogy that is most frequently drawn upon is the outbreak of the First World War in 1914. In many respects, writes Charles Emmerson, the world on the eve of the Great War seems not so much the world of a century ago as the world of today, curiously refracted through time: 'It is impossible to look at it without an uncanny feeling of recognition, ... telescoping a century into the blink of an eye' (Emmerson, 2013a). One of the most notable parallels between the world on the eve of the First World War and the world of today is the fact that so many leading thinkers felt that a great power conflict was as improbable in 1914 as many do today.

The causes of the First World War in 1914 have been the subject of an endless debate. The general consensus is that the Great Powers did not so much sleepwalk into war as blunder into it, in part because they thought such a conflict was so improbable. In the Balkan war of 1912, both Austria–Hungary and Russia mobilised parts of their armed forces near their common borders. 'Bluff, everything a bluff,' Alfred von Kiderlen-Wachter, the German foreign minister, wrote that year to a friend. 'War could only happen if one were so unfathomably foolish to bluff so badly as to be unable to back down ... I really consider none of the current statesmen an example of such oxen' (Afflerbach, 2007: 179). A few years earlier the director of British Military Operations had been asked whether it would not require 'inconceivable stupidity on the part of statesmen' to ignite a European conflagration. His response: 'Inconceivable stupidity is just what you're going to get' (Hastings, 2013).

One of the lessons that can be drawn from the war is the fact that the leaders of the Great Powers eventually took too many risks because they genuinely believed that great power conflict was unlikely. Jack Beatty, one of the leading figures in the 'new school' of historians, distinguishes three stances with regard to the origins of the war—avoidable, improbable and inevitable. War would only have been 'avoidable' if the political leaders had set out to do everything in their power to avoid it. They did not do so, in part because they thought it so unlikely. War would only have been 'improbable' if they realised how only remarkable crisis management skills could have kept the continent at peace given the tinder box nature of European politics. It therefore follows that war was largely 'inevitable' because the politicians did not take the prospect of war seriously enough (Beatty, 2012: 4).

Historians will never arrive at a 'final' agreement on the causes of the war. Some contend that the war resulted from political miscalculation, while others attribute it to the Central Powers' decision to risk a successful preventative war. However, the factor underlying all of the contending explanations is the fact that the politicians on all sides concluded that war was improbable with the result that they did too little to avert it.

The world is in danger of making exactly the same mistakes today, as we are telling ourselves the same stories we did in 1914. The prevailing complacency about great power conflict is much the same, as too is the misplaced liberal assumption that inter-state war has become almost 'extinct' or 'anachronistic'. This is exactly the kind of thinking that could lead to another conflict in the near future. This book aims to prize inter-state war from the grasp of the rational actor modelists with their narrow understanding of the world, and the economists and globalists who think 'distance is dead' because geography has been trumped by globalisation. History does not suggest that we are part of a process of continual moral improvement and ever greater progress. The course of international relations over the centuries is instead more akin to a pendulum swinging from good times to bad and from war to peace, and this pendulum may swing back once again.

Historical analogies do not exhaust historical experiences, and there are always exceptions to every rule. But analogies are all we have. When Lyndon Johnson was warned about the dangers of mission creep in Vietnam he replied: 'I haven't got time to fuck around with history.' Unfortunately, we do not enjoy that luxury if we wish to avoid making the same mistakes as our predecessors.

1

HISTORICAL ANALOGIES AND THE LOGIC OF HISTORY

'The chief practical use of history is to deliver us from plausible historical analogies.'

(James Bryce, cited by Yuen Foong Khong, 1992: 251)

Nothing is granted me, claimed Franz Kafka, 'everything has to be earned; not only the present and the future but the past, too—something, after all, which perhaps every human being has inherited. This too must be earned. It is perhaps the hardest task' (Kafka, 1999: 174). The only way to 'earn' the past is to learn the lessons it has to impart. If the right lessons are learned by studying the most suitable analogies, then there is at least a reasonable chance of preparing for unanticipated events in the future.

Analogies lend themselves to logical thinking. They are central to inductive reasoning, which assumes that the same regularities and correlations that have held in the past will continue to hold in the future. Inductive reasoning tends to move from instances of the particular (such as the specific causes of the 1914 war) to generalisations (the causes of all wars), or from generalisations (the contention that all great powers compete) to specific instances (the competition between the United States and China). People rely on inductive reasoning in their personal lives, which is partly why history is so popular. History is a guide that can be learned from, and in some instances the lessons learned enable us to make the future different from the past. But although analogies are the basis of inductive reasoning, they will not necessarily help predict the ways in which the future might resemble the past. The problem is the particular instance: the exception to the rule or the statistical anomaly.

There is also a more general problem with inductive reasoning. Induction is largely unproblematic in the natural sciences. Natural laws are sufficiently reliable for predictions to be made with a 99.9 per cent chance of accuracy. But the remarkably diverse nature of human societies means that the same does not apply in the social sciences. Societies have different cognitive styles, different cultural beliefs and different ways of perceiving the world and their own place within it.

This is why it is impossible to make general statements about the causes of war that hold for all times and for all cultures. If such statements could be made then it would be far easier to make accurate predictions. In Joseph Conrad's novel *The Rescue*, one of the characters claims that all the conflicts of the world can be blamed on women:

> I remember, we once had a passenger ... who was telling us a yarn about them—Greeks fighting for ten years about some woman. The Turks kidnapped her, or something. Anyway, they fought in Turkey; which I may well believe. Them Greeks and Turks were always fighting. (Conrad, 2006)

Despite the certainty of the elderly gentleman in Conrad's tale, the causes of war have been debated for thousands of years and are likely to be questioned for many years to come. Thucydides, for instance, prided himself on understanding the 'real' causes of war in a way that made his work different from Homer's account of the Trojan War, in which everything was blamed on the gods and, of course, a woman—Helen. Herodotus, on the other hand, had explained the Greek Wars against the Persians as the East's attempt to avenge the fall of Troy.

1914 and all that

When the First World War broke out in 1914 it instantly dispelled a widely held proposition, one which also prevails today, according to which violent inter-state conflict no longer paid dividends on belief.

Ortega y Gasset once claimed that intellectual effort sets us apart from the commonplace and leads us by hidden and different paths to the secluded spots where we find ourselves amid unaccustomed thoughts. That is why intellectuals are important—they establish trends in the way that people see the world. The Polish engineer Jean Bloch, who was one of the most famous intellectuals of his time, sought to approach the problem of war from a scientific perspective. In his study of the mechanics of war he concluded that war consumes the resources needed to fight it. It also burns insofar as it destroys resources as well as hopes. He estimated the resources available to the great powers on the eve of the twentieth century and concluded that another European war would be a catastrophe for the victor and the vanquished alike, thus making war unlikely or even 'impossible' (Luttwak, 2000: 182). His opinion was widely shared. For example, the respected historian G.B. Gooch wrote in 1911 that 'We can now look forward with something like confidence to the time when war between civilized nations will be considered as antiquated as the duel' (Mueller, 2011: 35).

Norman Angell is one of the most famous writers to have adopted the view that war had not only ceased to be inevitable but that it also ran counter to enlightened self-interest. In a speech to the Institute of Bankers in London in January 1912, Angell claimed that:

> Commercial interdependence, which is the special mark of banking as it is of no other profession or trade in quite the same degree—the fact that the interest and solvency of one is bound up with the interest and solvency of many; that there must be confidence in the due fulfilment of mutual obligation, or whole sections of the edifice crumble, is surely doing a great deal to demonstrate that morality after all is not founded upon self-sacrifice, but upon enlightened self-interest, a clearer and more complete understanding of all the ties that bind us the one to the other. And such clearer understanding is bound to improve, not merely the relationship of one group to another, but the relationship of all men to all other men, to create a consciousness which must make for more efficient human co-operation, a better human society.

A former editor of the *Financial Times* who was present at the meeting later reported that Angell had carried the audience almost to a man (Keegan, 1998: 11–12).

The belief that war is increasingly unlikely due to the ever growing complexity of the world is also commonplace today. Like many of today's analysts, Angell maintained that the complexity of the world defied the previous ordering power of war, a point he emphasised in his book, *Europe's Optical Illusion* (1909) (all subsequent editions were titled *The Great Illusion*, by which it is now widely known). The book argued that war would disrupt the flow of international credit, and mere knowledge of this fact should be sufficient to prevent war from ever being fought. Even if war broke out, a credit crisis would soon bring it to an end. Angell insisted that international finance was so complex and the world so interdependent that 'robbery' had become unprofitable and diplomatic 'dishonesty' profitless.

Angell had good reason to arrive at this conclusion. By 1914 the advanced European economies had become part of a continent-wide business cycle which extended across the Atlantic. But Angell and his contemporaries overestimated both the degree of this interdependence and its likely impact on inter-state relations. Although governments signed international postal, telegraphic and wireless conventions, and harmonised railway timetables, they continued to pursue protectionist policies and to engage in economic nationalism. Moreover, far from making war impossible, financial interdependence and the international bond market actually facilitated war finance when the conflict finally came (Stevenson, 2004: 6).

Angell's ideas were consistent with a prevailing system of thought. It was during this period that people first began to talk about global networking, although they did not yet use the term itself. By 1900 the world had gone global. The millions of Europeans who had emigrated from Europe to North America in the course of the nineteenth century were part of an Atlantic system, and the movement of money across the Atlantic produced a one-world economy. Prices and interest rates converged across markets. As the world financial system came into being, economic downturns in one country would quickly spread worldwide.

English, which had become the language of international trade, was already the world's lingua franca and it is probably true to say that the British were the authors of globalisation. When Bismarck was asked what he thought would be the most important factor in twentieth-century politics, he replied with the fact that the North Americans spoke English. The English language served to unite two fractious and disputatious powers, the United States and the UK, first against Prussian militarism, then against German Fascism and finally against Soviet Communism.

In Angell's view, the economic interdependence of the world in the early twentieth century, as well as the use of English in international trade, meant that war had become a dangerous anomaly, and he was far from alone in holding these beliefs. War had always had its critics, including Homer—'Would that strife would disappear from the world of the Gods and that of men'—but it had always been taken for granted as part of human existence. This changed as the causes of war started to be questioned in much the same way as other activities of life which had previously been viewed as inevitable. As Franz Boas writes, one of the fundamental characteristics of human development is that 'activities which have developed unconsciously are gradually made the subject of reasoning' (Wright, 2001: 239), and this is certainly the case with war. By the time Angell was writing there was a growing body of opinion that competition was becoming less useful than cooperation, and in no country was this held to be more self-evident than his own. Even Herbert Spencer, the father of Social Darwinism, concluded that 'From war has been gained all that it had to give' (ibid.: 238). As a devotee of Darwin, Spencer was claiming that the passions and emotions that had powered human progress and given rise to war had lost their adaptive value. This belief has been present in one form or another in much of the literature ever since, and most recently in Steven Pinker's book, *The Better Angels of our Nature* (2011).

However, while Angell was at one with the received opinions of the time, he did receive some criticism. Most importantly, his book was underwritten by a set of ideas which were quintessentially those of an early twentieth century liberal internationalist. Anything that was not relevant to his worldview was simply edited out. All he noticed were the risks rather than the opportunities of war.

Angell also ignored those who were making a powerful case for the benefits of war in imperial Germany. One notable example is Max Weber's famous address following his appointment to the chair in political economy at the University of Freiburg in 1895. The central idea put forward in the speech was that the science of political economy was a *political* science, the only purpose of which was to extend the national economy of states. None of this was especially new. But the aggressive language in which he couched his argument certainly was. His address was peppered with words taken directly from the vernacular of Social Darwinism such as 'survival' and 'selection', and expressions such as 'historical' laws and the 'struggle of nations'. Similar ideas can be found in the work of Weber's contemporaries, such as Werner Sombat. The latter was particularly dismissive of Spencer's argument that war had given 'all that it had to give', and claimed that such a belief was typical of the 'self-satisfied' spirit of a country that had achieved industrial pre-eminence. When war with

Britain eventually broke out, Sombat complained that 'often we can't help but feel we are fighting not a country, but a department store' (Joas and Knobel, 2013: 139).

Although it may be unfair to suggest that a belief in liberalism and progress was both a casualty and a cause of war, the liberals were undoubtedly guilty of wishful thinking. Historians still ask why Germany chose the path of war in 1914, with explanations ranging from the struggle for markets and nationalist sentiment to domestic political pressures. Yet though these undoubtedly played a part, none of these material factors usually 'cause' war: they simply set the frame of reference in which the struggle will be fought. Conflicts ultimately break out due to a given society's emotional response to violence and the benefits it expects to gain from engaging in war. When a sufficient number of people believe that war is a necessary part of the struggle for existence, a biological necessity of the first importance (that 'To supplant or be supplanted is the essence of life' (Hopkirk, 2006: 25), or when war is viewed as the staging ground on which a nation can fulfil its 'historical purpose', material explanations become superfluous.

The same is true for societies that conclude everything is to be gained from peace and nothing from war. Angell's ideas were particularly influential due to the fact they were grounded in the largely unacknowledged system of thought that prevailed in the Britain of his day. He firmly believed, for example, that the British Empire offered the ultimate behavioural model for humanity:

> It is to English practice and ... experience that the world will look as a guide in this matter ... *The extension of the dominating principle of the British Empire to European society as a whole is the solution of the international problem which this book urges.* The day for progress by force has passed; it will be progress by ideas or not at all. And because these principles of free human co-operation between communities are, in a special sense, an English development, it is upon England that falls the responsibility of giving a lead. (Ferguson, 1998: 22)

Economic ideas, like all others, are subjective opinions on how the world works, or should do, and economists are given to wishful thinking more than most. The world that went to war in 1914 was dominated by liberal precepts; behind the management of the world economy was 'the invisible hand' of Adam Smith. And there was the rub. The surprising enthusiasm with which Europe's youth went to war in 1914 was informed, in part, by a profound disenchantment with 'the dismal science' of economics which was just beginning its take-over of political life; as well as by the belief that the competition between nations would be determined not by the markets, but a social Darwinian struggle for existence with victory going to those who were willing to fight their corner and not settle for the easy life.

The story of the outbreak of war in 1914 is one in which an entire system of thought collapsed. Liberal thinking was progressively weakened in Germany and a competitive, zero-sum conceptualisation of political economy gradually emerged alongside a profound disdain for economics itself.

Despite the two world wars in the period that followed the appearance of *The Great Illusion*, Angell continued to hold the same views—that power politics was no longer a guarantee of prosperity and peace promised greater opportunities for wealth creation—until his death in 1967. As Britain was about to join the Common Market he had every reason to believe that he had been vindicated, even at the eleventh hour. But if he had lived until today, he might have been less confident in his opinions. His argument, after all, rested on the assertion that military conquest no longer guaranteed access to the forms of wealth that a modern economy produces because finance and credit markets demand peace.

A further problem with Angell's argument was the faith he placed in the idea that 'lines of division on moral questions are within the nations themselves and intersect the political frontiers' (Angell, 2010: 17). Although Angell recognised that there was a pro-war current in German thought and a strong protectionist tradition in the UK, he believed that the liberal tradition in both countries would ultimately prevail in any confrontation between the two. But he overestimated the strength of liberalism in relation to the forces of nationalism when that moment finally came. In Britain a large number of liberals who had previously opposed war simply stifled their misgivings in patriotic declarations when war broke out. In Germany, on the other hand, many prominent liberals, including Max Weber, Hans Delbrück and Friedrich Neumann, had never been opposed to war itself. All three were resigned to the fact that a general European war was probably 'inevitable'.

Angell discovered this when he took his peace campaign to Germany in 1913. Prior to the visit, 2,000 copies of the German translation of *The Great Illusion* were distributed to a select group of German professors and students. Angell's German sponsors believed that even if only a small number of students attended his meetings—and few did—then German universities would at least be exposed to his ideas. But Angell and his sponsors found the climate of opinion to be distinctly hostile. At the University of Gottingen, twenty-five students left the room when Angell began to speak in English and then proceeded to the police station to complain that a political meeting was being held in a foreign language. In Berlin the meeting ended in a fracas, with Angell complaining that some professors had goaded their students into heckling him (Supina, 1972: 164). Angell's tour was a failure. Germany was a nation whose youth were impatient to find a 'place in the sun', even if the promise of that dream turned out to be the greatest illusion of all.

Alternative rationalities

How little do we know our thoughts—our reflex actions, indeed, yes; but our reflex reflections!

(Samuel Butler, *The Way of all Flesh*, 1902)

The First World War remains a contentious issue. Although it is easy to describe the war itself, understanding and explaining the reasons why it broke out is a far from straightforward task. Historians are reluctant to blame Germany exclusively for the war and prefer to emphasise the long-term dynamics that set the stage for 1914, such as the intensification of economic and imperial competition; rampant nationalism in all countries, even liberal ones; Social Darwinist beliefs, which were strongly embedded in popular culture; and a system of alliances and first-strike strategies that made most of the Great Powers victims as much as aggressors. But one inescapable fact remains: in the last stages of the July crisis, two countries, Austria and Germany, decided to launch a war. There is no reason to think that the Germans were actually gunning for war from the beginning, writes Max Hastings, but they were certainly prepared to live with the consequences in the firm belief that they were in a stronger position to win a war against Russia and France in 1914 than they would be in the years to come. They were confirmed in this opinion by the importance that war played in their own worldviews (*The Spectator*, 2013).

Using the First World War as an analogy can help to identify parallels with a coming conflict between the United States and China. But material factors alone do not drive societies to war. Societies, like people, are driven by ideas of how the world works, or ought to work. They are driven by passions as well as beliefs.

The 'great illusion' in the title of Angell's book could equally refer to another illusion, namely our stubborn belief, all evidence to the contrary, in humanity's ability to behave rationally. We do not always appreciate what is in our own best interests because we are not as rational as we like to think we are. We are also chronically incapable of learning from experience or dealing with the recurring dilemmas of life. This is not a view, of course, which fits easily with the liberal worldview, and as worldviews are anchored to ideas about life they condition the way reality is viewed.

Angell won the Nobel Peace Prize in 1921. The following year's winner, the Norwegian historian Christian Lous Lange, extolled Angell's book in his own acceptance speech. What he found especially inspiring was 'a profound and warm belief in what he calls in one of his books, "the potential rationalism of mankind"'. Yet Angell's rationalism was largely devoid of human passion. Bertrand Russell, looking back on Europe's atavistic militarism, broke with convention by critiquing the extent to which his fellow liberals tended to overemphasise human needs and consequently to ignore human desires. If impulse and desire were important, he insisted, so too was the desire for activity and the need to excel: the sense of successfully overcoming resistance and the respect that success usually wins in the eyes of others (Russell, 2010: 54). Russell extended this analysis to that of nations (indeed, for those who could not excel individually, self-esteem of a sort could be derived from belonging to a nation that could command the respect of others).

Russell was greatly influenced by the work of William James, the American philosopher and psychologist. Prior to the war James had argued that military sentiments were too deeply grounded in human nature, and that they were likely to play a part in international politics until such time as better substitutes for national glory could be found than the returns of trade. While trade may lead to wealth, some societies aspire to achieve much more than wealth alone. Most liberal thinkers, James added, tended to gloss over this inconvenient truth because Europe had begun to find war rather embarrassing:

> At the present day, civilized opinion is a curious mental mixture. The military instincts and ideals are as strong as ever, but they are confronted by reflective criticisms which sorely curb their ancient freedom. Innumerable writers are

> showing up the bestial side of military service. Pure loot and mastery seem no longer morally allowable motives, and pretexts must be found for attributing them solely to the enemy. England and we, our army and navy authorities repeat without ceasing, are solely for 'peace'. Germany and Japan it is, who are bent on loot and glory. (James, 2013)

James's criticisms were not solely confined to liberals and liberalism. In 'The Moral Equivalent of War', from which the above passage is taken, James also attacked a number of Western militarists who sought to justify war with pseudo-scientific jargon. One example was *The Valor of Ignorance* by an American general who suggested that nations rise and fall into vitality or decrepitude, and that in any future conflict with Japan the United States was unlikely to prevail thanks to conceit, commercialism and (inevitably) feminism. Another was *The Philosophy of War* by a German writer who thought that war was ordained by God (it allowed Him to evaluate whether humanity was progressing or not in terms of heroism, tenacity, inventiveness and—inevitably—manly vigour).

These 'alibis of aggression', as the historian Peter Gay calls them, were also found in the heart of liberal England. Both the British and the Germans developed justifications for war which provided a sense of collective identification that was both inclusive and exclusive at the same time. They helped to solidify society by identifying the 'outsider' who was to be bullied, ridiculed or exterminated at will. They 'cultivated' hatred in both senses of the term—at once fostering and restraining it while providing it with a scientific veneer (Gay, 1993). Social Darwinism is a case in point. Its influence can even be found in the work of the great parliamentary commentator Walter Bagehot, who was not only inspired by Darwin's work but who, in turn, influenced Darwin when he was writing *The Descent of Man* (Crook, 1994: 49). Bagehot argued that 'the competitive examination of ... war' promoted progress because it improved the 'fitness' of the race. Similar arguments were put forward thirty years later when Chalmers Mitchell spoke of a nation as 'a species in the making' and saw Germany as a 'biological' rival to Britain and France (two 'commensal mates') (ibid.: 184–5). Such thinking persisted for longer than is often assumed. Some Americans, for example, viewed the Japanese as an inferior race and did not consider Japan to be a serious threat until after the attack on Pearl Harbor. In John Hersey's novel, *The Call* (1947), the narrator observes that the Japanese had been redeemed by their attack on the

United States: 'They had stopped being caricatures of themselves and had turned into real people' (Hersey, 1985: 47).

Social Darwinism proved just as persuasive as the liberal meta-narrative that the Great Powers would have to conform to the logic of the interdependent, symmetrical relationships that the market demanded. However, war did not break out in 1914 because of ideologies that justified war, such as Social Darwinism. What mattered most were not the ideological justifications for war, Gay's 'alibis of aggression', but the frame of reasoning into which they fitted.

James's work is important because he recognised that both the war party and the peace party were equally rational. He had argued that rationality is merely a feeling or emotion from the beginning of his career (*The Sentiment of Rationality*, 1878). James's work still appears in standard anthologies on logic because his argument is quite persuasive. Some beliefs cannot be settled by intellect alone. James accepted that since beliefs harm others (and sometimes those who hold them) they should be as rational as they can, but he also insisted that they should be life-affirming too. He recognised that the arguments for war had to be met directly, and that the failure to do so was a failure of the liberal imagination, a failure on the part of writers like Angell to grasp that ideas such as Social Darwinism tapped into deeply held human passions, and it was the passions rather than the ideas that were most important:

> Turn the fear over as I will in my mind, it all seems to lead to two unwillingnesses of the imagination, one aesthetic, and the other moral; unwillingness, first, to envisage a future in which army-life, with its many elements of charm, shall be forever impossible, and in which the destinies of peoples shall nevermore be decided quickly, thrillingly, and tragically by force, but only gradually and insipidly by 'evolution', and, secondly, unwillingness to see the supreme theatre of human strenuousness closed, and the splendid military aptitudes of men doomed to keep always in a state of latency and never show themselves in action. These insistent unwillingnesses, no less than any other aesthetic and ethical insistencies, have, it seems to me, to be listened to and respected. One cannot meet them effectively by mere counter-insistency on war's expensiveness and horror. The horror makes the thrill; and when the question is of getting the extremest and supremest out of human nature, talk of expense sounds ignominious. The weakness of so much merely negative criticism is evident—pacifism makes no converts from the military party. (James, 2013)

James insisted that a belief is always connected with the satisfaction of desires as well as needs. War did not serve any interests (and very few needs) for the British. For the Germans it served the need for greater respect. It was a palliative for a crippling sense of resentment and it was from this premise that he concluded that all truth is biographical. Reality is real if it is true for you.

Reality is not unitary but multiple. There are many ways of looking at the world and understanding life. No reality is more fundamental, let alone more 'real', than another. There are many worlds out there coexisting, sometimes uneasily. This is at one with the modern understanding that reality is mediated by language, by concepts and symbols and especially by metaphors. To insist that something is true, right or real, James insisted, will always raise the question—true for whom? True ideas are those a society can validate and corroborate from its own historical experience. Whereas previous theorists had thought of truth as a property possessed of the truth-bearer, James regarded it as a historical process. 'The truth of an idea is not a stagnant property inherent in it. Truth *happens* to an idea. It *becomes* true, is *made* true by events. Its verity *is* in fact an event, a process: the process namely of its verifying itself' (Goldstein et al. 2010: 75).

James argued that ideas about reality also explain very different styles of behaviour. Some people are more fearful of failure than they are of achieving success and hence prefer to be cautious. Others are more interested in finding the truth or meaning to existence than avoiding errors of judgement, and some will even be willing to take a leap of faith into the future (at some personal risk to themselves). In other words, some people are willing to take risks that others are not.

In *The Will to Believe*, James uses the example of a man climbing a mountain. The man suddenly finds himself in danger, which he can only escape by making a great leap into the abyss. Have faith, James insisted, and you will find the nerve to accomplish the leap successfully. Doubt and mistrust your ability to make the leap and you will probably fall into the abyss. 'Refuse to believe and you shall indeed be right, for you shall irretrievably perish. But believe, and again you shall be right, for you shall save yourself' (Ford, 2007: 148). Beliefs are manifest in feelings.

James was a respected psychologist as well as a philosopher. However, contemporary science now has a clearer understanding as to how the mind works. Risk-avoidance is not mediated in the thinking part of the brain, but largely in the emotional one. Feeling at risk and acting recklessly is a 'feeling' too. Rational thinking has little to do with risk-avoidance. What is rational is the way that people that will often try to justify the risks after engaging in a certain act, or to rationalise decision-making after the fact. Because the human brain is unable to 'compute' all the variables of our relationship with the world, we also tend to take emotional short-cuts (Taleb, 2001: 38). James's leap of faith is a good example.

To be in favour of war or against it in 1914 was much more complicated than deciding on the merits or otherwise of protectionism. A good argument could indeed be made that another great power war would be irrational (no one would emerge victorious; modern war in privileging defence over offence would be long and attritional). But rationality cannot win an argument if the arguments for and against are equally compelling, or if the evidence is not especially conclusive either way. The French went to war thinking that *elan* and *cran* (guts) would be sufficient to achieve victory. Many in Germany wrongly believed that the British would remain neutral, which would allow them to concentrate on defeating Russia. The British hoped that Germany would intervene to prevent the Austrians from provoking another Balkan war (the greatest illusion of all).

The problem of choosing 'who' or 'what' to believe is a challenge that faces everyone on a day-to-day basis and this becomes even more challenging when the matter exceeds our understanding. Given the complexity of the issues involved in climate change or nuclear energy, for example, many people have little choice but to rely on expert opinion. But experts are always at odds with each other, and certain beliefs, such as global warming, are influenced by scientific projections based on computer models that have to be taken on trust. In France the military experts just happened to be convinced in 1914 of the power of the offensive against the defence, anchored to the unquestioning 'logic' of national *elan*.

Where there is a possibility that two beliefs could be right, it might seem sensible to adopt a position of intellectual agnosticism. But in life, James added, choices have to be made all of the time. To be agnostic about the utility of war when another society is not may be dangerous, and could even invite attack. Britain chose to go to war in 1914 because it concluded that it would be more dangerous not to. Many British historians agree with that choice. The First World War might not be the 'good war', as the Second World War is known, but many historians now consider it to have been a necessary evil. Ultimately, the two sides were not morally indistinguishable. To argue, writes Max Hastings, that Britain should have accepted German hegemony in Europe, a very real prospect had it chosen neutrality, as a fair price for deliverance from the horrors to come, seems as simplistic and questionable as it seemed to most of those who volunteered or were later conscripted to fight (Hastings, 2013).

James's reasoning was itself biographical in that it reflected the spirit of pragmatism, the chief American contribution to philosophy, one that is still deeply entrenched in the way Americans tend to view the world. James recognised that different societies have different cultural constructions of reality, and the American construction is consequentialist (i.e.the morality of an action should be judged solely by its consequences) (Ford, 2007: 150). War is inevitable. Whether it is right or wrong (and, as a pacifist, James himself thought it was wrong) every society has to ask itself the question: what concrete difference will going to war make to my life? The meaning of war is to be found not in its origins, but its consequences.

James's critics have also found fault with his argument on other grounds (ibid.: 163–4). He failed to ask, for example, what we do when we cannot change reality—an optimistic outlook may help a man jump a crevice, but it will not help him overcome death should he falter and fail. He also neglected the question of intrinsic value. It is all very well to insist that truth is determined by the fulfilment of needs, but this does not tell us what needs should be met or the best way to fulfil them. Finally, he did not discuss the source of human needs, whether they are biological, social or cultural. This, surely, is the kernel of the problem. To believe that we are programmed to fight for survival is one thing; to believe that a nation's cultural DNA predisposes it to fight is another.

However, although James's ideas are certainly open to criticism, in many areas he was clearly right. War itself is not irrational, any more than Bloch's belief that it no longer paid dividends on belief. Although the war ended with Germany's defeat, the outcome could have been very different indeed. The Germans came close to defeating France in the early months of the war, and Britain could easily have chosen not to engage in the war at all. If Britain had stayed out of the war then Germany would have defeated Russia even earlier than it did, thereby securing victory at little cost to itself. One of the main reasons why it did not is that its calculations were not irrational, but unreasonable.

James was the forefather of what the American philosopher Charles Peirce called 'fallibilism'. Fallibilism is the epistemological thesis that a belief can never be rationally justified in a definitively conclusive way. Other fallibilists include Karl Popper, who distrusted all intellectual certainty; Friedrich Hayek, who distrusted government certainty; Herbert Simon, who insisted that all rationality is 'bounded'; and Daniel Kahneman and Amos Tversky who argue that human decisions are often based on irrational heuristics and biases.

Bismarck can also be described as a fallibilist in that he appreciated how easily people could be led to believe whatever they wanted to believe. In contrast to his successors as chancellor, Bismarck recognised that Germany was actually a much weaker power than Britain or France, and that defeat in a war would have disastrous consequences for the German nation. Even the prospect of victory worried him. As one diplomat wrote, Germany had had to pay for the victory of 1870 with universal suffrage: 'Another victory will bring us a parliamentary regime' (Kagan, 1995: 173). Success in war could unleash populist sentiments and ambitions that the state would be unable to contain.

German weakness did not stem from its economy but from its constitution and political system. The parliamentary system, though based on universal suffrage, was rendered ineffective by the limitations placed on parliament itself. Its most important power was control of the budget, but the military budget was only approved every five years, thus reducing its power of oversight. And though parliament was able to express a lack of confidence in the chancellor, it could not remove him from office. Germany, in short, was a democracy of sorts, but an illiberal one. It was a vivid example of 'reactionary modernism'.

This was to prove fatal in the years leading up to the First World War, as too did the fact that the Kaiser was responsible for assessing German war plans and policy. Almost fifty men had direct access to the emperor, but there were no routines to discuss or coordinate among or between them. Even information about the war plans was not shared between the General Staff, the War Ministry, the Admiralty, the Naval General Staff or the Foreign Office. This would be similar, writes John Keegan, to the US Strategic Air Command having the freedom to write plans during the Cold War for a nuclear war against the Soviet Union without reference to the Navy, the Army or the State Department, with the president being left to circulate details of the war planning within his administration as he saw fit (Keegan, 1998: 51).

One 'lesson' to be learned from the First World War is that investing hope in war is not necessarily irrational at all from a cultural point of view, although a belief in victory might well be. James was arguing that leaps in the dark, betting on luck or trusting to providence are perfectly 'rational'. Irrationality came from knowing, or suspecting, the fatal consequences of taking such a leap and still going ahead, and some in Germany were certainly aware of the possible consequences that would result from war. In a secret memorandum that was discovered in the 1980s, for example, Field Marshall von Moltke advised the Kaiser that war would not be short (as the generals publicly claimed) but would probably be long and would ultimately result in the exhaustion of all the powers. Equally 'unreasonable' was the German navy's decision to begin planning for a war with Britain at exactly the point that it abandoned the naval arms race as 'unwinable' (Kagan, 1995).

In 1914 the German Chancellor Bethmann Hollweg was so pessimistic about the eventual outcome of the war that he told his son there was no point in planting the family estate with new elm trees because the Russians would cut them down in thirty years' time (an accurate forecast, as it turned out—they did indeed arrive thirty years later and stayed for another fifty) (Stone, 2007: 16). Everyone is capable of acting irrationally, and much of the time rational people live unreasonable lives. We now understand much more about why this is the case than we did in 1914 as we are much more aware of what Francis Spufford, employing a simple formula, *HPtFtU*, calls the 'human propensity to fuck things up'.

Why the rational actor model does not always apply

Regardless of which interpretation for the outbreak of the First World war we choose to believe, the underlying reason for the war is the fact that Europe's leaders were simply too optimistic. Optimism is one of humanity's adaptive features in the biological sense of a trait that provides a survival or reproductive advantage. It has even been suggested that the adaptive nature of optimism is to be found in our hunter-gatherer past, in the evolution of warfare. If warfare was one of the most important selective pressures in evolutionary history then its persistence over time is likely to have had substantial effects on our psychological evolution (Johnson, 2004: 10–11).

But optimism also leads people to take more risks. The suppression of negative thoughts and feelings can enhance an individual's performance in a given task, and this also applies to war. As Clausewitz wrote, 'Boldness in war ... must be granted a certain power over and above successful calculations involving space, time and magnitude of forces, for wherever it is superior, it will take advantage of its opponents' weakness. In other words, it is a genuinely *creative force*' (ibid.: 13–14, my emphasis). If a positive illusion is adaptive, adds Richard Wrangham, and if those with positive illusions often tend to succeed, then it is hard to avoid the conclusion that it pays to hold such illusions (ibid.). A miscalculation may be the result of a trade-off between successful and unsuccessful bluffs rather than an inherent inability to assess a situation correctly. The lesson of 1914 is not that the miscalculations proved fatal but that if war usually has a winner and a loser, then false optimism and valid optimism are both true by definition (ibid.).

False optimism arises from an individual's inability to decide what is in their best interests. This characteristic of human nature is no different today than it was in 1914, despite the claims of those who adhere to the rational actor model which dominates much of American political science. In its canonical formulation the rational actor model presumes that individuals make economic choices aimed at maximising material payoffs based on all available information. The model is not wrong in presuming that people do indeed try to be rational, at least most of the time. The problem is that we are not very intelligent and people have great difficulty identifying their true interests.

One example of this is the financial crisis of 2008, which was partly caused by the failure of Alan Greenspan, the former chairman of the Federal Reserve, to persuade the US Congress to regulate the futures derivatives market. He later admitted that he had been 'shocked' to discover that financial houses and banks had not acted rationally in their own self-interest (in providing loans to people with no prospect of ever paying them back). It is an all-too-vivid example of what George Gilder calls 'the incalculable subjectivity' of economists and the resulting impossibility of 'calculable rationality' in human affairs (Gilder, 1981: 248).

Even if we were more intelligent, social psychologists claim that our intelligence is highly constrained. In the 1950s writers such as Herbert Simon and a small group at the Harvard Business School began to point out that our limited computational and predictive capabilities significantly constrain our ability to make utility-maximising choices. The Nobel Prize-winning economist Daniel Kahneman is an exponent of what Simon called 'bounded rationality'. Simon, who was also a Nobel Laureate in Economics, was the first to argue that organisations and people adopt principles of behaviour that allow them to make acceptable, but not the best, decisions. One of the most important examples is 'satisficing' (the melding of two words, satisfy and suffice). As people are unable to evaluate all outcomes with sufficient precision, they make do with the best available alternative. We stop when we arrive at a near-satisfactory solution to a problem. If we did not choose to do so it would take far too long to reach the smallest conclusion or perform the smallest act. We are therefore rational but only in a 'bounded' way—it is the best we can do (Banaji, 2013: 95). Economists generally accept Simon's ideas but tend to reject those of Kahneman. Although economists are willing to accept that humans are flawed, they are much less willing to acknowledge that we are imperfect machines—we are not very good at working out what is in our true interests.

Economists generally believe that governments should run economies on rational lines, and so they often pretend that they do. Economists also tend to oversimplify things by presenting the normal elements of any economy, such as strikes, corruption and tariffs, as aberrations. One of the fundamental problems with rational choice is that everything is forced to fit the model (every apparent anomaly or 'odd' case) with the result that the case gets mangled or mutilated. Economists do all this in the name of 'science' when economics is anything but scientific. A popular book which adopts this approach is Dan Ariely's *Predictably Irrational* (2008). But as John Kay writes, if people really are 'predictably' irrational, then perhaps they are not really irrational at all. Perhaps the real fault lies not with the world, but with our understanding of rationality (Kay, 2011: xii). We try to be rational, of course—we are in thrall to reason but we are simply not very bright. Our 'rational' decisions too often end disastrously for that reason. Many economists are well aware of this, which is why Kahneman was awarded the Nobel Prize. However, Kahneman's ideas also tend to be ignored for the same reason: it is impossible to factor irrationality into economic computer models.

The problem of rationality is not confined to economics. As Donald Green and Ian Shapiro point out, there is more to political behaviour than just incentives and opportunities. Systems of thought are not universal and culture is also important. As James argued, rationality is biographical. The rational choice model is unable to deal with biographical profiling—in other words understanding that people often have highly personal, even idiosyncratic reasons for their actions; trying to profile people is much too complex. When analysing political protests, for example, political scientists often ignore popular enthusiasm, or attitudes towards leaders in a movement, or feelings of personal inadequacy on the part of the protesters, or even the wish to participate in something larger than the individual self (Morozov, 2013: 41–2). This also applies to war, which often breaks out because decision-makers fall victim to cognitive dissonance or confirmation bias (the tendency to favour information that supports a certain belief or hypothesis). In Hans Joas and Wolfgang Knöbl's book, *War and Social Thought* (2012), the authors take issue with sociologists such as Charles Tilly and Michael Mann for rooting their models in rational action and not doing justice to social reality. They criticise them for taking insufficient note of societal processes that have unforeseeable and at times disastrous consequences and for failing to accept on the evidence of history that war can be provoked for its own sake (Joas and Knöbl, 2013: 255).

Rational choice, in James's words, is unable to 'plumb the thickness of reality' (Ford, 2007: 157). Economic models are not suitable for mapping actual human behaviour. The things people often prize the most are those that they will not exchange, the things that cannot be priced such as reputation. Unlike the world in 1914, it is now possible to 'plumb reality' in computer models. But even in the case of pure logic rather than rationality, it is impossible to design an error-free computer program. In principle, a computer program should be as near as one gets to 'pure thought' unsullied by day-to-day reality. Yet in practice errors arise all the time; they are inevitable (Hearst, 2013: 226).

Behavioural models can lead to complacency in that they can encourage us to believe that 'one size fits all' or what is true for us must be true for others. James argued that many of the decisions people make are arrived at by faith rather than argument. Individual beliefs are 'adopted faiths', and the holders of such beliefs can often misconstrue them as 'logical'. Cultural preferences, especially the 'will to believe', or to take a bet on chance, James's leap of faith, are strongly reinforced by a sense of self. If rationality is biographical, it probably counts for much that some societies feel they are owed more by history than others. A belief in a country's exceptionalism may even encourage risk-taking. Angell's contemporaries also held to a pre-theoretical version of rational choice only to find that all their versions of reality were only 'a passionate affirmation of the desire in which our social system backs us up' (James, 1956: 9). In other words, the thesis Angell put forward was true for him, as a liberal, and doubly true for him as an early twentieth-century Englishman.

This is not to deny the validity of the material explanations for why war broke out in 1914, including the still widely held view that it was a consequence of several behavioural factors—political mistakes, uninformed anxieties, major misjudgements and irrational drives. This is why behavioural economics and the rational choice model continue to play such a central role in how the war is understood. But it is rationality itself that ultimately underlies all of these explanations: our perceptions of the world, our worldviews. A focus on rationality does not mean a reduced emphasis on behaviour, just a richer understanding of it.

Conclusion

Analogies are paradoxical and dangerous instruments. Historians often quote the words of Bishop Butler: 'everything is what it is, and not another thing'. History is unique or atypical, yet it is also typical at the same time. If it were entirely atypical there would be no point in studying it. '(Historical) developments are sometimes the result of accidental conjunctions ... the concatenation of particular leaders with particular contexts, and of particular events with other events is always a matter of chance, never of necessity.' So writes Jack Beatty (Beatty, 2012: 201). In other words, we must analogise with care as the exceptional event is as important as the larger pattern.

Secondly, history is also always written backwards. Hindsight is its essence. That is why even the best maps and projections of the future based on our understanding of the lessons of the past are likely to prove little more accurate than a medieval *mappa mundi*.

Thirdly, we need to question where the author is coming from. Is he cherry picking? Or to mix metaphors, is what is left on the cutting floor more important than what appears in the final movie? Why has he chosen the 1914 case in the first place as opposed to any other? Even disinterested experts tend to suffer from what psychologists call the availability heuristic: we tend to judge the probability of events according to how easy it is to think of examples (usually recent and close to hand). At best, such thinking is lazy; at worst it is intellectually dishonest. Variations are often as important as themes; noise often matters more than signal; we should sometimes focus more on variability within a trend rather than the trend itself. War may be what you expect; peace is what you may get.

The main conclusion to be drawn from 1914 is the fact that none of the Great Powers actually wanted war but some were ready enough to seize the moment when it came. They allowed the moment to escape control because no one really thought that the summer crisis occasioned by Archduke Franz Ferdinand's death would end in a European conflagration. The real explanation then is the peculiar optimism that lulled the European political elite into a false sense of confidence that peace would hold come what may, and the peculiar optimism that seized the Germans in particular that they could risk all in a war and still prevail.

In the case of Germany all the usual explanations are still important—the naval arms race, the country's strategic autism, the independent role of the military and the absence of democratic accountability in Berlin. But although crucial, these are all second-order explanations. The chapters which follow examine some of these factors in order to explore whether there are parallels with American and Chinese examples today, beginning with the challenge that China may pose to the American world order. Unlike imperial Germany and the British Empire, China may be seeking only a 'gradual modification of the *Pax Americana*' (Schweller and Pu, 2011: 53). But should we find this reassuring?

We are still telling ourselves the same stories that the statesmen told themselves in 1913. One is the comforting view that globalisation has made war even more unimaginable than it was in 1914. National markets are even more interconnected and war between advanced economies would be 'counter-productive either as a mechanism for resolving inter-state conflict or as a mechanism for transforming the international status-quo' (Held and McGrew, 1998: 222). But this story is only as compelling as your belief in it. In some respects the world was even more interdependent on the eve of the First World War than it is today. Economic interdependence will not prevent war if a power concludes that it has a chance of success should the right circumstances present themselves. While recourse to violence in such circumstances may be unreasonable it is not necessarily irrational.

Economists argue that consistency is the essence of rationality and that maximisation and consistency of choice, in mathematical terms, should be seen as the same thing. It is generally assumed that people want to maximise their wealth and improve their quality of life, the basic human desires that would be inconsistent with any decision to go to war. But consistency in itself is not necessarily rational. To commune every night with fairies at the bottom of the garden, writes John Kay, is to be consistent, but it is hardly rational. Yet if it is possible to be consistent but not rational, then it is equally possible that people can behave rationally but not consistently. Sometimes people seek to attain things that are not necessarily compatible—to be respected and rich, for instance. In seeking to attain these ends, it is possible that people will demand to be esteemed by others even when this presents a risk to their economic well-being. As we shall see, the German demand for respect was partly responsible for its diplomatic isolation and the same could be true of China. Indeed, Xie Tao (the co-author of *Living with the Dragon*) believes that China is on a collision course with the United States because it is pursuing two incompatible objectives. 'If you respect me, you won't challenge me; if you challenge me you clearly don't respect me'—the idea of earning respect by meeting another power half-way is becoming as difficult for the regime to grasp as it was for the imperial German government (*New York Times International*, 12 Dec. 2013).

Kay was arguing that inconsistency can be perfectly rational, which is certainly true. He quotes Walt Whitman: Do I contradict myself? / Very well then I contradict myself, / (I am large, I contain multitudes.)'. It is impossible to lock a country into a permanent state of being. As James understood, the world is too complex for consistency to be possible all of the time. On the whole, nations do indeed prefer peace and wealth creation to war. But we are emotional creatures, too, and although economic models are important, they should ultimately be used to arrive at a better understanding of the complexity of the world and our interaction with each other (Kay 2011: 176).

The prevailing complacency regarding another great power war is due in large part to the emphasis placed on the rational choice model and the assumption that people consistently behave in a rational way. Lieven and Hulsman argue that the fundamental question in US–Chinese relations is whether the United States should deal with Beijing with carrots and sticks, or just sticks. They claim that the answer is easy. America should not seek to democratise China but to make it what a Bush administration official in 2005 called 'a responsible stakeholder' in the system. China can be 'socialised' and reason dictates that it cannot be contained. China is not a global power, yet. It has global interests which should not be mistaken for global responsibilities. Indeed, its unwillingness to share those responsibilities is becoming an increasing irritant in US–Chinese relations. Reason, the authors insist, must surely convince the Chinese that it will not be possible to replace American domination in East Asia with its own unilateral hegemony. Reason should also dictate that Japan and Vietnam can be relied upon to oppose it themselves. However, whether the Americans have any reason to trust the Chinese management of North Korea any more than the Europeans in 1913 could trust Germany's management of Austria–Hungary, or Russia's management of Serbia, is very much open to question.

Lieven and Hulsman maintain that the 'Americans and Chinese must recognise that no possible gains to either from a clash between them could compensate for the damage that such a clash would do to both [of them]' (Lieven and Hulsman, 2006: 171). Such a conflict would probably wreck America's capacity for global leadership, possibly for decades, and end China's hopes of emerging as a great power. But they are far too optimistic about the capacity of states to reason out their own best interests. The United States palpably failed, as they themselves point out, in its own over-reaction to 9/11. There is no 'reason' to suspect the Chinese of being any more sophisticated in reasoning out what is in their best interests.

The idea that another great war is improbable is also proposed in Noah Feldman's *Cool War: The Future of Global Competition* (2013). Both sides, he contends, have too much to lose. War would simply cripple the economies of both countries, and it would also endanger Party rule in the case of China. It would 'simply be irrational' to go to war. But just because something is irrational does not mean it cannot happen. There are many examples in history of intelligent governments being right for the wrong reasons, and when driven by their anxieties and demons, wrong for the wrong reasons. People are rarely right for the right reasons. There are plenty of flashpoints that could provoke a conflict (Taiwan for one), and there are many real obstacles to cooperation, however open-minded the protagonists.

Feldman is probably right on at least one point: in suggesting that American exceptionalism may prove a problem. From the perspective of the Chinese leadership, it must be frustrating to negotiate policies with a government that views CCP rule as illegitimate because of the undemocratic nature of China's political system, and which would like to see the entire regime come to an end. As Feldman observes, this is not a good starting point for mutual trust or respect. But the United States is unlikely to alter its position in the near future, and the two societies will find themselves on a collision course if neither can earn the trust and respect of the other.

As Lee Kuan Yew remarked in 2013, 'competition between the US and China is inevitable, but conflict is not' (Allison and Blackwell, 2013). It is a comforting thought and not one to be dismissed lightly, but wars are not always triggered by intelligent design, but by accidents, mishaps and miscalculations, as well as passions such as nationalism. War is unpredictable for that reason. Indeed, reason often has little to do with it.

The philosopher John Gray once wrote that if there is anything unique about us as a species it is our ability to know more than ever while being chronically incapable of learning from history. Torture returns as enhanced interrogation; slavery as sex trafficking. War does not end either: it fades away from our imagination but it lies in wait, waiting to be summoned back to life by the usual 'ancestral voices'. When we invoke the idea of progress we are mixing together two different myths: a Socratic myth of reason and a Christian myth of salvation. 'If the resulting body of ideas is incoherent,' writes Gray, 'that is the source of its appeal.' We believe that humanity improves along with the growth of knowledge but the belief that an increase in knowledge results from advances in civilisation is an act of faith. He ends with a depressing but largely incontrovertible conclusion: while human knowledge may increase, human rationality remains the same (J. Gray, 2013: 81–3). This also means that even if we were to 'read' a historical analogy correctly, we would not necessarily learn much from it.

As the Japanese and Chinese once again drifted into another diplomatic spat in 2012/13, US Vice-President Joe Biden pronounced that China was at an 'inflexion point', a moment of dramatic change. The extraordinary economic growth of the past decade has made China increasingly over-confident at the same time that it is becoming resentful of its diplomatic isolation. The country has few friends. When commenting on Biden's remarks a Chinese professor, Zhang Lifan, argued that the system in China would have to change if the country was to avoid a conflict with the United States—the Party would have to become less paranoid and suspicious of the outside world, and more amenable to change within. Chinese society would have to become more open. The alternative, he added, was not desirable: China might want to reset the rules of the international system as it had shown by its provocative behaviour in the South China Seas (*New York Times International*, 12 Dec. 2013). This is a sobering conclusion, particularly as most of the great power wars of the past 300 years have resulted from a rising power's ambitions to alter the norms and rules of international politics.

2

DOMINANT CONFLICTS AND THE LOGIC OF GREAT POWER CONFLICT

While sheltering in a bunker during an air raid on the capital of nationalist China, Chongqing, the American writer Owen Lattimore overheard a conversation between two Chinese officials. Although allied with the United States and fighting a common enemy, they were not discussing the war with Japan, but the coming war with the United States. They saw America as a far more formidable threat because of its ambition to 'Americanise' a world much older than itself (Thorne, 1988: 67).

In practice, the rise of American power and its increasing cultural influence throughout the world took place in tandem with the rise of Asian nationalism, which served to delineate the differences between Asian societies and the West in the popular consciousness. It also led Asian societies to rediscover the ways in which they were different from each other. It was in this context that Asian countries, such as India and China, began to rediscover what made their societies distinctively Indian or Chinese.

Despite the misgivings Lattimore overheard, and the ensuing rise of a distinct Chinese nationalism, the Chinese in fact owe a great debt to the United States. In the period prior to the US entry into the Second World War, some of Roosevelt's advisers had urged him to reach an agreement with Japan. They argued that the real enemy was Nazi Germany and that it would thus be far more sensible to offer Japan a free-hand in

China so as to allow the United States to engage in war with the Third Reich before becoming involved in a separate conflict with the Japanese. The proposal was not entirely unreasonable. But Roosevelt refused to abandon China. In the United States local churches were vocal in their support of China. In his book *One World* (which inspired the creation of the United Nations in 1942) Wendell Willkie, the 1940 Republican presidential candidate, defended the idea of an international order based on democracy and the rule of law. The Americans were the true internationalists of the time, opposing protectionist blocs such as the British Empire, the Nazi Festung Europa (Fortress Europe) and the Japanese idea of a Greater Co-Prosperity Sphere. The United States sought to create an international economic order based on free trade and China was expected to play a central role in this. According to a Rockefeller Foundation report published during the war, China was 'plastic in its democratic possibilities'. China lived in the American imagination as much as America lived in China's (despite the fact that as much as 60 per cent of the US population, according to one survey undertaken half way through the Second World War, were unable to locate China on a map (Cantril, 1951: 265)).

Stories can have different endings, and the world would undoubtedly be a very different place if Giuseppe Zangara had succeeded in assassinating Roosevelt on 13 February 1933, and John Nance Garner, a Texas conservative with no commitment to internationalism, had become president for the next eight years. Would the United States have done a deal with Japan and traded China's fate for its own interests? War with Japan was probably inevitable anyway. The dominant conflicts of the modern age are 'fuelled' by national interests, but they are also fired by contending visions of the future. This has been especially true of the modern era.

When examining the history and factors behind great power conflict, as Niall Ferguson argues, too little importance is attached to the wars that did not take place (Ferguson, 1998: 41). The British came near to war with the Russians in the Balkan crisis of 1877–8 and with France in the Fashoda Crisis (1898). The overriding reason why Britain did not engage in war with either Russia or France after 1870 is the fact that Germany was a much greater danger to all three powers in terms of what former US Defence Secretary Robert Gates called 'the rules of the road'—the rules and protocols of the international order. What I shall attempt to show in this chapter is how the importance the dominant power of the day attaches to those rules largely dictates whether it will go to war to defend them; and whether a rising power is willing to consider war either because it doubts whether the dominant power can any longer enforce them, or because it wishes to revise them in pursuit of its own interests. This too, is part of the logic of great power conflict.

Dominant conflicts

The great power conflict of 1914 had a main theme and several variations. The variations included the balance of power (essentially a struggle between France and Germany over which power would be hegemonic in Europe). But the real conflict—the 'dominant conflict', to adopt George Liska's term—was between Britain and Germany. Liska defines a 'dominant conflict' as one in which a rising power intends to transform the international system in pursuit of its own interests.

The international system in 1914 was in part a product of Britain's victory in the Napoleonic Wars. Although British power had started to decline in the intervening period, with the United States and Germany overtaking Britain in terms of industrial production, it still remained the 'dominant power' until the outbreak of the First World War. Sterling was the world's reserve currency, and Britain towered over its rivals in terms of financial services, banking and insurance. It continued to manage the global financial system as no other country could. While much of the globe may have been coloured red, British power depended on much more than the sheer size of its empire. Many or even most of the features that characterised the world prior to 1914 originated in Britain, from steam power to the belief in progress and evolution. With the exceptions of Spain, Portugal and Russia, every European country adopted the railway gauge Robert Stephenson had introduced. In some countries, such as France and Italy, trains kept to the left (and still do) due to the fact that it was British engineers who laid the tracks. It is the British who initiated what we today refer to as globalisation, in the process establishing English as the language of international trade. Britain also played a central role in spreading liberal ideas, including the extension of the political franchise, throughout the world. All the Great Powers ultimately chose to grant their citizens or subjects the vote (Russia, the only exception, would pay the price for its miscalculation by becoming the only Great Power to experience a revolution during the twentieth century).

Although Anglo-American thinking continues to underpin the current international order, the system itself is not without its critics. The extension of liberal thinking to a policy of liberal internationalism (known in the United States as 'liberal interventionism'), for example, has received only lukewarm support. As Pierre Rosanvallon argues, once we stop thinking of liberalism as a doctrine and see it instead as a mode of thinking or a field of vision then everything connects up. Economic liberalism (the open market), democratisation (open minds) and nation-building (open government) appear so intertwined that they are inseparable (Trouillot, 2003: 54). The Austrian novelist Robert Musil coined a pithy phrase for this in the 1930s when he called freedom 'a philosophical appendix of free trade'.

The Chinese were the first to be subjected to a policy of liberal internationalism during the Second Opium War (1856–60). The Liberal government in London, which faced criticism from the opposition for taking the country to war for the principle of free trade rather than for narrowly defined geopolitical interests, countered that free trade would open Chinese minds and help integrate the country into the international community. When the war broke out, a stringer for *The New York Daily Tribune* reported that he had witnessed a new principle of international politics: 'the preachers of red hot steel'—with their vision of what the Americans would later call a 'new world order'—were now liberals rather than conservatives (Hurd, 1967). The journalist was none other than Karl Marx.

The first cold war (1871–1914)

The period between 1871 and 1989 involved several dominant conflicts. When Woodrow Wilson took the United States to war in 1917, he viewed the conflict as being fought in opposition to an idea, 'Prussian militarism', rather than Germany itself. British writers also held this belief, including H.G. Wells who viewed the war as an example of 'sanitary engineering'. The liberal democracies would similarly find themselves at war with another principle twenty years later, namely fascism, and some years later again with Soviet Communism during the Cold War.

A cold war had in fact broken out between the liberal powers of Europe and imperial Germany long before 1914, yet in contrast to the Cold War between the West and the USSR in the second half of the twentieth century, this cold war actually went 'hot'. Prior to 1914, Max Weber viewed the Anglo-German conflict as a cold war in embryo, a 'dry' or 'latent' war, in the words of two of his contemporaries (Dehio, 1959: 76). At the root of this conflict was an ideological divergence between Germany and the other European powers, one which can be traced back to the Franco-Prussian War of 1870–1. From the French perspective, its defeat in the war had revealed that the 'value orientation' of German development was fundamentally different from that of France. In Louis Dumont's words, it 'taught [them] a hard lesson, i.e., that contrary to what they fondly believed, the Rights of Man were not the alpha and the omega of politics' (Dumont, 1994: 227). Germany's aspirations for humanity were not the same as those of France.

This is not to say that the First World War broke out solely due to the normative factors discussed above. These factors simply served as the background against which the material factors came into play. In the case of Britain, war resulted from several more immediate factors such as the British–German naval race, colonial conflicts and the prospect of a Europe in which Germany would have a hegemonic position over a defeated France, and probably Russia too. But the decision itself to enter the First World War was ultimately made due to the British fear of what a German-imposed peace would involve, including the prospect of living in a German-dominated Europe that no longer adhered to the 'liberal' rules of the European diplomatic system.

The French entertained similar fears. Writing in self-imposed exile in Zurich in 1917, the German liberal writer Hugo Ball was able to shed light on the opposing German and French worldviews through a comparison of two nineteenth-century political manifestos:

> I recently compared the Declaration of the Rights of Man of 1789 with German Fundamental Rights of 1848 [the respective bills of rights adopted by the Constituent Assembly of the French Revolution and by the Frankfurt Parliament of the 1848 Revolution]. The difference is very striking.
>
> 1. The Declaration contains a philosophy (of man and of the state); the Fundamental Rights contains nothing of the kind.
> 2. The Rights of Man establishes a sovereignty of the people over the state in a universal sense and assigns the state only the negative right of watching over such a constitution. The Fundamental Rights on the other hand, contains no decision in principle on the limitations of the state, or even on the dependence of the state on the nation.
> 3. The French Constituent Assembly establishes certain inalienable rights of the individual (safety, property, equality before the law and the right of

opposition to suppression of all these laws). The Constitution is guaranteed by the whole and by each individual. It recognises only human beings (implicitly including the Proletariat) and addresses itself to those human beings. The Fundamental Rights, however, speaks only about the rights of the citizen and subject, not about the rights of man.

4. ... [T]o characterise the Fundamental Rights one must ...
5. not forget to mention that it was drawn up half a century after the French Revolution with all the experiences of the interim period and all the results of German classicism. In spite of that, there is not much trace in it of German humanity and German philosophy. (Ball, 1996: 138–139)

This document has been quoted at length because it captures the essence of Germany's challenge to the liberal order as represented by Britain and France respectively: although the former played a central role in creating the contemporary international order, France has also left a distinctive footprint on today's international system with the notion of human rights and laissez-faire economics. But neither laissez-faire economics nor human rights had a central place in the German worldview. Germany was a communitarian rather than a cosmopolitan country, one which emphasised primary-group loyalty to the exclusion of everything else. According to the prevailing German worldview, a nation derived its values from the community and its meaning in life from membership of a group. The dominant German view was that life was inherently social and embedded in culture. In the words of Thomas Mann's notorious essay, *Reflections of a Nonpolitical Man* (1918): 'to [a German] to transfer his allegiance ... to what the peoples of Europe call *freedom* would ... amount to a demand that he should do violence to his own nature' (Dumont, 1994: 54). Germany did not have any specific idea as to what it wanted to replace the international order. German policy-makers simply disliked it. Germany was a resentful power, a spoiler.

The mutually exclusive nature of the normative codes that the major European powers held on the eve of the Great War was identified in the work of the sociologist Norbert Elias. According to Elias, the French philosopher, Henri Bergson, had stated the problem most clearly. Bergson maintained that the French sought to uphold the dominant rules of the system during periods of war because they reflected France's cosmopolitan values. When invoking the principles of morality, Bergson had asked, to what should one refer: to humanity as a whole, or to the country in which one is born? 'A moral philosophy which does not emphasise this distinction misses the truth ... when we lay down that the duty to respect the life and property of others is a fundamental demand of social life, what society do we mean?' (Elias, 1996: 155). Bergson subscribed to the ideas of the historian Jules Michelet. As far as he was concerned, to be born French was to be born a citizen of the world, to ground one's very being in the Rights of Man.

However, during the course of any war, the demands of an individual society will inevitably be prioritised over those of 'humanity'. Indeed, Elias added that the increasing democratisation of states and societies had led to a corresponding nationalisation of worldviews and national sentiment, with the moral demands of society almost becoming categorical imperatives that were deeply rooted in popular feelings and emotions. As Elias also argued, norms are not always benevolent and inclusive. While they may bind people together, the same process can often encourage people to bond in opposition to others. When the Great War began, it quickly became clear which countries had internalised liberal norms and which had not. 'The German policy—and policy it was—of seizing large numbers of hostages and murdering them wholesale in response to resistance, largely or wholly imagined,' writes Max Hastings, 'was unmatched in scale in Western Europe.' The treatment of British Prisoners of War (POWs) tells its own story. The official figures list just over 11,000 British POWs who died in captivity, yet many thousands more, reported missing, were worked to death as slave labourers. From October 1917 to September 1918 the death rate for British troops in the trenches was 4 per cent. Among British POWs it was 5.2 per cent (Lewis-Stempel, 2014). The German policy towards POWs was widely regarded as an inevitable outcome stemming from the violation of norms and the suspension of rules in the name of 'necessity'.

Elias was less clear with regard to why the British were able to retain their liberal values during the war, something which he sought to explain by invoking British 'pragmatism' and the famous British 'spirit of compromise'. Although neither is definitively 'British', both ideas reflect Britain's historical experience. Truth, as James claimed, is indeed biographical. Safe from invasion, behind their 'wooden walls' now policed by Dreadnought battleships, the British could afford to be more moralistic. The public expected Britain's foreign policy to be conducted in accordance with the principles both they and the British elite professed at home. Yet the British could be illiberal too. Three quarters of a million people died in Germany from starvation in the war years, for instance, many of whom were victims of the British blockade which sought to ensure that Germany surrendered its merchant fleet to the Allies. The blockade continued into the summer of 1919, months after Germany had surrendered. Two American historians have concluded that the suffering of women and children was greater under the continuing blockade than prior to the armistice (Loewenberg, 1996: 556).

However, although Britain's record in following what can be described as the British worldview is slightly mixed, the greater penetration of liberal bourgeois opinion into political life, and the more active political role taken by the middle class in the making of British foreign policy, allowed Britain to profess a universal morality which allowed it to 'win the narrative'. This was especially the case with respect to the country which mattered most after 1915, the United States.

By the end of the war the United States had displaced both France and Britain in the German imagination. As Andrew Gamble argues, the United States was drawn into the order that the British had done so much to construct, and in so doing it came to see the preservation of that order in the face of those nations that sought to challenge it as its paramount national interest (Gamble, 2009: 9). The German historian and philosopher Oswald Spengler had once claimed that an 'Innere England' (an 'inner England', or liberal fifth column), contaminated by liberal ideas, existed in imperial Germany. Alfred Weber, writing in February 1945 in the ruins of Hitler's Reich, concluded that the only way Germany could save its soul was by allowing this (now American-inspired) liberal core to have a voice in the future order (Watson, 1992: 60). The Federal Republic's subsequent integration into NATO and the European Common Market served to embed it in the contemporary world system. By 1960 the Germans had thus internalised liberal norms, thereby limiting Germany's foreign and security policy options, including the recourse to war against other liberal powers.

In June 2013 President Obama reaffirmed the values of the United States at the Brandenburg Gate by invoking the words of the German philosopher, Immanuel Kant, who claimed that freedom is the 'un-originated birth right of man and it belongs to him by force of his humanity'. The point Obama was seeking to emphasise in the speech was the fact that the Americans had already inscribed these words in the Declaration of Independence some years before Kant spoke of them in 1796: 'We are not only citizens of America or Germany,' Obama told his audience in Berlin, 'we are also citizens of the world' (*The Financial Times*, 22/3 June 2013).

Sinologists will perhaps find few parallels between the illiberal German states of 1871–1945 and today's China and subscribe more readily to the belief that the United States and China can avoid another 'cold war' confrontation. The world of 'dominant' conflicts only works if it has a rigid and immutable structure. If it lacks such a structure then it does not work. The stories we tell can overwhelm all sense of judgement: we can be traduced by the manipulative power of storytelling. It is the frame for conflict that creates the narrative, regardless of which country is under discussion.

If Zhang Lifan is right, however, then the only way that another challenge to the dominant normative order can be avoided is through internal change in China itself as part of a process that will transform Chinese society into one that is more sympathetic and attuned to liberal values. Whether China, as a rising great power (even if it is not necessarily revisionist), will allow itself to remain constrained indefinitely by the rules that the dominant power is intent on policing when these clash not only with its national interests but also its own ambitions and desires remains an open question.

But does the United States even remain committed to enforcing the rules? In the immediate post-Soviet period it appeared that the international order would grow ever more democratic. In the words of James Baker, the former US secretary of state, the world seemed to have become 'a hub-and-spoke system' in which everything depended on the United States. Now that the optimism of the 1990s has dissipated, the world looks rather different. According to Fareed Zakaria, the world has entered a 'post-American' era which may lead to a 'governance gap' in the event that the United States chooses to forfeit its role as the 'indispensable' nation (Zakaria, 2011: 39). One recent critique of Obama's foreign policy argues that the United States is following a path where this outcome will ultimately be realised: it has lost its 'exuberant desire to lead in the world' and is about to yield its strategic advantage to China (Nasir, 2013).

A different way of interpreting contemporary US policy, one which would appear to be borne out by the US 'Pivot to Asia', would involve distinguishing between what one writer describes as 'democratic globalism'—the project of refashioning the external environment to make it more amenable to democratic values—and the more modest goal of policing and where necessary enforcing the rules of the international system (Drolet, 2011: 124). The United States still regards the latter as a global public good. One of the main aims of the Pivot to Asia is to sustain what the Pentagon calls America's 'global leadership' (Tow, 2001). By re-animating regional alliances the rules can be policed more effectively.

The success of the United States in maintaining its position in the international system can be attributed to its adoption of a demand—rather than supply-side model, much like nineteen-century Britain. US policy has met with general international support when the United States has sought to police the system, or has chosen to enforce the rules. When the United States has acted unilaterally, on the other hand, or when it has supplied services for which there is no demand, the result is predictable: it quickly forfeits its international legitimacy. The invasion of Iraq in 2003 is a case in point. Whereas the international coalition that the United States assembled in order to dislodge Saddam Hussein from Kuwait was mandated by the United Nations, the invasion itself went ahead without receiving a Security Council Resolution explicitly authorising war. The US refusal to accept the validity of critiques of its practices in this and other instances (including Guantanamo Bay and the policy of extraordinary rendition) has greatly tarnished the way America is perceived throughout the world.

As John Ruggie argues, the problem with US policy is that America's leadership of the international system has often been accompanied by US 'exemptionalism', or a dogged refusal to be tied by the rules it has put in place (Ruggie, 2005: 305). This sense of 'exemptionalism' has frequently found expression in the reaction of writers in the United States to the creation of international institutions that would limit America's freedom of action. The historian Moorhouse Millar, for instance, sought to justify the US decision not to join the League of Nations by declaring that: 'Of course if America is to serve the cause of peace, it will only be by a clear and generous proclamation of her own true principles and not by bartering them for an international security based on mere utilitarian expediency' (Millar, 1928: 110). Twenty years later, Dean Acheson despaired that if that the United States chose to subordinate itself to the UN it would abdicate responsibility for its own history to a body that could not possibly comprehend that its first responsibility was to fulfill its covenant with history (Acheson, 1966). For the most part, however, these voices have been in the minority. The America First School has, too. Most Americans are internationalists of a kind, not because they love the world but because the institutions which presume to speak for it from the World Bank to the IMF were designed by the United States and are still inspired by liberal ideology.

To be sure, America's expectations are now much more modest in scope than they were in the immediate aftermath of 9/11. In US policy discussions the emphasis is now on the notion of a 'higher liberalism', which would balance a commitment to liberal principles with what John Ikenberry calls an 'appropriate regard' for the 'historically rooted interests and aspirations of other great powers' (Ikenberry and Deudney, 2009/10: 55). The US foreign policy establishment feels sufficiently confident to share power with others. And you do not need to be a neo-isolationist to value the importance of prudence. In the words of John Dewey, 'Right is only an abstract name for the multitude of concrete demands in action which others impress upon us, and of which we are obliged, if we would live, to take some account' (Rorty, 1999: 73). Condoleezza Rice expressed a similar sentiment in 2006 when she called for a more secure, rather than a better, world: 'We strive to make the world ultimately safer. Not perfect, just better' (*Washington Post*, 26 July 2007).

Realism inheres in that understanding just as prudence inheres in the belief that history is on your side. America's success in the Cold War owed much to its belief that it was marching in step with History. In the same way in which our ancestors once said 'God will know his own', so the post-Second World War generation often used to say that 'History will know its own'. I was born in 1953 (the year Stalin died) and completed my first degree twenty or so years later when the North Vietnamese Army triumphantly entered Saigon. At the time it did not appear that America's destiny was running with the grain of history. However, countries that tell themselves such stories are usually confident enough to stay the course, even following setbacks in the field. Yet self-belief can also lead countries to overestimate their power, as the United States did in the aftermath of 9/11 when it exercised what one conservative commentator called 'an unapologetic and implacable demonstrations of will' (Lieven and Hulsman, 2006: 38).

The United States is not as assertive today as it once was, in part because of China's growing power and influence. China's rise has encouraged many Americans to question whether the United States is still riding the tide of history. If the twenty-first century will not be American, can US citizens and policy-makers derive any comfort from China's apparent disinterest in challenging the United States' 'dominant' position?

In *Confront and Conceal*, David Sanger writes that part of America's continuing appeal results from the values it embodies: US policy continues to reflect America's commitment to liberal principles (Sanger, 2012). This is a typically American claim. But it is unclear whether it is still true, if it ever was. It is questionable whether China, as Sanger claims, will limit its ambitions to acquiring more power and wealth within the framework of the current international system. Indeed, China frequently criticises the system's lack of 'justice' and 'harmony', and even expresses enthusiasm for introducing 'Confucian' norms into international political life. Should China begin to pursue a revisionist policy towards the international order inspired by its own values and ideas, then this would again raise certain parallels with the period immediately prior to the First World War. In 1902 the Kaiser called for the 'world supremacy' of the German mind, and when war eventually broke out a significant number of German scholars represented it as an ideological struggle which would assure the victory of the 'German ideas of 1914' over the 'western ideas of 1789' (Kohn, 1964: 306). Although Imperial Germany itself didn't seem to know what it wanted in place of the international system the British managed, there were plenty of Germans who did. The same would seem to be true of China today where the government appears to be supportive of the system but many intellectuals would like to see some Confucian 'reforms'. The future may witness a similar conflict of ideas, another struggle for the high ground of history. At the present time the world remains largely content with US leadership of the international system. In research published in *The Economist*, for example, only twenty-six out the 150 most populous countries are classified as leaning against or opposing the United States. There is broad support for America's global role, and that support is likely to persist. But it is worth pointing out that China was the most powerful of the twenty-six countries identified (*The Economist*, 2013a).

Is America in decline?

Be assured, my young friend, that there is a great deal of ruin in a nation.

(Adam Smith, 1777)

On 11 September 1990, exactly eleven years to the day before the attacks on the World Trade Center, President George Herbert Bush called for a 'new world order' in an address to a joint session of Congress: 'A hundred generations have searched for this elusive path to peace, while a thousand wars raged across the span of human endeavour. Today that new world is struggling to be born' (Mead, 2008: 12).

After al-Qaeda's attack no one promised the American people a new world order. The United States simply tried to shore up the old order, confident in its strength as the world's only remaining superpower. After the financial crash of 2008–9, however, many Americans felt that the country was in decline, and outsiders thought they spotted the symptom—a sense of bereavement. A standard response to grief is initially either shock or denial. During the acute stage the sufferer may still have the illusion that the deceased person is still around, if only in his or her dreams. The next stage is anger at the loss and the effect it has had on our lives. We then look for people and institutions to blame—in the case of America, the banks or the neo-conservatives, or George W. Bush, or simply rising powers like China. Grieving becomes fixed during the phase of anger or depression. Only with time do the bereaved move on to a state of sullen acceptance of their loss. Is the same happening to the United States? Are the Americans coming to terms (or failing to do so) with their own 'decline'?

If the United States is indeed in decline, then it would clearly be at a disadvantage in policing the rules of the international system. However, many have been arguing that the United States is in decline since the 1960s, when it looked as though the American Century was quietly ebbing away on the battlefields of South East Asia (Hacker, 1970: 230). According to one writer, the curtain had come down on the *Pax Americana* even faster than it had on the *Pax Britannica* (Steel, 1967: 45), while another concluded that the Vietnam War meant that it was time for the United States to 'come of age' and reconcile itself to becoming an 'ordinary' country like every other (Brandon, 1966: 269).

The terms of the debate over US decline have not changed. Edward Luce's book *Time to Start Thinking* (2012), for example, provides a snapshot of what the subtitle calls 'an age of descent'. In doing so the book charts the 'hollowing out' of the middle class, the diminishment of primary and secondary education, the nation's loss of leadership in innovation, its increasing un-governability and the corrupting role of money in politics (Luce, 2013).

Similar ideas are put forward in George Packer's *The Unwinding* (2013), which views the Great Recession of 2008 as a sign of both economic and moral decline:

> [A] decadent kleptocracy in rapid decline, abetted by both political parties—America's masses fed on processed poison bought with the food stamp swipe cards, low-skill workers structurally unable to ever contribute again and too dumb to know their old jobs weren't coming back, the banks in Gotham leeching the last drops of wealth out of the country, corporations unrestrained by any notion of national interest, the system of property law in shambles, the world drowning in debt. (Packer, 2012, 18)

Packer is adept at unpicking intricate details and *The Unwinding* is an honest and interesting attempt at analysing what has gone wrong. Yet its message is not entirely devoid of hope. 'There have been unwindings every generation or two ... each decline brought renewal, each implosion released energy, out of each unwinding came a new cohesion' (ibid.).

For those who seek to promote this view, there is certainly plenty of evidence that suggests the United States is indeed in decline. The United States is less innovative than is commonly believed. Its lead in innovation in fact only dates back to the massive R&D investment in industry after 1940, and China is quickly catching up. Although Americans still account for most of the Nobel Prizes awarded in the sciences and have done so since 1956, an increasing number are now being awarded to Chinese scientists. The proportion of scientific research papers written by US authors declined from 26 per cent in 1993–2003 to 21 per cent in 2004–8. China is second only to the United States in the number of published articles and peer-reviewed scientific journals (Royal Society, 2011).

However, a shift in economic gravity is not the same as a historical power shift, and that is the main difference between Britain's decline after 1870 and America's today. Economic changes do not always lead to changes of hegemony. The Asian Century has not necessarily dawned, and it is possible that it never will. The population of China comprises 20 per cent of the world's population and the country generates around 14 per cent of global GDP. With only 6 per cent, the US generates 20 per cent and its standard of living is six times higher. In other words, the US economy is more productive than the Chinese economy, and this is likely to remain the case when China eventually overtakes the United States as the largest economy in the world. China no longer appears able to attain annual economic growth rates of 10 per cent, as it had in the past. It is also possible that it has entered a middle-income trap (i.e. a situation in which middle-income countries are unable to compete with the low-income, low-wage countries and highly skilled, innovative and advanced economies (Kharas and Kohli, 2011)). Only thirteen countries have succeeded in escaping this trap since 1960.China is rapidly losing its advantage in labour-intensive industries due to rising labour costs, but it has not yet gained a comparative advantage in technology and capital-intensive industries owing to its inferior technology and a deficit in human capital (Cai, 2012). The middle-income trap usually applies when GDP per capita reaches $11,000 or $15,000 (Eichengreen et al., 2012: 4). If China continues to grow at its previous rates it will reach the slowdown thresholds in 2015 and 2018 respectively (World Bank, 2013).

It is also important to take into consideration some of the more intangible strengths of the United States, many of which stem from its founding principles. Although there are acute signs of social inequality and declining levels of social trust in the United States, the country's social fabric is quite different from that of China (Murray, 2013). This does not make the United States exceptional, but it does make China different. The two are also very different in other areas. China does not rank, for instance, in the top twenty of Transparency International's 'Corruption Perception Index' (that is, in the twenty countries perceived as least corrupt), and corruption is one of the reasons why emerging markets rank far behind developed markets in terms of size, inequality and depth. Most private investable capital still originates in the Western world (70 per cent of the $80 trillion in pension, insurer and mutual funds is based in the United States, Europe and Japan), and despite the global recession the stock markets of the West have still performed better as a group than the BRICs. Whereas the equity of companies in the developed world has risen 6 per cent over the past few years, the equity of companies in emerging markets has decreased by 10 per cent (*The Times*, 29 Nov. 2012). One possible reason for this is the fact that the developed world still holds a decisive advantage in terms of normative rules, such as the rule of law, property rights and anti-corruption laws.

The United States has also been extremely fortunate in that it stands to benefit from new technological developments such as the 3-D printing revolution and the shale revolution. Economists often refer to 'present bias', or the temptation to exaggerate the impact of recent developments or technological advances in relation either to established patterns of behaviour, or longer-term systemic trends. However, the shale revolution could prove to be of substantial significance because the United States is better placed than any other country to exploit it as it has far fewer regulatory hurdles to cross. The construction costs of shale gas wells are cheaper than in any other developed country. Two other countries which are rich in shale oil, Mexico and Canada, are also members of the North American Free Trade Area. The importance of the shale revolution was emphasised in a report by Leonardo Maugeri, 'The Shale Oil Boom: A US Phenomenon', which points out that US oil production has increased significantly after falling for thirty years. In 1995 the US Geological Survey estimated that the Bakken field contained 151 million barrels of recoverable oil. In 2008 this was revised upwards to nearly 4 billion barrels, and in 2013 that number was doubled again. The figure is likely to be revised upwards in the future too (*The Times*, 4 July 2013). In other words, there are still grounds for defending the resilience of American power on material grounds. Indeed, the shale revolution may lead to a fundamental reassessment of the material basis of American power (Hastings and McClelland, 2013: 1427).

It would consequently be premature to describe the United States as a declining superpower. It should also be noted that the US manufacturing industry is experiencing something of a revival due to the fact that the US labour base is becoming cheaper, more productive and more flexible. The point at which manufacturers return their manufacturing operations to the United States has nearly been reached in several product areas including computers, motor parts, plastics and rubber.

Yet many Americans continue to feel acute anxiety about the future. It was none other than Alexis de Tocqueville who predicted that the US moment in history would most likely end not in economic collapse or defeat in battle, but with the expiry of its energy. It would decline, if at all, because of 'the mediocrity of its desires', and its power would gradually ebb away only for 'want of ambition'. Ambition would lose its vigour, passions would abate. Society would simply become less aspirational. There are many who fear that America's career as a great power will end not on a high note but on the downside of a dream as its power slowly and surely ebbs away.

Predictions, especially with regard to political, economic and moral decline, rarely come true. The best way to become a futurist, writes

Bruce Sterling, is to wait until tomorrow, by which time tomorrow will be promptly dismissed as the present (Strathern, 2008: 275). The United States still has its exceptional aspects, writes Charles Murray, but it is no longer 'the unique outlier that amused, amazed and bemused the rest of the world from its founding to the first half of the twentieth century' (Murray, 2013). But its resilience is likely to be enduring. De Tocqueville saw its democracy as a political faith, not only in the value of democracy itself but also in the greater American project. He recognised that power consists of more than just a crude measurement of material circumstances. It encompasses ideas and aspirations and national visions. The United States will only lose its ambition to lead if it loses faith in what others still think makes it exceptional.

Existential angst?

In the Western world the idea of exceptionalism can be dated to the sixth century BC, when the Greek poet Phocylides wrote that a single Greek *polis* (city-state) was superior to the 'folly' of Nineveh. Coleridge said much the same of Chinese history: a century of Europe was worth more than a 'cycle of Cathay'. The Chinese, for their part, have tended to be dismissive of every other people since they first claimed to be 'the Middle Kingdom'—exceptionalism is not specific to a particular culture. We are all, Nietzsche told us, value-esteemers, and the more powerful demand more esteem from others.

Yet to claim that exceptionalism is a fiction does not necessarily mean that it is untrue, but that it is something constructed or made—'*fictio*', from which the word 'fiction' is derived. The idea of exceptionalism is fabricated, and like all fabrications it is persuasive only when it accords with reality, or what is widely held to be real. The way things appear at a given point in time is largely a function of how we are predisposed to see them. That is why some fictions lose their explanatory force over time.

National fictions are necessary, of course, as long as we insist on attributing meaning to life, and even if they are illusions, not all illusions, Freud reminds us, are errors, especially if they are life-affirming. An illusion, he argued, is not the same as an error so long as it never becomes a delusion, one so improbable that even others can no longer believe in it.

The idea of US 'exceptionalism' has now lost much of its lustre, as is suggested in the title of William Pfaff's book *The Irony of Manifest*

Destiny, as well as in Andrew Bacevich's *The Limits of Power: The End of American Exceptionalism*. According to Bacevich, the idea of exceptionalism has become the refuge of a section of American opinion that seeks to deny the real state of the world. Behind the claim lies anger as the country's relative decline becomes more marked with stagnant or falling incomes, massive debts and rising new centres of wealth and power. And the belief in its own special place in the world looks to be increasingly unsustainable as a large gap opens up between the professed aspirations of the nation's political class—still all but unanimously committed to the United States asserting its 'global leadership' and the means available to fulfil those aspirations (Bacevich, 2009: 27). In re-reading the work of Reinhold Niebuhr, Bacevich rediscovered this passage written in 1937:

> One of the most pathetic aspects of human history is that every civilisation expresses itself most pretentiously, compounds its partial and universal values most convincingly, and claims immortality for its finite existence at the very moment when the decay which leads to death has already begun. (Bacevich, 2008: 24)

The interdependence of the twenty-first-century world has made it even more difficult to sustain a belief in any single nation's exceptionalism, including China's. It is hard to view a nation as exceptional when every major problem it faces, from terrorism to nuclear proliferation, requires joint action. According to Roger Cohen, if the idea of exceptionalism is taken to extremes then a country will simply be left without allies or influence, and little understanding as to the risks involved in pursuing a particular course of action (*The International Herald Tribune*, 24 Sept. 2008). The only form of exceptionalism that can be sustained over the longer term is one based on values and ideals embedded in a narrative fiction. America may still remain an unusual country in that respect and it may even be an 'indispensable one'. For its allies this may be what matters most.

Narrative fictions allow actors to weave a story about who they are and what they may yet become. This is why ideas are important. America itself was born of an idea, and in many ways it remains the last ideological great power. China's influence and power is certainly increasing, but the ultimate aims and aspirations of Chinese policy are far less clear than those of the United States. The United States will remain 'dominant' in the collective imagination as long as it subscribes to a national myth. Myths change over time; no one now believes in the country's 'Manifest Destiny' and fewer than before think of it as the 'beacon of liberty.' But the oldest myth of all still rings true for many, 'the Shining City on the Hill'. To speak of a national myth is not to accuse it of being a false story—it merely means that it is given a symbolic power which is independent of its possible or proclaimed truth (Midgley, 1985: 33). It is our experience of the world that constitutes its reality. 'Reality' is what we imagine it to be, and what we choose to imagine is often what we secretly want to be true (Vattimo, 2005: 10).

The American 'reality' is at one with what George W. Bush called 'the non-negotiable demands of human dignity' in his 2002 State of the Union address. When speaking of dignity he was invoking yet another fictional order of reality because history does not provide any empirical or scientific evidence of the fact that human dignity is important. We tell the story first and invest history with a meaning from the stories we choose to tell: it just happens to be the case that the Americans have told a very compelling story. It is at the heart of the American 'creed', a word first popularised by Gunnar Myrdal in 1944. Despite their racial, religious, ethnic and regional diversity, wrote Myrdal, Americans acknowledge that they hold in common 'a social ethos, a political creed'. Scholars have defined creeds in various ways. Myrdal himself spoke of the 'essential dignity of individual human being'.

Dignity is also at the heart of Western humanism insofar as it is human beings who insist on giving others dignity and the freedom which is a condition of being able to achieve it. By implication, we consider that the source of value is to be located in our own humanity. An understanding of one's national history as 'meaningful' is the same as being able to refer events to a teleologically bounded order, or to what, even if it is not humanity's goal, is nevertheless its destiny, which is either already being actualised in history or which demands such actualisation in the future. As one Western philosopher wrote:

> Each time I raise my voice against the conditions which insult human dignity; each time, even unknowingly, I project my own voice towards reasons which are rooted in what human dignity *truly* is, then each time I demonstrate that I know what a realised man would be, or what the demand to be human is. (Kolakowski, 1989: 31)

In other words, the demands of human dignity can only be 'non-negotiable' if we know what they ought to be, and we can only postulate the latter, not by analysing the historical record which suggests that we are 'owed' nothing, but by returning to the myths that help us order history and give it the shape and meaning it has. It is only through story-telling, after all, that history actually happens—history renews its energy from the stories we choose to tell.

The journalist Gilbert Adair was reminded of this during a visit to Ellis Island. The island is one of New York's greatest landmarks, the gateway to successive waves of immigration from Europe from the mid-nineteenth century until it was finally closed in the 1970s. It is now a museum. While walking around its corridors Adair was struck by the snapshots on its walls showing the uncomprehending faces of Central European immigrants herded into anonymous mobs; pictures of bewildered infants with improvised name-tags stitched to their coat lapels, and of hastily packed middle-class suitcases jostling battered, string-entwined cardboard boxes. He was nagged by the thought that he had seen all this before. Then he remembered that he had: he had glimpsed it in Steven Spielberg's movie *Schindler's List*. 'Ellis Island was a benign Auschwitz, a Holocaust in reverse, a positive Final Solution' (Adair, 1997: 179–80). The question is: will a United States transfigured by immigration be any less exceptional than the United States we know so well? And will it be any less confident that it has something to say to the rest of the world?

Immigration brings with it many social and economic challenges, of course but it also brings one enduring source of strength. Combined with a higher birth rate it will ensure that the country retains a fertility rate above 2.0. According to Joel Kotkin the population of the United States will rise by 100 million by 2050, thereby ensuring that the country not only continues to prosper but that it will keep ahead of the debt curve in a manner that most European and many Asian countries will not be able to emulate (Kotkin, 2010: 1–6). The United States will be the youngest post-industrial economy in the world, at a time when China will be one of the oldest. The fertility rate promises to reinvigorate cultural life and reanimate the American brand.

In his book, Charles Murray makes much of the fact that the United States has left behind the Founding Fathers, whose great achievement was to translate an ideology of individual liberty into a governing creed. No government restricted its own power as much as that of the United States in the two centuries that followed, but that great achievement no longer defines the nation—the social contract is crumbling, as is the social trust that underpins it. The dream is over: the United

States is special but no longer exceptional (Murray, 2013). But that is to miss the point. The brand is being updated in defiance of the odds. 'We are a 19th century people,' complained Dean Acheson, 'our minds are our great-grandmother's and father's minds. We aren't a 20th century people. Our ideas are inherited ideas' (Acheson, 1973: 26). A famous English visitor to the United States in the 1920s, the author G.K. Chesterton, had already arrived at much the same conclusion. America's ultimate test would come at the end of the century, when 'Eighteenth century ideals, formulated in eighteenth-century language, [had] no longer in themselves the power to hold all those pagan passions back' (Chesterton, 1922: 296).

Around one in five American adolescents is already Hispanic. By 2040 the proportion will be nearly one in three (*The Economist*, 2013b). This influx is likely to be a game changer. America is indeed being challenged to 'reinvent itself', the term Bill Clinton evoked in his inaugural address. He was probably unaware that this was one of the central messages of the country's greatest philosopher, John Dewey. Dewey was not opposed in principle to national fictional narratives: he was only opposed to them when they were life-denying, not life-affirming. If a fiction gave rise to spirited actions and useful initiatives it was socially useful. It was also, in his eyes, essentially true, for truth lay in its intrinsic value as a spur to action. Truth was not a cause of success, but was an effect of holding to a belief. In other words, Dewey judged the rightness of all beliefs by their effects rather than their causes.

Dewey's ideas had great appeal outside the United States, and especially in Japan. In the lectures he delivered at the University of Tokyo in 1919 (later published as *Reconstruction in Philosophy*) he told his Japanese hosts that they would have to revalue their own traditions in order to keep in step with the modern world. Their success in reinventing themselves would depend upon their chances of rising to the challenges of modernisation (Dewey, 1982: 201). This challenge confronts all modern societies, and it now faces America too. There is no reason to question whether the next generation of Americans or for that matter the generation after that will not be assiduous in promoting and defending the norms and rules of the international system that they chose to shore up after 1945 in institutions of their own making.

The belief in the American brand even underlies the denunciations of what America has become—George Packer's voice is so different from the Englishman Edward Luce's, which expresses a defeatism that many Americans would probably find distinctively 'European'. There is something more in 'the American grain' (as William Carlos Williams called it) than immigration: it is the energy which de Tocqueville found to be so quintessentially American. There is nothing to suggest that America's insistence on dreaming for the rest of us will diminish as its enemies or even some of its allies seem to suppose. There are of course always signs of weariness. But there is little evidence of any willingness on the part of the United States to relinquish the role of 'dominant' power, let alone to allow any other country to challenge the rules of the road.

However, it is certainly true that the United States has grown increasingly weary of foreign entanglements. A 2013 Pew Research Center poll found that 52 per cent of Americans felt that the United States should 'mind its own business' and stay out of the world's concerns, while only 38 per cent disagreed (the most lopsided balance for the United States staying at home in the fifty years in which the polls have asked that question). But the poll also showed that Americans still want to defend the norms and rules of the international system, especially the commercial ones, and a majority think that Asia is the 'business' of the United States (*Financial Times*, 21 Jan. 2014). Indeed, the United States has a long history of involvement in Asia and has always been committed to Asia's future. It is in essence—and always has been—an Asian power (even if the Chinese are unwilling to acknowledge this).

The problem is that China is in the process of reinventing itself too, even if the Chinese Dream is of a much more recent vintage. The Party has set out to achieve the two '100s': the material goal of China becoming a moderately well-off society by 2020 (doubling its 2010 GDP per capita) on its 100th anniversary, and the far more ambitious goal of becoming a fully developed nation by 2049 (the 100th anniversary of the People's Republic).

Regardless of whether these goals are achieved in practice (or are even achievable), in the future Chinese politicians will be much more confident and assertive. The next generation of leaders is coming to political maturity at a time when the country has known nothing but rapid economic growth. And nationalism may be in the ascendant once again in the years ahead. Collective human identities, though multiple, have become primarily national in the modern era (Canadine, 2013: 54). In the post-modern societies of the West this is no longer necessarily true: in most 'mature national communities' there is a crisscrossing of loyalties that make up the fabric of people's individual and collective lives (ibid.). But this is not necessarily true of China, nor is it likely to be true for some time to come because the country is the last major power which is in the process of becoming a fully fledged nation-state.

This inevitably begs the question: to what end? Every society, the Nobel laureate Octavio Paz insists, involves communication; every society has something to say. But this in turn raises a further question with regard to what a given society actually wants to say. A social discourse can be reduced to one simple phrase: 'I am.' However, there are also numerous variants of this phrase: 'We are the Chosen people', or the 'master race' or the world's number one power. In the pre-modern age humanity thought in terms of people, tribes or ethnic groups. In the modern era the principal conceptual unit has been (and still remains) the nation state. Nationalism is merely the most recent expression of the verb 'to be' (Paz, 1990: 157).

Yet as Aristotle once observed, something only 'is' when it realises itself though an attribute: 'I am stronger' or 'I am a believer in a particular religious creed'. I am strong because the group to which I owe allegiance is strong; I am different because I worship a different God. Everyone finds safety in the power of the particular group to which they belong. And we still put a premium on security.

Nationalism is not always dangerous, or even problematic. Nations can sometimes look beyond their own sectional interests and parochial concerns and situate themselves in the history of humanity as a whole, and the history of any country is as much about cooperation as it is conflict with its neighbours. Chinese nationalism, however, is pervaded by the memory of national humiliation in the two Opium Wars (1839–42/1856–60) and the unequal treaties imposed upon China in their wake. Conflict is the major theme of Chinese nationalism and it is hard-wired into the patriotic education courses the Party promotes to justify the historical 'inevitability' of its own rule, and it will continue to remain important as long as the Party treats history as an issue of political management.

Wang Fei-Ling claims that history in China has been monopolised by the state ever since the time of the first emperor who burned the history books and dated China's existence to Year Zero (the first year of his reign). The last imperial dynasty even nationalised history writing. Chinese historians have always written under government license (F.L. Wang, 2011). History is important because the way in which a country remembers its past can profoundly influence and shape the way it moves forward into the future, and because there may be politicians ready to summon history into the service of the present to reshape the world itself.

Opium Wars and China's historical entitlement

> Truly, though our element is time,
> We are not suited to the long perspectives
> Open at each instant of our lives.
> They link us to our losses ...
>
> (Philip Larkin, *Whitsun Weddings*, 1964)

A British writer tells of a friend whose visit to America did not quite turn out as he had expected. He was set to marry a Chinese-American whose parents had emigrated from mainland China many years before. But when he arrived at the family home he immediately felt uncomfortable. The welcome was polite but not as warm as he had expected. There was a distinct chill in the air which seemed to grow as the evening wore on. Finally, the father asked a question: 'Will you before marrying my daughter be good enough to apologise?' 'For what?' he asked. The answer surprised him: 'For the Opium Wars' (Webb, 2013).

Memory is elastic. People tend to remember history for what it has to say to them at a particular point in time. This is how historical memory works: the events of the past are shaped in such way as to invest them with a meaning they did not have at the time. This includes the 'humiliations' visited upon China in the nineteenth century, even though the First Opium War was ultimately of little importance to the ruling dynasty at the time. There were some violent battles, such as Zhapu and Zhenjiang (1842), when Manchu soldiers were outgunned and little quarter was asked for or given by either side, but as James Polachek shows in *The Inner Opium War* (1992) the Qing state did not act as if the engagements were of any consequence, or for that matter that the country had even lost a conflict.

The European military engagements with China (including the most important, the Second Opium War, 1856–60) only played a minor role in destabilising the Qing dynasty. The real cause of the dynasty's downfall was in fact internal dissent. China was not a unified state (as Westerners understood the term in 1840) but an empire made up of many heterogeneous and often competing parts. There was a significant degree of ethnic diversity; indeed, even the dynasty was foreign. One historian describes Qing rule as 'a Manchu occupation' (Paine, 2003: 377). There were several attempts to secession including the Miao Peoples' Revolt in the south in Hunan and in Guizhou in 1850–70 and a Muslim revolt against Chinese rule in Yunnan and Xinjiang in the period between 1862 and 1873. The anti-dynastic rebellions were far more dangerous, such as the Red Turban Revolt (1854–5) when Canton almost fell to the rebels, and the most destructive rebellion of all, the Taiping (1851–64), which devastated more than 600 cities and resulted in the death of 20 million people (which makes it by far the costliest civil war in history). Chinese historians are encouraged to label all of these as 'rebellions', but many were more than that: some were independence movements (one of the leaders of the revolt in Yunnan even wrote to Queen Victoria offering to submit to British rule) (ibid.: 27).

The danger of concentrating on such a short historical perspective, to quote Larkin, is that it is being used to fuel a sense of history that is deeply misleading in emphasising continuity rather than discontinuity. Chinese history is not monolithic. Far from being governed as a strong, unified empire, for 600 years the country was divided between two or more regimes. For some periods of its history it was weak (the nineteenth century merely being one of these) and for long periods the dynastic house was not even of Han ethnic origin (Yuan, 1271–1368; Qing, 1644–1911). The importance of the Western incursion into Chinese history resides in the fact that it broke the previous pattern of political change in China, which was based on a long-standing assumption that change resulted from repetitive cycles of history. With the arrival of the British, that belief could no longer be sustained. Change was now produced—as it was everywhere else—in a linear fashion and could only be brought about by exposure to the outside world. Little of this appears in Chinese history textbooks. Just as the Party cannot confront its own past, especially its record in the Great Leap Forward and the Cultural Revolution, so it cannot admit to some of the historical facts which precede its own rule. The European incursions of the nineteenth century did indeed kill thousands of Chinese but the insurrections (both secessionist and anti-dynastic) killed tens of millions. Entire provinces were devastated. Most of those killed lost their lives at the hands not of foreigners, but their own countrymen.

The real importance of the First Opium War is that it was followed by the infamous 'unequal treaties' which the European states negotiated with the Qing dynasty. The Western powers seized upon the decline of China to demand a number of treaty ports, freedom of navigation of inland rivers and uninhibited travel into the interior, all of which were won under the threat of further military action. By 1920 there were sixty-nine ports in total. The Treaty Port system played an essential part in bringing China into a single international system. Over the course of time it became a far-reaching arrangement of interrelated rights, interests and privileges within which foreign nationals enjoyed their own tax and legal judicial systems, exempt from Chinese jurisdiction. The system was not international at all, of course, but was neo-colonial. The privileges that foreigners enjoyed included their own administered bureaucratic services such as the Postal Service and the Maritime Customs Service, and the right to station troops in the capital city and at strategic points along the railway network from Beijing to the sea.

But China was always too large to be partitioned, annexed or occupied, as was Africa in the same period. It is clear that the Europeans recognised that the country was different. Its age together with the unity of the civilisation made partition unattractive and colonisation unthinkable. China's sovereignty was never questioned. 'We have given the Chinese a most exemplary drubbing,' wrote Britain's Foreign Secretary Lord Palmerston after the First Opium War, 'but we must stop on the very threshold.' Any further military action would only be taken if there were any more 'attempt[s] on their part to treat us otherwise than as their equals'. As John Darwin adds, the irony was that the pursuit of equality (rather than dominion) did indeed lead to 'unequal treaties' (Darwin, 2012: 123). But the unequal treaties were a product of the internal implosion of the imperial dynasty and not only a consequence of European expansion. Moreover, the system did not last very long. It was finally renounced in 1942 when China became allied to the United States and Britain against imperial Japan. It had become increasingly unsustainable long before then as China had slowly been incorporated into the international system. A Chinese representative attended The Hague Peace Conferences in 1899 and 1907; China joined the Universal Postal Union (UPU); and international law courses taught at universities including the Imperial College of Tongwen Guan introduced the Chinese to the idea that the international system was contractual and egalitarian at the same time—even if some states were more equal than others. Indeed, after the League of Nations court system had been established, China was the first country to appeal for the revision of the unequal treaties on the basis of equal sovereignty. Only the civil war that soon engulfed it, followed by the long war with Japan, kept the treaty system in place as long as it did.

The Sino-Japanese war

Chinese hegemony was shattered from the outside not only by the Europeans. It was also destroyed in the Sino-Japanese War (1894–5). This war was even more devastating than the Opium Wars because it fractured the harmony of the Confucian world system and left a territorial legacy with which we live today: the disputed status of Taiwan and other islands. Only now is China restoring its status as a major naval power which it lost in 1894 at the battle of the Yalu River (the first time in Asia that iron-clad battleships and rapidly firing guns were used in naval combat).

What followed was even more of a shock. When in 1938 W.H. Auden and Christopher Isherwood visited the city of Xian in Shaanxi Province they found a gigantic walled city whose 'penitentiary walls' reminded them of a gaol and its guards of gaolers. Behind the walls arose a broken line of savage bandit-infested mountains. Xian, they wrote, smelled of murder. In 1926 the city had endured a seven-month siege by local warlords. Now it was being bombed by the Japanese, an episode which seemed to capture China's unhappy interface with the twentieth century (Auden and Isherwood, 1973: 124–6). In Auden's deservedly famous sonnet sequence *In Time of War* (penned following his return to the West) there is a poignant line about a dead Japanese soldier: 'Far from the heart of culture he was used'. It is often forgotten that the Sino-Japanese War was as much a race war as was the Russo-German war for the Nazis. It was not merely a territorial conflict, or a traditional political contest between two contiguous powers intent on displacing the other as the leading power in the region. Nor was it simply a struggle to subvert a regional balance of power. Instead, the two societies found each other engaged in an existential conflict. The Japanese chose to think of themselves as being in Asia without being Asian, and in explaining their uniqueness, they incorporated many of the worst elements of Western thinking. The Chinese people were deemed to be inferior, not, as they had been during the first Sino-Japanese War (1894–5), because they were technologically or politically backward, but because they were racially inferior. The Japanese word for the Chinese, *chankoro*, was the equivalent of the British term 'chink'.

This war does not feature as prominently or as often in Chinese Communist Party propaganda as the Opium Wars with Britain, and one reason for this may be that its own war record is so ambiguous. The Communist Army fought only one major battle against the Japanese. Nearly all the fighting was done—ineffectively, for the most part—by the nationalist forces under Chiang Kai-Shek. The latter forces were most effective in retreat, rather than in open combat, as was the case when they flooded the Yellow River to block the Japanese advance, even though hundreds of thousands of peasants drowned. During the war Mao's capital at Yan'an was the home of terror, not resistance. A TASS representative, Peter Vladimirov, recorded 'an oppressive atmosphere' where people sought to redeem themselves from non-existent sins (as they were to do during the Cultural Revolution). In other words, the terror that Mao was to unleash many years later started early (Mitter, 2013).

All nations have a selective memory. Karl Popper once argued that there is no 'history', but only a series of 'histories', an insight in which he was anticipated by eighteenth-century novelists who wrote of the 'histories' of their heroes such as Tristram Shandy and Tom Jones. But even if history will always be disputed, it is important to avoid regressing into myth. If all history is part fictional, then it is important to remember that fictions serve the purpose of discovering and understanding new things. Fictions degenerate into myths when they are not consciously held to be fictive. Myth, writes Frank Kermode, presupposes a total and adequate explanation of things as they are and were. They are the agents of stability compared with fiction, which is usually an agent of change (Kermode, 1967: 39). In the case of the United States the fiction of exceptionalism will help it to adapt to the demands of a new century. In the case of China the memory of national humiliation may play a much less constructive role.

The falseness of an opinion, as Nietzsche acknowledged, is not an objection to it. The only relevant question is whether the opinion is life-furthering or life-preserving. The problem with the Chinese Communist Party's rendering of the past is that it encourages the Chinese people to remain frozen in a time of humiliation which, though certainly real, was largely the result of their own internal weakness, as some Chinese historians readily admit (see Mao Haijian, *The*

Collapse of the Celestial Empire (2005)). In its determination to patent the past the Party has drained the nineteenth century of its colour. The black-and-white demands of politics have reduced the Opium War to bite-sized chunks of propaganda for Party rule. This is what makes it so advantageous. 'Forgiveness means giving up all hope of a better past,' writes Lily Tomlin, and in lieu of a better past, the Party is at least offering a better future. From primary school to university, China's youth is taught a selective narrative which is underpinned by the recent investment in historic sites and museums. One example of this is the National Museum of China, which opened in 2011 and has a permanent display narrating 'The Road to Rejuvenation'. The last item on display in the Museum offers a future in which there is an iPhone for all. China's future aspirations would thus appear to be rather modest, and this might seem somewhat reassuring. However, the past will continue to cast a long shadow on how the future is imagined, and this is dangerous because it allows the Party to escape responsibility for its own crimes or 'mistakes', such as the Great Leap Forward which cost the lives of 30–40 million people and the catastrophic ten years of the Cultural Revolution, as well as the disastrous and unnecessary war with Vietnam in 1979 in which more Chinese soldiers died in a matter of months than the number of American soldiers in ten years of war in Indo-China.

In an essay in *The International Herald Tribune* in April 2013, the Chinese writer Yan Lianke discusses the subject of memory-deletion. A truly great people, he writes, are those who have the courage to remember their own past; a truly great nation is one that has the courage to record its own history. In the absence of both, there is only resentment (*International Herald Tribune*, 2 April 2013). As the following chapter explains, resentment may become a major problem in relations between the United States and China. Although resentment arises from many different factors, one of the most significant is an inability to move on or to move out of the shadow of the past; it blocks the exit to the future.

Sinosphere

Long before the West forced it into the international system China had run a very successful regional hegemonic system. It was the 'dominant power' in East Asia for well over 700 years. If China seeks to re-establish its own regional pre-eminence and change the local rules of the road, or to challenge the United States by reshaping the international order in a way that is consistent with its own values and traditions, then this would almost certainly set it on a collision course with the United States.

In the words of the Sinologist Warren Cohen: 'In the Beginning There Was China' (Cohen, 2000: 1). Although not literally true, this description captures China's long-standing regional importance. In some ways China was the equivalent of Athens in the fifth century BC. It was the 'school' in East Asia, the one to which everyone else looked, and unlike Periclean Athens its hegemonic role lasted for centuries. The periodic tribute missions to the capital which were organised along accepted routes under a Chinese escort were at the heart of the Chinese system. One of the most well-known customs to emerge during this period was the kowtow (three total prostrations with the forehead touching the ground). The kowtow was a ritual, and Confucians expected rulers to rule by means of ritual; ritual and order were closely interlinked (Mitter, 2003: 209). Children kowtowed to parents, parents to grandparents (and the ancestors); ministers to the emperor; and the emperor to heaven itself. The Confucian classic *The Great Learning* described the indivisibility of the order thus: 'Rectify yourself; put your house in order; regulate the kingdom; and there will be peace under all the heavens.' Peace under all the heavens began with a kowtow at home (Gong, 1984: 174). But the kowtow was only the sharp end of the system. China's cultural dominance in Korea and Vietnam was not the product of a conscious campaign to spread Chinese culture beyond its borders. Instead, China's chief concern was stability within its own borders (Kang, 2010: 2). The adoption of Chinese culture seems to have been purely voluntary, with scholars viewing the dominant power as *wen xian zhi bang*, or 'ruling through texts' (ibid.: 34). The Koreans, for example, beginning in the early fourteenth century institutionalised, assimilated, internalised and practised Confucianism for more than half a millennium with very little encouragement from their neighbour (Haboush, 1991: 86).

It was a regional rather than a global system. The only attempt to break out of East Asia came in the early fifteenth century when China, which had earlier launched an extensive ship-building programme, dispatched seven expeditions into the Red Sea and the Indian Ocean before the programme was abandoned, probably for financial reasons.

The expeditions were called off, and even the records of the voyages themselves were later burned in an act of scientific vandalism. By 1500 contact with the outside world had ceased altogether. It became a capital offence to set sail in a ship with more than two masts without special permission. It would be another 300 years before a Chinese vessel made its way to Europe—on a visit to the Great Exhibition in London in 1851.

If the ship-building programme had continued, it is quite possible that the Chinese could have reached the Americas across the Pacific, passing via Japan and across to the North Pacific to the Aleutians and Alaska, and from there to what is now the Californian coast. They might have used the trans-Pacific routes at lower latitudes, the same ones, in fact, used by Magellan in 1521. It is unlikely that their encounter with pre-Columbian America would have been quite as transformative as the Spanish. There would have been no forced conversion to Christianity, no settler societies and no enslavement of the local population, though the encounter would almost certainly have been violent. The Chinese like to think of themselves as less violent than the Europeans. But even the great Admiral Zheng who voyaged several times to the East fought a war in Ceylon and executed the king of Sumatra for not showing due respect to the emperor. In contrast to the claims of today's Chinese leadership, Zheng's voyages were not peaceful but were an early example of 'gunboat diplomacy', coercion and recognition of Ming dominance. Even so had Zheng actually reached America it would have produced a great historical challenge; China would have encountered a civilisation very different from any it knew, several centuries before the Industrial Revolution. The establishment of a trading system across the Pacific would have opened minds to the variety of human societies and to different social experiments (Cook, 2001: 87–99). It would have widened China's cultural horizons.

The difference between the Sinosphere and the Westphalian system which the Europeans established in 1648 is instructive because today's international order is modelled on the 'normative rules' the Europeans devised first for themselves and then for the rest of the world. Whereas the former was agent-centred, the latter was rule-based, and if the rules were often flouted and states misbehaved, the assumption was that they would be punished. Although the means for enforcing the rules externally were comparatively weak, the rules themselves were largely internalised by the Europeans in relations with each other. There was a degree of internal motivation not to break them. The system included resident ambassadors, a feature of inter-state relations since the Renaissance. After the mid-seventeenth century states accepted the absolute demand of sovereignty, including freedom from interference in another state's domestic affairs. With very few exceptions (the partition of Poland being the most egregious) states recognised the right of every other to exist. This system became so entrenched that by the mid-eighteenth century the Europeans regarded it as a universal norm.

The Chinese agent-centred system was very different. Its sustainability depended on whether the chief agent, China, was sufficiently powerful to be able to promote its own interests and exercise its power in accordance with certain moral principles (such as the Mandate of Heaven) (Geuss, 2010: 50). But an agent-centred system is entirely dependent on the relative power between the hegemon and its allies. In the Chinese worldview, 'order' was inherent in the process of existence itself. When the centre was strong, tribute moved in to reinforce it; as the centre weakened, the periphery had the power to exert influence, reshaping and even subverting the centre itself (Ames and Hall, 1995: 278).

The 'rules' of the system were ultimately an epiphenomenon in that they were not part of the system's basic structure. Moreover, the Sinosphere relied far more on soft power than hard power. The Chinese emperor demanded tribute, but what he gave back in the way of quality goods (silk) was always far superior to the goods he received. This was the whole point of the exercise as it reinforced the cultural superiority of the Middle Kingdom. But it did not work against the nomads who were beyond China's cultural reach. The horse peoples of the Central Asian Steppe were greedy, parasitic and destructive, and they continued to haunt the Chinese imagination until they were finally tamed in the eighteenth century. But just when the horse Nomads had been tamed, another group arrived by sea in the early nineteenth century. Like other nomadic people the British were equally predatory and ruthless. The Chinese soon learned that soft power had no appeal to a people who were culturally immune both to the medium and the message.

The Sinosphere survived the Mongols, but it did not survive the British. Just as the rule-ordered Westphalia system replaced the agent-ordered Christendom which was destroyed by a combination of religious polarisation brought about by the Reformation and the 'gunpowder revolution' that made wars far more devastating than before, so in East Asia a regional order that had been run for centuries by the country that had invented gunpowder was soon shattered. The industrialisation of warfare by the Europeans after 1800 ended China's 'monopoly of violence' in East Asia and devalued its legitimacy as the regional hegemon at the same time.

Andrew Phillips argues that all international orders are normative. They are informed by a heightened awareness of the sacred and the mundane and they recognise the existence of a fundamental tension between these two worlds. This tension is usually expressed in their constitutional structures, which rest on an ontological recognition of the appropriate relationship between the spiritual and social worlds. The Sinosphere was dependent on the Mandate of Heaven. The pre-Westphalian order of Latin Christendom, by contrast, was anchored in Augustinian political theology, which preached that power was both temporal and spiritual. The church had its own sphere of jurisdiction—the care of the soul—and there was also a public sphere policed by the state and concerned with the maintenance of public order and the protection of property. In due course canon lawyers began to fashion a system of law that included rights inhering in the individual. The fifteenth-century Conciliar Movement sought to restrict the power of the papacy and to introduce something similar to representative government in the church. Though it failed, the Protestant Reformation and the religious wars which followed in its wake ultimately led to a more systematic separation between church and state, and to secularism with its assumption that religion is a matter of conscience. The European state system that replaced the Augustinian was instantiated in a purely secular system of legal conventions and rules.

Such Western conceptions of international order were superficially egalitarian and legalistic in character, given their emphasis on notions of sovereign equality, and were quite foreign to Chinese hierarchical assumptions including the tribute system upon which the East Asian order was based. The Chinese were eventually forced to renounce the paternal moralism characteristic of East Asian diplomacy, and to accept that diplomatic relations should be mediated through a depersonalised, formal, rationalised corpus of international law (Phillips, 2011: 180). When drafting the country's very first formal trade treaty with China in 1871, Japanese conservatives wanted a broadly worded agreement without specific provisions, which were deemed to be unnecessary between two fraternal countries with a shared cultural heritage. The Japanese Foreign Ministry insisted upon a precisely worded European-style treaty which cast Japan in the role it wanted, as the legal guarantor of trade rights in East Asia (Kim, 1980: 138).

In its propaganda the current Chinese government frequently refers to the two Opium Wars and the 'unequal' treaties that the Europeans imposed. But the disintegration of any order starts from within. Outsiders merely exploit domestic vulnerabilities. What really killed off the Sinosphere was not commercial adventurism but the challenge of other norms and rules of behaviour—for example, in the Taiping Rebellion. Its eventual collapse was marked by widespread rural unrest, a period of social anarchy that was just as chaotic as that of mid-seventeenth-century Europe. When the city of Nanjing fell to the Qing imperial forces in 1864, it ended history's bloodiest civil war but not before it had claimed 20 million lives.

The Sinosphere will never be revived in its original form. However, old ideas rarely disappear altogether, and the Chinese might have every reason to revisit the principle if not the practices that provided stability in East Asia for so many centuries when the empire was strong and Confucian culture in the ascendant. Should they feel blocked from taking their place in the sun, they might think of other options—a more networked East Asian relationship system. The Chinese leadership is aware that most Asian countries will oppose any attempt by the United States to make them choose between partners (Zakaria, 2011: 173). Most have moved closer to Beijing in the past few years, recognising perhaps, in the words of the Japanese Prime Minister Shinzo Abe, that borders and exclusive economic zones are determined by national power and that 'as long as China's economic power continues to grow its sphere of influence will continue to expand'. Andrew Krepenevich's article in *The Wall Street Journal* struck an especially alarming note when he talked of China's 'Finlandization' of the Western Pacific (*The Wall Street Journal*, 11 Sept. 2010).

Owen Lattimore, writing in 1940, noted that China's frontiers had constantly shifted. A linear boundary was never established as a geographical fact: 'that which was politically conceived as a sharp edge was persistently spread by the ebb and flow of history into a relatively broad and vague margin that signified the optimum limit of growth' (Lin, 2011: 15). As we have seen, the Sinosphere was a system based on the shifting power of the centre. When the centre was strong its influence expanded. In the future it is possible that China will seek to impose 'unequal' practices of its own (in all but name) including, perhaps, some that threaten freedom of navigation, a core interest for the United States. The United Nations Convention on the Law of the Sea (UNCLOS), of which China is a signatory, challenges China's indisputable 'sovereignty' over Exclusive Economic Zones (EEZ). The Chinese have also marked out an Air Defence Identification Zone (ADIZ) which lies between China, Taiwan, Japan and South Korea. The East China Sea is now primed for one-off clashes of military ships or aircraft or even an escalation into more widespread conflict. There is also the prospect of conflict over the Spratly Islands, where sovereignty is contested by several countries, those who claim the entire cluster (Vietnam and the People's Republic of China (PRC)) as well as those who only claim part (Malaysia and the Philippines). China is both the most distant and the most powerful claimant, and the possibility of energy reserves beneath the South China Seas may translate a local irritant into a 'core interest'.

Chinese support for the principle of non-interventionism is almost taken for granted. However, its adherence to this principle could change over time. Non-intervention in the sovereign affairs of other states still remains one of the main principles of its foreign policy. During the Maoist era it was one of the five principles of peaceful coexistence. But the PRC has intervened in a number of countries in the recent past: in Korea, Tibet, India and Vietnam. It provides the largest number of peacekeeping troops for UN operations, and is now the largest provider of loans, both of which may be creating an interdependent network of relationships: the 'pull' factor of political and military intervention.

The 'push' factor may be provided by history. The Sinosphere always allowed for military intervention. Throughout its history China has been frequently at war with its neighbours. Old instincts may well be rekindled. Great powers, after all, earn the right to call themselves such because of their capacity to intervene in the affairs of other states. Chinese interventionism may differ from the Western model, but interventionism, though it may take a different form, is unlikely to be renounced. Political realities usually prevail.

China and the international order

How resilient is the present international system? One of the main difficulties in answering this question is the fact that experts in different fields use the term 'resilient' in very different ways. In engineering, resilience means the extent to which a structure such as a building can return to its baseline state after being disturbed. In ecology it refers to an ecosystem's ability to avoid becoming irrevocably degraded. A common definition is the capacity of a system to maintain its core purpose and integrity in the face of dramatically changed circumstances. This capacity requires a system that can adapt quickly to strategic shocks while still retaining its core purpose (Zolli and Healy, 2012: 6). The core purpose of the present international order is to prevent war between the great powers, and much will depend on America's ability to adjust to the rise of China.

The belief in the end of great power conflict is anchored to the idea that the present international system is resilient enough to survive, or that it can be reformed without recourse to war. Unlike imperial Germany and Japan (the only countries that William James accused of being interested in 'plunder'), no country in the contemporary international system really expects to make a profit from war. But this should not be a source of complacency. The rise of China will be as disruptive as the rise of Germany after 1870, in part because China may have difficulty coming to terms with the nature of its own power. In the same way, the United States will find it difficult to adjust to its own decline. Do we really expect it will be easy for either power to adjust to the increasing complexity, volatility and inter-connectivity of the twenty-first-century world?

In posing that question I am greatly influenced by Henry Petroski's classic study, *To Forgive Design*. One of the book's main observations is that 'A single failure ... is a source of knowledge we might not have gained in any other way'. 'The best way of achieving lasting success is by more fully understanding failure' (Petroski, 2013: 36–7, 360). This is why the logic of history is important, as it is the only way in which lessons can be learned from mistakes. Although Petroski's book is primarily concerned with engineering disasters, it also discusses the social systems that humans engineer (such as international orders), which occasionally reveal 'weaknesses in reasoning, knowledge and performance'.

Systems have to be improved all the time, and endless improvement, Petroski argues, is what engineering is all about because unfortunately failure is built into everything humans build. All we can do is build on the basis of the lessons learned from the past. But what, he asks, if we can no longer invoke the past as we once did? This is certainly becoming true of engineering. Engineers predict the probability of occurrences for certain events such as a 100-year storm in such and such a percentage on the basis of historical experience. But we are leaving behind the Holocene Age—the 10,000-year period of benign climate stability. Global temperatures are rising. The amount of energy in the atmosphere has increased dramatically, which has accelerated every process that feeds off this energy. Why is this important in engineering? Warm air holds more water vapour. We have already increased the moisture in the atmosphere by about 4 per cent, which increases both the danger of drought (because heat evaporates over surface water) and of flooding (because evaporated water eventually turns to rain). Both are proving to be an engineering nightmare for the resilience of the existing structures that we have built. What was once a 100-year event is now becoming a fifty-year event, and a fifty-year event, in turn, could become one in every twenty-five years (Petroski, 2013).

Is the same true of the international system that was designed in the late 1940s? Systems have always had to be re-balanced in accordance with changes in the distribution of power, but we have never witnessed changes in peacetime as dramatic as those which are taking place today. Five years ago Goldman-Sachs forecast that China would overtake the United States in 2042. A few years later it revised the estimate to 2020. Today, economists are predicting that China will become the world's largest economy in 2014. This inevitably raises a number of questions. Will the United States lose the power to enforce the rules? Will it lose its self-belief, its existential certainty? Will China even want to challenge the system?

It is always possible that China will simply accept the current rules. Fareed Zakaria argues that the United States, like the UK in the nineteenth century, still has a strong Protestant mission. China is not a proselytising nation and it may never acquire a similar sense of destiny. 'Being' China at the same time as becoming a world power may well fulfil its historical ambition (Zakaria, 2011: 125). But the talk in China itself is very different. Many in the Chinese military now openly talk of the United States as being in terminal decline, which may leave a political vacuum that will have to be filled. Writers like Yan Xuetong describe China's decline as a 'historical mistake' which will need to be corrected (Leonard, 2008: 83). Competition between the two countries is no longer about land, resources or markets, but about rule-making, and Yan believes China urgently needs 'to set the global rules' itself (ibid.: 94). Others see China's rise as an opportunity to forge a more just world order. Such an order, writes the philosopher Zhao Tingyang, would guarantee sovereignty, world interests and world rights, rather than just material rights and interests. This is a vision of family rights rather than individual human rights. It is deeply normative in its own way, and Confucian in inspiration.

However, some Chinese writers have expressed concern at the possibility of the United States losing interest in managing the system as they believe that China is not ready to assume this role. The controversy between those in China who believe that the country should seek to refashion the international system and those who believe it is not ready to do so publicly erupted in 2006 following the publication of a provocative newspaper article by Wang Yiwei, a young scholar at Fudan University, who asked 'How can we prevent the US from declining too quickly?' For Shen Dingli, who believes that Beijing is not yet ready to assume a leadership role, the goal should be to 'shape an America that is more constrained and more willing to co-operate with the world' (ibid.: 116).

The challenge for the United States as the 'dominant power' is that China also has ambitions and a vision for the future world order. These were stated by a leading Central Committee official, Yang Jiechi, following the Annenberg Meeting between President Obama and Xi Jinping in the summer of 2013. Jiechi posited a 'new model' for the relationship between the two most important global powers, one that the Chinese call 'win–win co-operation'. The model, which would be based upon non-conflict and non-confrontation, would entail abandoning the zero-sum mentality of the past (Jiechi, 2013). Jiechi also called for 'innovations in diplomatic theory and practice', though what these might be were not spelled out.

Chinese policy-makers and analysts maintain that the 'Chinese Dream' is different from the American Dream in that the country's ambitions are neither imperialistic nor hegemonic. But other Asian countries do not necessarily view Chinese policy in the same way. For China's neighbours, it remains unclear whether China's 'Royal Way' will be any different from the hegemonic way of the West, or for that matter the Imperial Way of Japan in the 1940s with its message of 'Asia for the Asians' (Hughes, 2010: 619).

Where is China heading?

According to Ye Zicheng, a professor of international politics at Peking University, the best strategic choice for China would be a partnership with the United States. Unfortunately, however, the two countries have different interests and ideologies. The prospect of another cold war is not attractive either, and should only be entertained if the United States defines China as an enemy that needs to be countered or contained. Ye is reluctant to envisage the possibility of a Sino-American war, but he is much less sanguine about the possibility of avoiding some kind of eventual showdown. The best option would be a workmanlike relationship, which would combine elements of cooperation and confrontation. The closer relations that China holds with Russia when compared with the United States, and the latter's close relationship with Japan, could serve as a stabilising factor in US–Chinese relations (Ye, 2011).

Ye is a liberal. In his view further economic development and domestic political reform is the key to avoiding confrontation with both the United States and China's neighbours. China's continued economic development has increased its power and influence, and democratic reform will make it a more legitimate power in the eyes of the rest of the world. Both will help China adapt faster and more effectively to changing events, and thus give it a more powerful voice in redesigning the present international system. In 1994 Nixon concluded that the lectures the United States was prone to deliver on human rights were already imprudent. Within a decade, China's growth would make them irrelevant. Within two decades it would make them laughable (Huntington, 1996: 195). But will it also make them unnecessary? Will China evolve its own brand of democracy as Ye hopes?

Democracy may well be the question on which confrontation or cooperation will eventually turn. As Singapore's former ambassador to the UN remarks, 'The great paradox of the twenty-first century is that this undemocratic world order is sustained by the world's most democratic nation-states, the Western nations' (Mahbubani, 2008: 104). This is America's challenge: can it come to terms with the need for change? But equally can China move forward into a more democratic future? If it fails to do so, some commentators warn that it will run the risk of becoming a delusional power. As Timothy Beardson writes, environmental degradation, cyber warfare and the avoidance of historical truth in China give the impression that the country is a threat to world peace. Analysts also ask whether China is building a society devoid of real culture and moral standards (Beardson, 2013). The fact that such questions are asked so often reflects a profound uneasiness in the United States and elsewhere about what might replace the normative order that still governs international affairs.

It is unclear if China will become more or less democratic in the future, although it is clearly becoming more unstable, with social polarisation between rich and poor, workers and the middle class, the seaboard and inland areas. These polarities are fuelling differences of opinion that will need to be aired if they are not to be expressed through violence. In its official proclamations the Party continues to claim that it is committed to 'democratic decision making', 'democratic management' and 'democratic supervision'. The official position is that the gains that have allowed China to modernise could be lost if the political system is not reformed. Although many Western commentators are understandably cynical about China's commitment to reform, this might not be entirely fair. China, after all, holds more elections than any other country in the world. Its 1 million villages elect committees every three years (600 million voters). According to research undertaken by Robert Benewick from the University of Sussex, elections have been growing more competitive, with the use of more secret ballots and the appearance of more independent candidates. Based on a study of forty villages over a sixty-year period it has found that spending on public services has gone up by 20 per cent while spending on 'administrative costs' (a euphemism for corruption) has gone down by almost the same percentage. The government had originally intended to adopt the village system for the towns, but these plans have now been abandoned (Hill, 2011).

There is also the possibility of increased internal democracy within the Communist Party itself. Competitive elections are now held for Party posts at lower levels. In the Provincial Party Congress there are already 30 per cent more candidates than posts, and this in a party which has over 83 million members.

Any democratic development in China will be distinctively Chinese. In Confucian thinking power should be derived from three sources: the legitimacy of heaven (the sacred or transcendent); the legitimacy of earth (the wisdom gained from history and culture); and the legitimacy of the human (the popular will). It is by no means self-evident that the popular will should always override the other two. Should a government have only one source of legitimacy: the people? Even Western philosophers have warned against majoritarianism—the dictatorship of the majority that has often fuelled racism, fascism and imperialism. Western scholars have similarly questioned whether the short-term interests of the populace should override the long-term interests of society.

A democratic China could prove to be a real competitor for the United States, especially in the realm of soft power. But this scenario is unlikely to unfold in practice. In the 1990s, Chinese bureaucrats estimated that by 2020 China would have reached a stage in its economic development—a 'moderately prosperous society' (*xiaokang shehui*)—where it would be able to implement democratic reform, and this may be why China agreed to implement universal suffrage in Hong Kong in 2017. China now seems to be backtracking on the latter promise, and given its current social tensions and inequalities it is unlikely that leading figures in the Chinese Communist Party will contemplate democratic reform in the immediate future.

Increasing Chinese competition with the United States may also prove an obstacle to the realisation of the hopes of liberals such as Ye. In August 2013 a memo referred to as 'Document No. 9' bearing the unmistakable imprimatur of Xi Jinping was sent to Party leaders across China, warning about Western influence and the threat of American soft power, including Western constitutional democracy which is top of the list. Other 'threats' include the promotion of universal values (liberal internationalism); an ardently pro-market neo-liberalism; and the 'nihilistic' criticism of the Party's appalling historical record (Mao's 'egregious mistakes'). The document ends by warning of the 'Western infiltration' of ideas hostile to Party rule (*International Herald Tribune*, 21 Aug. 2013). Thus it is much more likely that the United States and China will drift even further apart ideologically, in a similar way to Russia and the United States since 2000.

Moreover, it is equally possible that China will not follow a more democratic path but will pursue a different political trajectory, one which may involve returning to the practices of the past. In the absence of a national debate on the horrendous years of the Mao era, the Communist Party is hardly in a position to prevent a similar system of repressive and arbitrary rule returning in the future. Unless the excesses of the past are fully accounted for, it is quite possible that a politician could adopt much the same tactics as Bo Xilai, the disgraced Party secretary in Chongqing. The policy he pursued was called the *Changhong*

Dahei—singing red, striking black—a combination of attacking corruption at home while promoting populist Maoist policies. In the end he overplayed his hand. But his fall does not necessarily spell the end of this type of politics in China.

As Wang Zheng argues, there have often been periods of continuity in Chinese policy from one period to another, despite the emergence of new leaders who have been ostensibly committed to different policies. After the Empress Dowager Cixi cracked down on the reform movement in 1898, for example, she carried out much the same programme as the reformist movement she had suppressed. Similarly, after China's leader Deng Xiaoping removed Zhao Ziyang as Party secretary in 1989, he still pursued Zhao's market reforms. Now they have removed Bo Xilai it is possible that the next generation of Party leaders may pursue much the same policies (*International Herald Tribune*, 25 Aug. 2013). Party infighting is likely to grow worse. The battle between Xi Jinping and Bo Xilai is possibly a foretaste of things to come. The revolution's children may be forced to turn on each other simply in order to ensure the survival of the system that spawned them.

The Chinese people's desire for a better life and for their lives to be more valued will undoubtedly persist and democracy would seem to be the only way that lives can be fulfilled. All life-forms, writes Simon Blackburn, inhabit a Darwinian jungle. The best predictor of which life-forms will survive is the sense of satisfaction people have with their own lives. The evidence suggests that the Chinese are more dissatisfied with their lives than most Americans. This does not necessarily mean that the United States has reached the future first. China's rise may be what history has in store.

Indeed, there is another argument that Blackburn goes on to reject, namely that a country's own experiment in democracy is the 'realisation' of human progress, or the apex of an evolutionary triangle, or the 'end' to which everyone else is marching. This is a very Hegelian understanding of history. It assumes that everyone has the same capacity for ethical truth because truths such as democracy are 'self-evident'. But they are not self-evidently true. Even if they were, he cautions, a universal capacity for ethical truth would not offer a great power a selective advantage over another in the competition of life (Blackburn, 2013: 12).

A democratic China would undoubtedly be a dramatic development. The twenty-first century might well prove to be 'Chinese' rather than

American. However, the 'China Dream', the 'China Way' and the 'Confucian Wave' could all prove stillborn without an underlying meaning, other than revenge for the past, to underpin them. All that will prevail is that other Western export—nationalism.

Ye's contending and pragmatic vision of the future, as discussed above, clearly conceals a deep anger about China's humiliating past. Ye wants China's status to be redefined in a way that is commensurate with its size. This should not be difficult to attain in principle because the institutions of the present international order are easy to join and hard to overturn. They have what Ikenberry calls 'intra-institutional mobility', which means that member states can rise—and wane—within the existing institutions (Ikenberry, 2011). But it is possible that China wants to achieve much more than this. The current world order was in crisis a few years ago paradoxically because the United States, free from all constraints on the exercise of its power following the Soviet collapse, came near to undermining the rules of the very order it had created. Although Ye is a 'moderate', his grand strategy involves holding the line until such time as the 'correlation of forces' works to China's eventual advantage. It is only in that sense that he can be considered a 'pragmatist'. Yet it is possible that he is wrong and the United States is not in terminal decline, and it is just as possible that China will not rise at the pace it expects to do so. If the Asian Century proves to be something of a mirage, what will happen if Chinese resentment continues to fester?

Ye fears that the United States would object to any Chinese attempt to restructure the international system into which it was forcibly integrated after 1840. Would it be prepared to change the financial system and give Beijing a greater voice? Or allow it to use its navy in the Pacific as a 'stabilising force'? He is willing to accept that the United States has not sought to contain China's rise, but rather to hedge against it, but what if China bids not only to increase its stake, but to change the international system? Rules rarely outlast the power of the powers that created them. The world's first 'globocop', as Ian Morris describes post-1815 Britain, eventually cracked under the weight of its global responsibilities; the next, the US, may do the same (Morris, 2014: 25). All the lessons of history suggest that the US needs to share the burden with China if both countries are to avoid a conflict; the two sides urgently need to enter into a dialogue to also decide which if any of the 'rules' need to be changed.

In the absence of such a dialogue the international system may gradually be hollowed out, or China may evade assuming responsibility for its management. Declining international orders, as Andrew Phillips points out, involve enormous risks and can result in enormous losses. The worst prospect would be that of a polycentric international system in which there is no hegemon, just a series of regional powers in which balance of power politics operates without the nineteenth-century value system that underpinned it and in which alliances shift on an issue-by-issue basis, informed by short-term interests, not deeply rooted values. Such a world could generate a governance gap. Global government structures such as the World Bank and IMF might be unable to deliver many of the international public goods citizens will demand. The failure of any state to dominate the system might create its own problems (in the event that no single power was responsible for setting the agenda or enforcing the rules). One Chinese critique of the system is that it embeds Western power and does not recognise the true redistribution of power that has taken place. Furthermore, for many in China it is simply unjust and disharmonious (Zhai, 2010). But a world that is not dominated by a Western agenda of human rights and democracy promotion could be devoid of any sustaining ideas of what public goods are best and what norms should be policed. A value-free international system might well prevent conflict between the great powers but prove incapable of addressing other global challenges such as climate change and attacks by militant non-state actors.

Both great powers confront a twofold challenge. One is to avoid coming into conflict while still competing as great powers always will (the word 'status' after all, is partly derived from the word 'state' as well as from the the Middle English 'estate'). The other is to work together to adapt the system to China's rise, and the relative reduction in Western power. Both powers have a chance, if they can enter into a genuine strategic dialogue, to make the world a little better than it is.

Culture-shock?

In 1943 the sociologist Karl Mannheim referred to a new 'normative consensus' and this is precisely what the world currently needs. Much of Mannheim's life and work was spent trying to alert his colleagues to the need to provide democracy with 'moral depth', and this remains a pressing challenge today given the fact that so many are disenfranchised within the current international order. Although many have benefited from globalisation, the same process has also worked to the detriment of many others and their numbers are rising.

In an ideal world the United States should not be defending the rules so much as seeking to finesse them with the Chinese; both powers will be making them for everyone else for the next few decades. If they can't agree to share power they may find themselves in conflict soon enough. They really do need to agree on what values count for most and which should be defended from revisionist powers, including Putin's Russia. Mannheim's main criticism of the democracies of his own day was that they did not place enough emphasis on values in the inter-war period (and had lost out to the totalitarian regimes with their deep moral certainties). As one of Mannheim's contemporaries wrote at the time, Fascism and Communism both posed as 'political religions' which offered hope of redemption to millions. Both were '"fundamentalist" revolt[s] against the whole tendency of rationalization in the Western world' (Furedi, 2013: 122).

But it is unclear if two powers who are so fundamentally different from each other as China and the United States will be able to work together to achieve this. As one of the characters in Henry James's novel *The Europeans* observes, it is not what an individual does or does not do that determines their life, it is their general way of looking at it. The worldviews of China and the United States differ from each other. Both have developed sophisticated ways of seeing that filter their experience of the world. As Henry James's brother William grasped, all reality is 'biographical' in that it is shaped by collective experience. Or as the futurist Richard Neville remarks in *Footprints of the Future*: 'nobody owns the truth'. All we own are our respective worldviews (Watson and Freeman, 2013: 178).

However, although the Chinese and US worldviews are self-evidently different, such claims must always be treated with a degree of caution because the uniformity of thinking that is observed in one culture may merely be the product of the distance from which it is viewed. In 1947 F.S.C. Northrop argued that there was a clear contrast between Western and Eastern knowledge. Whereas the former is expressed in logically developed scientific treatises, Eastern knowledge is a form of knowledge in which 'the individual concentrates attention upon the immediately apprehended aesthetic continuum of which he is part'. He also claimed that Western knowledge arrives at 'concepts by postulation' whereas Eastern knowledge forms 'concepts by intuition'

(Northrop, 1947: 77–101). Henry Kissinger has made similar claims with regard to the difference between the Chinese and US worldviews. Kissinger claims that while Americans tend to think in terms of concrete solutions to specific problems, the Chinese tend to think in terms of the stages involved in approaching a subject, a process that has no precise culmination. Americans tend to believe that international disputes result either from misunderstandings, or simply ill-will, with persuasion or coercion being the most suitable remedy. The Chinese approach is more impersonal and patient. To Americans, good will and good faith are the lubricants of foreign policy. To the Chinese good personal relations are not considered to be particularly important in the conduct of diplomacy (Kissinger, 2011: 137–8).

In *The Geography of Thought* (2003) Richard Nisbett argues that the East tends to see and interpret the world by noting patterns and connections rather than attempting to impose its own reality (a factor the Chinese call *shi*—adapting to the propensity of things, a point to which I shall return at the end of the next chapter) (Nisbett, 2003). His research with Shinobu Kitayami at Kyoto University claims that Westerners focus on individual needs, whereas Asians focus more on context and relationships. To Asians the world is understandable in terms of the whole rather than in terms of its individual parts, and it is subject to collective rather than personal control. When asked to describe her day, a six-year-old American child will make three times more references to herself than a Chinese child. When shown a picture of a mother and child arguing, American children tend to take sides whereas Chinese children tend to see merit in both positions (Brooks, 2011: 141–3).

According to the developmental psychologist Bruce Hood, when Westerners are asked to define the 'self' they will often invoke a purely personal perspective such as the statement 'I am tall', whereas Asians tend to stress relationships: 'I am taller than my sister'. The Chinese prefer to see themselves in a social context (Hood, 2011: 156). Like Nisbett he believes that developmental processes shape the way individuals pay attention to the world. The plasticity of the brain enables it to encode relevant experiences, and even to shape the way that language is used (ibid.: 158–9). Western and Eastern mothers, for example, talk to their children in different ways. The former are much more likely to focus their children's attention on the properties of a toy, while Japanese mothers are more likely to engage their children in exchange relationships—handing a toy to a child and then asking it to hand it back.

Most striking of all, perhaps, is the observation that Claude Levi-Strauss made in a series of lectures which he delivered in Tokyo in 1986. The aggressive individualism of a culture like the West, he argued, is explained by the extent to which the 'I' is an autonomous, already constituted entity. By contrast, the Japanese construct the 'I' from outside in relation to the larger community. It is not an original entity but one in constant process of being fashioned. He was confirmed in this thought on realising that Descartes' famous proposition, 'I think therefore I am', is strictly untranslatable in Japanese (Levi-Strauss, 2013: 25).

If China and the United States are to work together to forge a fairer international system they will have to take each other's perspectives on life into account, and it is not clear whether this will be possible. Although the world faces many shared problems, such as climate change, the responses to these issues in the West and the East are framed very differently. The following outlines three ways in which a certain issue can be framed.

1. Narrow framing within a culture. People tend to frame risks differently in terms of their individual experience. This is called the availability heuristic. People are inclined to compare one risk with another (the other usually being the last that we have met with). Then there is saliency: the immediacy of an event in the imagination (the Americans quite naturally drew an analogy between 9/11 and the Pearl Harbor attack in 1941). People are also influenced by what John Stuart Mill called 'learning by experience the tendencies of actions' (Mill, 1871: 34). What one considers probable as opposed to possible is likely to be determined by our own history. All of these cohere into what Daniel Kahneman calls a 'narrative fallacy'—a preference for stories over truth, as well as a desire to compress a series of unconnected events into a single story. Mallarmé actually got there first when he talked about 'the dialect of the tribe'.

Zbigniew Brzezinski is particularly concerned by the extent to which the Chinese debate about international politics is being framed entirely in terms of the post-1840 experience: victimisation. He cites an article from the publication *Liao Wang* from August 2012, which claims that the strategic objective of the United States is 'to ensure its leading status in the entire Asia-Pacific region' and to 'build a trans-Pacific order centred on the United States' that would enable it to continue to dominate the Pacific. This objective can only be realised by dismantling the East Asian Regional Corporation framework. In other words, the article accuses the United States of deliberately promoting discord between China and its neighbours. Brzezinski also quotes a passage from an article in another newspaper, *Renmin Ribao*, from January 2013: the US 'is boosting old military alliances, damaging the political foundation of East Asian peace, sharpening the territorial sovereignty contradictions between China and countries around it, building a united front aimed at China'. It argues that China should respond by allying with Russia to prevent America gaining 'total control of the Eurasian Continent'. Similarly, another article, from the *Jiefangjun Bao*, urges China to cast away its 'pacifism and romanticism' and prepare for an inevitable war with the United States.

Brzezinski argues that the use of the present tense in articles such as these imports a sense of credibility, couched as though it is describing a reality rather than a possibility. The adoption of a single tense (the present) to describe both the present and the future helps to entrench in the minds of the readers (and even some experts) the illusion that what might happen one day is already happening today (Brzezinski, 2013b). Such a belief, if it is widely held in China, is clearly a dangerous one.

Brzezinski is illustrating the availability heuristic at work. Chinese newspapers tend to promote the Party's agenda by repeating its favoured messages: tapping into the collective consciousness of past wrongs and the memory of European imperialism, thereby influencing the way the public thinks regardless of whether the message bears any relation to the facts.

2. Anchoring. People tend to anchor their actions on narrative fictions. The West usually anchors its military interventions on the need to protect human rights. But it is we who insist on giving ourselves those rights as well as the freedom which is a condition of achieving them. When speaking of rights we are actually invoking a fictional order of reality, and fictions are biographical. History does not provide any empirical or scientific evidence of the fact that humans have rights. We tell the story first and then invest history with a meaning. The story of human rights just happens to be a very powerful one which is based on an understanding derived from Western humanism that it is an obligation of being human to draw the best from, and the best of, life in the frame of our lifetime—in this world, not the next. The Chinese, by

contrast, tell themselves very different stories which also bear on the concept of human dignity. Indeed, back in the third century BCE the Chinese understanding of what made us human was not our capacity to reason (the Greek definition) but our capacity to live a moral life (Lloyd, 2012: 15).

The fact is that value attribution is hardwired into us by natural selection. All societies value fairness. People seek to right wrongs and to win a measure of self-esteem. We all dislike betrayal and disloyalty, or in other words, anti-social behaviour. The values we prize are all pro-social for that reason: they are designed to promote cooperation. We have language for another reason, too, so that we can evaluate the behaviour of others. We honour some people for being dependable and trustworthy, and devalue others for being unworthy of our trust.

3. Coherence. There is no such thing as an objectively secure world. Whether we feel secure or not is largely a matter of the stories we tell ourselves. When you change the way you look at things, the things you look at often change. As Donald Rumsfeld said of the weapons of mass destruction that were suspected to exist in Iraq, the Coalition did not act because it had discovered new evidence for their existence; it acted because it saw the existing evidence in a new light, through the prism of its experience of September 11. He later insisted that 'absence of evidence' was not 'evidence of absence' when it clearly was. This is a striking example of cognitive dissonance, a term coined by Leon Festinger in 1957 to describe a peculiarly problematic state of mind, like Rumsfeld's in the period prior to the invasion. Dissonance encourages us to think that we have been successful when we have clearly failed.

Kahneman argues that a genuine dialogue between the United States and China would allow for more rational decision-making. A genuine dialogue would be free of all of the above: narrowing, anchoring and excessive (associative) coherence. In all likelihood, the most that can be expected of two countries as different as China and the United States is that they will find a way of developing better habits of cooperation. They might be able to reduce errors in decision-making on the understanding that the normative illusions of one's own society are more difficult to recognise than those of another. The voice of reason is often much fainter than the loud voice of tradition. 'The upshot is that it is much easier to identify a minefield when you observe others wandering into it than when you are about to do so' (Kahneman, 2012: 417).

But it is questionable whether such a dialogue will take place. Starting from different places it is unlikely that China and the United States will reach a similar destination. It is much more likely that they will confront each other in a strategic stand-off. Their continued prosperity calls for peaceful coexistence at the very least, and cooperation at best, but both countries are prone to suspicion and anxiety. Though they appear to accept that war is 'not on' (at least, for now), it is still unclear whether the two powers can live together in peace. Can China accept and continue to negotiate with a country that wants the Chinese regime to change and considers any government model but its own largely illegitimate? Can the United States deal constructively with a China which is so resentful of its past and confident about its future? Both want peace, but coexistence requires that most elusive state of being: it requires them to be at peace with themselves.

Conclusion

One of the chief lessons to be learned from the 1914 analogy is that the violence released was probably encoded in the DNA of the pre-war world—in the domestic violence over Irish Home Rule in Britain and the struggle over votes for women as well as workers' demands for a living wage. It was encoded in the barely suppressed revolutionary tensions in Russia which had already been made manifest a few years earlier in 1905. It was expressed in the latent hostility of the army and parliament in Germany, and the angst of workers and the middle classes crammed into the cities, both looking to nationalism or socialism for salvation. It was implicit, above all, in European imperialism which made it possible for white men to inflict the same violence on other white men as they had on the 'lesser breeds' they had earlier subdued. The pre-1914 world, in other words, may well have been fated to die of its own internal contradictions and a war between the United States and China may arise from the contradictions of our own world: its glaring and growing social inequalities; the continuing violence that mars the political landscape of much of Africa and the Middle East; the resurgence of nationalism in the world at large. All of these could generate a climate of opinion that renders war less improbable than economists and liberal thinkers suppose.

In practice there is little hope that the two rivals can work together to reconstruct the system agreed at the Big Power conference in Yalta in 1944 and bring justice to Asia as a region (Zhang, 2006). The international order has failed to achieve a 'transition' from *la raison d'état* to *la raison du monde*. China remains rigidly regional in its outlook, even though a number of Chinese writers have visions of a networked world, a *guanxi wang* (or relationship system), a subordinate system of power in which China can link up with the 'subaltern' states of Africa and Latin America and reduce their dependency on Washington-dominated institutions such as the World Bank and IMF (Pei, 2012).

The present world order may be unsustainable as resource scarcity and austerity begin to affect societies around the world. A zero-sum economy may engender a competitive and conflict-prone zero-sum mentality. The prospect of de-globalisation and the progressive questioning of Western liberal norms may lead to further fragmentation. However, it is also possible that power will be redistributed and shared between states and NGOs, which may mark a veritable paradigmatic shift from 'governance by club' to 'governance by hub'. None of this will necessarily bring into question the logic of great power conflict, but it might create a new context within which the dynamic may work itself out, and that could make the difference between war and peace. But all this will take a long time to work itself though the system, and meanwhile, as critics of globalisation from Joseph Stieglitz to Masao Miyoshi contend, more and more of the world's people are being integrated into a geopolitical system that denies all but the most powerful a voice in their own future.

'Insecurity about the present and uncertainty about the future are our constant companions in our journey through life.' The future itself is just a shorthand expression for 'anything might happen, but nothing can be known or done for sure'. It is the 'doing' that is important. We make the future what it is through the choices we make. Antonio Gramsci insisted that the only way of 'predicting' the future was to join forces and pool our efforts to cause future events to conform to our desires (Bauman, 2010: 109–10). There is no guarantee that these efforts would help us to win out against uncertainty, but it is the sole strategy that gives us a chance. There is, alas, no certainty that two countries as different as China and the United States can join forces and pool their efforts on behalf of the rest of us.

3

STRATEGIC NARRATIVES AND THE LOGIC OF STRATEGY

Norman Mailer's Second World War novel *The Naked and the Dead* (1948) ends with its chief protagonist General Cummings concluding that he is unlikely to be 'in' the next war with Russia. The novel is set in the Pacific theatre, where Cummings has made his reputation. He recognises that the future belongs to younger men as wars are always changing in character. There would have been no role for him in the Cold War with its proxy battlefields and nuclear weapons. The war he imagines would have been a reprise of the Second World War. The fact that nuclear weapons were never used during the Cold War owed everything to America's ability to craft a successful grand strategy.

The purpose of grand strategy was best summed up by Edward Mead Earle, whose seminal book *Makers of Modern Strategy* provided one of the first comprehensive examinations of the concept. Earle did not explicitly associate the work with the ordeal of his time, but as he was writing in 1943 the Second World War is an unavoidable presence in the background. Earle argued that grand strategy should aim to integrate the policies and armaments of nations so as to make resort to war unnecessary. If war does break out, then a sensible grand strategy should ensure that it is undertaken with a reasonable chance of victory (Earle, 1943: viii).

Every state engages in grand strategy. But the grand strategies of the great powers also involve a geopolitical vision. The link between the two is profound since the former is based on assessing which interests are not vital and which are, and those assessments are usually based on a country's geopolitical priorities (Brands, 2012: 5). Both China and the United States are currently crafting grand strategies on the basis of how they interpret each other's intentions. Obama's Pivot to Asia is seen as a containment strategy in all but name and not as the administration itself sees it, a belated correction of the fact that the United States under-invested in Asia due to its preoccupation with the war on terror (Sanger, 2012: 412). China sees the Pivot as further evidence of America's decline. From the Chinese perspective, the strategy is a desperate attempt by an ailing country to reinsure while it still has time. It is viewed as evidence of a nation turning inwards while flexing its muscles abroad. Some Chinese strategic thinkers believe that the main danger the United States poses is its weakness, which translates into what they call 'meddling' (in the South China Seas) and unnecessary 'provocations' (such as the decision to beef up America's presence in the region by rotating a US Marine force in Australia).

All great powers live an interpreted life. Grand strategy allows them to make sense of their past experiences and lends coherence and meaning to their present existence. However, some of the stories the great powers tell themselves are more credible than others. Some are more compellingly told and a few are even a good match for reality. The human race is a species of story-tellers: archaeologists piece together historical artefacts in order to tell the story of prehistory; historians have been telling stories since the time of Herodotus and Sima Qian; business executives create stories about the products they sell, pitching them in a way that is likely to appeal to specific markets; lawyers have been crafting their cases in narrative form since courts of law first came into existence; and, more recently, the military has been told that success and failure depends on 'winning the narrative'. It is the stories that states and societies tell themselves and others that lead to conflict, or which allow a different, more peaceful path to be pursued.

In *Alice's Adventures in Wonderland*, the Duchess remarks that everything has a moral if you know where to look for it. The moral of the war that never was, between the United States and Britain after 1890, is an instructive one. Britain was able to design a grand strategy which stood the test of time, and arguably still does. Liu Ming, a PLA colonel and professor at the National Defence University, claims that it is possible that the United States could follow Britain's example and simply vacate the role of world leader to China (Wang, 2010). But this is not going to happen because the United States is unable to create a similar story to that which Britain told itself after 1890.

What I shall show in this chapter is another aspect of the logic of great power conflict; the need to weave strategic narratives that are believable. And the need to grasp that in the absence of a compelling grand strategy, nations can find themselves sleepwalking to disaster as happened in 1914. Above all, strategic thinking is merely a grand term we give to social intelligence—the capacity to devise a set of options that take into account the opponent's view of the world. What Edward Luttwak calls 'strategic autism' was clearly in evidence in Imperial Germany's failure to see itself through the eyes of others; social intelligence was what accounts for Britain's relative success in managing its own decline as the 'globocop' and thus avoiding an 'inevitable' war with the United States.

The war that never was: the United States versus Great Britain

In May 1913 a British delegation visited New York to discuss plans for celebrating the anniversary of the Anglo-American peace. The last war between the two countries had ended in 1815 (though the peace treaty had actually been signed the year before the last battle, a definitive American victory which launched the political career of Andrew Jackson). At their final meeting in the Plaza Hotel the representatives of both sides agreed to observe a five-minute silence across the English-speaking world on 17 February 1915. There was one voice of dissent: a Harvard professor astounded the delegates by claiming the two countries were planning to join together in a war against Germany. He happened to be of German-American descent. A member of the committee stepped in to reassure him that neither country was contemplating war. Indeed, every nation would soon be members of a universal brotherhood of men. Everyone applauded. This, as we have seen, was a widely held belief in the period prior to the First World War (Emmerson, 2013a).

Yet only eighteen years earlier Britain and the United States had come close to engaging in conflict over an obscure territorial dispute between Venezuela and a British colony, or what is now Guyana. The US secretary of state had chosen to redefine the Monroe Doctrine unilaterally and retrospectively. 'Distance and 3,000 miles of intervening ocean make any permanent political union between a European and an American state unnatural' (Roberts, 2003: 164). In a counter-factual essay, the historian Andrew Roberts imagines how such a war might have panned out, given that the British seemed to hold all the cards. He points out that the US Eastern seaboard had virtually no coastal batteries with which to defend cities like New York, Baltimore or Boston. The US Navy had only one first-class battleship, with a further three under construction. The Royal Navy had twenty-nine first-class battleships, twenty-two more second-class battleships and fifteen more armoured cruisers. But the reality, of course, was that the UK could have done little to defend Canada, whose possession the Colonial Secretary Joseph Chamberlain insisted, contrary to Overy's claim, rendered Britain a 'natural' American state with a land area actually greater than the United States. In Roberts's scenario, the Americans would take Montreal and Toronto, forcing the Royal Navy to go from a blockade of the coast to a bombardment of coastal cities. Four well-armed shots would dispose of the Statue of Liberty. But the government of Lord Salisbury stops short of bombarding Manhattan.

What Roberts captures is the realisation among British policy-makers that their country could not win a protracted war. War in 1895, at best, would probably have concluded with Britain conceding the province of Quebec. The British were realists. As the Prime Minister Lord Salisbury acknowledged in 1902, the time to contain American power had been the Civil War. Only a Confederate victory forty years earlier would have reduced the power of the United States to 'manageable proportions', and, in his words, 'two such chances are not given to a nation in the course of its career' (ibid.: 165).

The war with Venezuela should have happened but it did not. The British never really contemplated a war with the United States in the period that followed. But rising states tend to be more bellicose than status quo powers, and the United States continued to regard Britain as its most likely adversary well into the inter-war period. Under the US war plan known as 'War Plan Red' (1930), which envisaged a hypothetical war between the United States and Britain, the United States would have eliminated all British land forces in Canada and driven the Royal Navy out of the North Atlantic. An invasion of Canada would have begun with massive bombing raids on key industrial targets, and it might even have involved the use of chemical weapons. This plan was signed off at the highest level by none other than

General Douglas MacArthur. Using the available blueprints for such a conflict, modern-day experts now believe the most likely outcome would have been a massive naval battle in the North Atlantic which the Royal Navy might have won, but which would have ended with Britain handing over Canada in order to keep its vital trade routes open. Only in June 1939, a few months before the Germans invaded Poland, did an internal US memo conclude that such plans were wholly inapplicable 'in the new circumstances'. But they were still placed in the archives for future use (Gerrie, 2011).

The 'moral' that the Duchess would find in this story is that declining powers should be pragmatic. The British had resigned themselves to surrendering their leadership position to the United States long before the First World War, and British leaders had little inclination to engage in further conflict after 1900. The Boer War (1899–1902) had brutally exposed Britain's isolation. Much like China today, Britain had almost no allies (the United States was the sole country to support Britain in that conflict, just as the British had been the only people to support America in the war with Spain two years earlier). Threats from Russia and fears of France (before 1904), as well as Britain's failure to strike a deal with Germany, forced Britain into America's embrace faster than might otherwise have been the case, even though they had been moving in that direction for some time. Complaints were made in Canada about British accommodation at the expense of Canadian interests as early as 1871. These complaints were revived by the settlement of the Alaskan boundary dispute on terms which the Canadians believed were unduly favourable to their neighbour. As the First World War loomed, Winston Churchill advised Australia and New Zealand that, if it came to the worst, 'the only course of the five millions of white men in the Pacific would be to seek the protection of the United States' (Barraclough, 1967: 73). In the Caribbean the 1901 Hay–Pauncefote Treaty waived British objections to American control of the Panama Canal. The United States was effectively given a free hand in Central America, which allowed it to gain financial control over the Dominican Republic and Nicaragua and to intervene militarily in Haiti and Mexico.

The British thus came to terms with the fact that war with the United States was no longer imaginable after 1900. One of the main explanations for choosing the path of appeasement is that they had engaged in one of the earliest exercises in trend analysis. One of the trends the

British identified earlier than anyone else was what the influential English journalist W.T. Stead called *The Americanisation of the World* (1902). His pamphlet's subtitle was: *The Trend of the Twentieth Century*. Trend analysis is not predictive. A trend is an unfolding event or disposition, but we know nothing of its direction or velocity. It is not fool-proof because the world is networked and influences interact with each other in complex and surprising ways (Watson and Freeman, 2013: 4). Despite these limitations, trend analysis is the best way to form strategies.

People usually mould trends into a discourse that reflects the language of the time, or its authentic idiom. A few years earlier Stead had written to Lord Morley that the 'centre of the English-speaking world' was shifting westwards, just as four years before Conan Doyle had conceded that 'the centre of gravity of the race is over here, and we have to readjust ourselves as best we can' (Barraclough, 1967: 75). Phrases such as 'the English-speaking world' and 'the centre of gravity of the race' were part of the strategic narrative. It helped, of course, that the two societies were English-speaking.

The American historian John Lukacs captures this change of attitude at one particular moment in the twentieth century. He writes of an Englishman braving the extremes of a harsh winter in New York in Christmas 1907 before travelling on to Philadelphia to visit his sister. The first skyscrapers had already been built and he will leave with the impression of a very large country whose presence in the world is larger than the people of England might think (Lukacs, 1998: 74). But Lukacs also captures how an Englishman of his time could come to terms with Britain's impending displacement by the United States as the 'dominant power' without feeling threatened, or even diminished by the prospect. For around that time a change in the reciprocal sentiments of Americans and Englishmen began to crystallise: 1907 was the 300th anniversary of the settlement at Jamestown from which many Americans dated the 'foundation' of their country. It was the year that the Anglophile Goodwin Archer spoke of an Anglo-American symbiosis (his son would later die in Britain in 1943 while serving in the US Air Force). It was also the year in which Frances Hodgson Burnett published a novel that was illustrative of the way that some Americans began to cling to their English heritage in the face of a stream of immigration from Eastern Europe.

Lukacs acknowledges that 'while on one place the shuttle was reweaving, on another plane the threads were unraveling, for the fabric of the American people was becoming less and less Anglo-Saxon' (ibid.: 76). It was a fact that Henry James noted with alarm in *The American Scene*, which constituted a farewell address to a country which he would never visit again. According to the National Census of 1910, the proportion of the population that could not speak English was nearly 25 per cent. James was not alone in worrying about the effect 'such a hotchpotch of racial ingredients' would have upon the American character. It was one of the reasons why so many East Coast Americans readily identified with England. In strategic and political terms the relationship between the two countries was never as close as the British would have liked, but many Americans invested in the relationship too—in English culture and language and literature and from the very first in English 'style'. All of this fed into what one writer calls 'a cult of Anglo-Saxonism' (Kupchan, 2011: 2–4).

Lukacs is not a sentimentalist. He acknowledges that politicians such as Woodrow Wilson, though thoroughly 'Anglicised' in terms of culture, were suspicious of British motives. When Woodrow Wilson took his country into the First World War he refused to call Britain an ally and referred to it as an 'associate' instead. If there was a partnership of sorts it was the British who had to invest much more. It was the pressure of outside events that forced 'the English and the American peoples ... to reknot their ties, to reweave their joint destinies, closer and closer together' (Lukacs, 1998: 76). The weaving continued into the inter-war years and beyond, which saw the publication of George Catlin's *Anglo-American Union* (1943) and Clarence Streit's *Union Now* (1939) which proposed a federal union of the two Atlantic democracies.

The British and Americans not only spoke in similar terms. Of possibly equal or even more importance was the fact that they were both heirs to a liberal tradition that emphasised reason and an empirically verifiable view of life. The intellectuals of both countries were intent on demystifying politics and sought to challenge the existence of 'World Spirits' or the 'historical absolutes' that had inspired their twentieth-century adversaries. The Anglo-American vision of modernity was peculiar to themselves with its juxtaposition of opposites for resolution. Both insisted on objectifying the subjective, on rationalising the irrational, conventionalising the extraordinary, intellectualising the emotional and secularising the spiritual. Neither was inclined to take seriously the more arcane notions of the German Idealists or the metaphysical speculations of Marx (Bradbury and McFarlane, 1976: 48).

In short, Britain's appeasement of the United States was normative. It had little to do with the balance of power and everything to do with intrinsic beliefs. This was especially the case in the period leading to the Second World War, when the British found themselves confronting an even more dangerous Germany. In his classic account, *War and Change in World Politics* (1981), Robert Gilpin discusses the case for peaceful accommodation with Hitler, which was put forward most famously in E.H. Carr's *The Twenty Years' Crisis*. Carr contended that appeasement was necessary to bring the system into conformity with the reality of international power. Nazi Germany's increasing strength required territories to be exchanged and for power to be redistributed in order to avoid another European war. Appeasement ultimately failed, of course, because the Germans interpreted the policy as a sign of weakness and kept raising the ante. But as Gilpin remarks, a close reading of Carr's text reveals that not even he was willing to sign away Britain's 'dominant position' in the system. Carr's preference was instead for an Anglo-American alignment, or even a *Pax Americana*, which would at least underpin the value-based 'rules' of the international system. From this analysis Gilpin concludes that the great powers have always placed values before peace and have been prepared to go to war in order to secure the rules of the international system (Gilpin, 1981: 209).

Reference was made earlier in this chapter to the hope of a Chinese colonel that the United States would emulate Britain and simply abandon its position of leadership in the international system. Unfortunately, British appeasement of the United States did not help the weaker party to preserve its dominant position. Though it may not have hastened its end, it did nothing to prevent it. Towards the end of the Second World War Churchill cut a rather pathetic figure by continuing to talk about a union of English-speaking peoples when his country's political capital had all but been exhausted. At the Bretton Woods Conference in 1944 the chief villain of the piece from the British point of view was the US Treasury Secretary Harold Dexter White, and the chief victim the most famous economist of the age, John Maynard Keynes. Both men battled for the right to establish the economic architecture that would ensure their respective post-war economic dominance. The British fought hard to keep London as the world's main financial centre and sterling as the world's principal reserve currency, and the empire as a protectionist bloc for British exports. The Americans ultimately won, writes Geoffrey Owen, because they held all the cards: by this stage Britain was practically bankrupt. White got what he wanted—two American-dominated institutions, the World Bank and the IMF, and he also managed to coerce the forty-four other nations who attended the conference to accept the US dollar as the world's reserve currency (Owen, 2013).

The United States had two agendas. The first was economic—to prevent the British from impeding an export-led recovery from the war (by favouring their own imperial markets)—while the second was political (to impoverish the UK by way of forging an American–Russian 'commission' that would run post-war Europe). Fortunately, the Cold War meant that Britain regained its importance from a US perspective. The Russians would not accept an American-dominated order, nor agree to play by the 'rules'. Truman subsequently re-established Britain as the United States' principal ally. But even Truman ensured that Britain remained an economic satellite by insisting that it repay its war debts (they were only repaid in full in 2006).

Could there have been an alternative ending to the story for the British? Happy endings are usually fantasies, and fantasy, as Freud warned, is merely 'the correction of an unsatisfying reality'. This is why novelists are always conflicted in the endings they want to give their stories. The romantic final scene of *Great Expectations* has Pip and Estella's shadows joined together, but in the original they meet on a street, exchange small talk and move on with their respective lives. The point to be drawn from this is that literature can hide ambiguities from the reader. Reader and author can both pretend that their favourite characters live happily ever after. In real life this is not usually an option. Survival is sometimes the best that can be hoped for.

From a US perspective, the analogy of Britain's loss of leadership in the international system provides little by way of comfort given the absence of a similar kind of cultural affinity between China and the United States as that which existed between the latter and Britain. The United States is unlikely to surrender its position willingly. But the fact that the United States and the UK managed to avoid war at least counters the claim of Halford Mackinder, the great geopolitical thinker, that democracies cannot think strategically except in wartime (when it is often too late). On the contrary, democracies are much better at strategic thinking than autocracies, in part because they have greater social intelligence. Because they are open societies, they tend to be more self-critical and therefore socially intelligent. It may be the case that the behaviour associated with imperial Germany and Soviet Russia—an extraordinary fixation on power relations and repeated lapses of judgement—were not incidental deficiencies but key elements of their political culture.

Strategic narratives

It is unlikely that the United States will follow Britain's example because the story that it is telling itself does not end in the same way. From the perspective of strategy, the main danger is not that the United States is telling itself a different story, but that it is telling itself so many.

In *Good Strategy/Bad Strategy*, Richard Rumelt argues that states should identify and draw upon two sources of strength when formulating a strategy. The first of these is coherence: coordinating policies and action allows an existing strength to be exploited, and for a new strength to be created through the coherence of its design. The second source of strength is the ability to reframe a competitive situation in order to create new patterns of advantage (Rumelt, 2012: 3). This was the British achievement. Once Britain had identified Germany as its principal enemy, the British pursued the only available policy option: to 'appease' the United States in order to ensure that it would remain, in the worst-case scenario, a neutral observer if war broke out. Britain reframed its strategic narrative by introducing ideas such as 'English-speaking unions', 'racial cousins' and later 'special relationships'. An Anglo-American war became improbable because it was impossible to imagine.

In Daniel Dennett's words, there are inevitabilities in life but the list of such inevitabilities has consistently grown shorter (Dennett, 2003: 54). We have more and more choice because we can discern patterns of avoidance and prevention; life as a consequence is becoming more 'evitable'. Dennett quotes Nicholas Maxwell who defines freedom as 'the capacity to achieve what is of value in a range of circumstances' (ibid.: 302). Circumstances really did change for the British. Not only were they displaced by the United States, but the rise of Germany also forced Britain to rethink its commitment to Europe. Disputes can be taken to arbitration, as was the case with Britain during the Venezuela crisis of 1895. Life can always be looked at in different ways, and it is always possible to break with familiar habits of thought such as the balance of power which had been central to British strategic thinking for centuries.

However, every action almost always leads to unforeseen consequences, and the solution to one problem can often result in new problems emerging. Dennett is not an optimist. People always have the ability to tell themselves a less positive story.

In his comparison of the two dominant powers of the past 200 years, Fareed Zakaria argues that Britain's decision to abandon the balance of power and to yield primacy to the United States enabled it to continue to succeed in winning its wars, and that Britain retained some political influence long after surrendering its economic position (Zakaria, 2011: 237). As Thomas Brimelow put it in 1946, the Soviet Union knew that Britain was not yet out of the game; if not the strongest of its opponents it was probably the most astute. 'The one quality which most disquiets the Soviet government is the ability which they attribute to us to get others to do our fighting for us ... They respect not us, but our ability to collect friends' (*The Spectator*, 15 Nov. 1986). This boast was not without some foundation. 'There was no other government,' Henry Kissinger later recalled in his memoirs, 'which we would have dealt with so openly, exchanged ideas so freely, or in effect permitted to participate in our own deliberations' (Kissinger, 1982: 282).

But as Zakaria concedes, twenty-first century America is very different from late nineteenth century Britain. Its economic base is far stronger than Britain's was. All indicators suggest that it will remain strong even after it has been overtaken as the largest economy in the world by China, and even once it has been overtaken by India (though this is not likely to happen for many years to come). The real challenge is political: there is no other western partner (not even Germany) on which the US could rely to share the burden of being the dominant power; it will have no real incentive, as a result, to yield first place to China as gracefully as Colonel Liu Ming hopes. In these circumstances the demands made upon it are likely to prove far more challenging than the demands faced by the British, and it is unclear whether the United States will willingly adjust and adapt to other powers as they grow in influence, or whether it will be able to respond to new shifts in what Hillary Clinton called the new 'geometry of global power' (Sanger, 2012: 423). 'Can Washington truly embrace a world with a diversity of voices and viewpoints? Can it thrive in a world it cannot dominate?' (Zakaria, 2011: 38). The United States has identified the main trend in world politics, the rise of China, and it has not sought to oppose it. But to return to Rumelt's critique, it has failed to re-frame a competitive situation in a language intelligible to everyone else.

One of the problems with contemporary US policy is the fact that the United States has viewed China in several different lights since the late 1980s, and as a result it has told itself many different (and often conflicting) stories. After Tiananmen Square the United States emphasised the ideological challenge that China posed, as well as its rejection of democracy, its state-directed model of capitalism, and apparent Chinese 'opt-outs' from the normative consensus on human rights. Max Boot accused China of reaping a 'dictatorship premium' which allowed it to invest in countries and to trade with regimes that were criticised internationally for their 'crimes against humanity'.

After 9/11 China became a partner in the war on terror. But when the Bush administration first came to power in 2001 it had identified the country as one of the main threats to the United States, and this cast a shadow over US–Chinese relations. Some neo-conservatives talked of the long-term goal with regard to China as 'regime change'. The mantra in Washington after the invasion of Iraq was: 'After Baghdad, Beijing' (Kagan, 2003: 38). One influential Pentagon spokesman, perhaps half in jest, even spoke of the invasion as a 'warm-up for China' (Tertrais, 2004: 106). As they faltered in Iraq the Americans told a less confrontational story and even coined a new term 'Chinamerica'. China saved half of its GDP; America borrowed money to pay for its global ambitions. Both powers were locked in a cynical but mutually useful embrace. When the economic crisis of 2008 threatened the US economy, the China Banking Regulatory Commission was asked whether it would continue to buy US government debt. '[T]here is nothing much we can do,' replied one of its officials, 'for everyone, including China, it is the only option' (Prasad, 2014: 117). All emerging markets need safe liquid assets with which to defend their own currencies from volatile capital flows: the more troubled the times the greater the need for assets that can be turned into cash. While it may seem unwise for China to buy so much US government debt, the absence of a better alternative makes for a perverse kind of stability.

However, the interdependence and cooperation suggested in the term 'Chinamerica' was an illusion which was bad for both countries (it encouraged the United States to overspend and China to take the United States for granted). Since the financial crisis of 2008 the Chinese have been looking to non-Western markets and hedging against the dollar by investing in countries and assets outside the United States. The 'great decoupling' may already have begun. When Washington came close to defaulting on its debt repayments after Congress shut down the government for several weeks in September 2013 it was the Chinese who stood to lose most. With more than $3 trillion of dollar foreign exchange reserves, $1.3 trillion of which are held in US treasuries, Chinese officials openly began talking of the need to build 'a de-Americanised world (*The Telegraph*, 2013). Economic nationalism in the United States is also on the rise, with Chinese multinationals such as the telecommunications giant Huawei now forbidden from buying into the US market, and the veto of a take-over of an American oil major UNACOL by China's state-owned China National Offshore Oil Corporation (CNOOC). One particularly egregious example of American nationalist rhetoric was a film released in the summer of 2012, *Death by China*, and its warning: 'China is the only major power that is systematically preparing to kill Americans.' The film featured a map of the United States stamped in the centre with a dagger engraved with the words: 'Made in China' (Leonard, 2012: 19).

There are also some less than encouraging signs that the world is moving towards greater protectionism. As *The Economist* has noted, multilateral governance is growing progressively weaker. Russia is instituting new measures to circumvent World Trade Organisation (WTO) rules despite being a member of the WTO. The United States is seeking to establish a trans-Atlantic Free Trade Area and a Trans Pacific Partnership (TPP), a free-trade agreement intended to bolster trade with its allies and non-Chinese partners including Vietnam, the most vocal of China's critics.

In July 2013 *The Economist* expressed grave misgivings about this proliferation of regional trade agreements on the basis that they signalled the fractionalisation of the global economy. It warned that a slowdown in China, India and Russia could lead to the sort of international tensions that countries traditionally displace by engaging in conflict:

> A century ago the world's last great era of trade integration ended with a war and ushered in a generation of economic nationalism and international conflict ... Whether or not the world can build on a remarkable era of growth will depend in large part on whether the new giants tread a path towards greater global co-operation—or stumble, fall and, in the worst case, fight. (*The Economist*, 2013c)

The 'Pivot' is at the centre of contemporary US policy in Asia—an attempt to revive America's alliances in Asia and to rebalance its naval presence in the Pacific, partly due to its fears with regard to the modernisation of China's armed forces. However, China's modernisation programme was likely to have been prompted, at least in part, by the apparent success of the invasion of Iraq which had been preceded by what the Chinese took to be a series of 'provocations' such as the Taiwan Straits Crisis (1996), the bombing of the Chinese embassy in Belgrade (1999) and the Hainan Incident in April 2001 when an American EP-3 spy plane collided with a Chinese fighter jet and was forced to land.

The Pivot is intended to redress the imbalance of power that arose as a result of the Bush administration's pursuit of the war on terror. The Bush administration became more focused on Central Asia than the Asia-Pacific region, leading US experts to complain that this was the 'lost decade', echoing Churchill's famous description of the 1930s as 'the years that the locusts had eaten'.

The United States is re-engaging with its allies and re-animating its alliances and adding to its existing military assets. F-35s are being despatched to Japan (2017), attack submarines will be based in Guam and the number of ships in-theatre will be increased from fifty to sixty by 2020. The rebalancing is not intended to create a pretext for China to overreact, but is instead designed to assure the United States' allies that it will enforce the rules of the road. Its present policy thus seeks to hedge against any attempt to challenge freedom of navigation, a key interest of the US Navy since it first engaged the Barbary pirates in the 1790s. Its purpose is clear: the United States intends to remain in the Western Pacific as well as to remain an East Asian military power. However, the Obama administration has done little to refocus its attention on what a real Pivot would probably demand: scaling down military commitments in the Middle East and coming to some agreement with a re-assertive Russia (the Bismarckian ploy—the 'grand bargain' that might rob China of a key strategic card). It thus remains to be seen whether the Pivot can achieve the objectives it is designed to realise.

At different times since the end of the Cold War the United States has consequently chosen to see China as a trading partner (fast-tracking its membership of the WTO), a strategic partner in the war on terror and a potential global partner in a G2 world. Hopes of the latter rose when Obama held a meeting with Hu Jin Tao for the first time in

2009 from which the rest of the world was excluded (other states were also excluded when the two met again at the Copenhagen Environment Summit). But hopes of US–Chinese cooperation in a G2 world faded early in 2011 as tensions between the two powers mounted and the Chinese became more assertive regionally especially in the East and South China Seas. It is now unclear which of the two powers would be willing to be the junior partner in such a relationship. Both powers recognise that they are strategic competitors, but both remain fearful of where the competition might lead. The most probable outcome is that China and the United States will try to agree to disagree on some issues, while working together on others.

In the absence of mutual trust between the two countries it is difficult to see how a partnership could ever arise. Trust has to be earned. Few great powers have ever trusted each other. But some were able to find ways of working together for the common good. There is an enormous disparity of views about the potential for US–Chinese cooperation. Commentators like Henry Kissinger believe that the United States and China can be part of a 'common enterprise', and the former US Treasury official Fred Bergsten has even proposed a US–China condominium to run the global economy. Yet it is difficult to see how two of the world's greatest polluters will be able to cooperate on climate change. Some Chinese analysts, on the other hand, claim that the international system has already become bipolar, something which could encourage cooperation between the two powers. However, the same dynamic could also provoke a protracted conflict between them, particularly as both states hold an exaggerated sense of their own exceptionalism (Leonard, 2008: 19).

The main priority from a US perspective is that the normative rules of the system continue to be upheld. As Obama stated in 2011, although the United States has welcomed the rise of China, it wants to ensure that China rises in a way that reinforces international norms and rules, and enhances security and peace (Condon, 2011). The problem is that there is a growing disbelief that China has much interest in underwriting those norms, still less promoting them. This concern can be found in the Pentagon's 2011 'Annual Report to Congress', a large part of which provides a detailed description of the threat that China poses. The Department of Defense (DoD) does not expect China to reinforce international norms, and if China fails to do so then it will inevitably be regarded as a threat to US interests. There has been little change in US strategy towards China in the twenty-five-year period since it began to hedge against China's rise. The 2012 'Quadrennial Defense Review' posits a world in which the post-war order continues to dissolve slowly and great power competition returns, probably framed by a return to the balance of power politics the British abandoned in their own relationship with the United States after 1900.

In search of a grand strategy

The lack of coherence in US decision-making has further compounded the problems raised by the absence of a consistent strategic narrative. Gary Hart defines coherence as a single framework of purpose and direction in which "random, and not so random, events can be interpreted, given meaning, and then responded to as required" (Hart, 2004: 33). If this definition is accepted, then American policy is clearly incoherent at the policy-making level.

This is all the more surprising because the United States developed a coherent strategy for dealing with China's rise. The problem of incoherence has only emerged now that it has risen. With the end of the Cold War no administration thought it either desirable or possible to contain China. Instead, the United States decided to hedge against its rise. In the words of 'The National Security Strategy' (2006): 'we seek to encourage China to make the right strategic choices for its people while we hedge against other possibilities' (Tunsjø, 2008: 42). In its 'Annual Report to Congress', the DoD insisted that the United States must 'hedge against the unknown' (ibid.: 43). If the unpredictable is now a permanent factor in international politics, as was not always the case during the Cold War, what is unpredictable by definition must be hedged against. The United States sought to accomplish this by folding China into the existing security architecture. This was the logic behind 'fast-tracking' its entry into the WTO. Its intention was to encourage China to become a responsible stakeholder in the international system. Stakeholders may not be allies, but they do share common interests.

The problem with hedging is that it cannot eliminate risks even though it is able to reduce them. Companies tend to hedge against risks that are important to their central business, such as currency fluctuations. They hedge in order to improve or maintain their own competitiveness, but the competition between companies is different from that between countries (ibid.: 107–19). When they fail to compete, companies often go out of business; countries rarely do. But whether hedging policies are long term or short, prudential or opportunistic (whether they involve hedging against the bad or exploiting the good), a society is usually only as secure as it feels itself to be.

Despite coming to terms with China's rise, there is little agreement in the United States with regard to how to deal with China now that it has risen. Rumelt believes that the United States is simply marking time. His main criticism is that while the United States is good at articulating strategic goals or sub-goals it is not good at thinking of ways to achieve them, leading to 'incoherence'. A 'strategy' becomes incoherent when a government mistakes goals for the strategy itself. Every strategic objective set, insists Rumelt, should involve a specific understanding of what is needed to succeed, or a country will merely end up setting itself a series of performance goals.

Obama's first 'National Security Strategy' (2010) was largely a list of rather vague aspirations. These include 'promoting a just international order', 'investing in the capacity of strong capable partners', 'accelerating suitable development' and 'strengthening the power of our example'. The 2012 'Quadrennial Defense Review' was even more ambiguous. Although the review claims that it is 'strategy-driven', the section on China merely concluded that the United States should adapt to its rise and monitor whether its rise threatens international norms. The DoD has chosen to adopt a 'watching brief' on China's Armed Forces modernisation programme. It hopes to 'encourage' Beijing to make the right strategic choices by reducing distrust and increasing the dialogue between the two militaries. Thus, on the basis of this documentation at least, there does not appear to be a great deal of coherence between the State Department, the DoD and the White House.

It is difficult to assess the quality of a strategy if a challenge is not adequately defined, and if a strategy's quality cannot be assessed then it is impossible to reject a bad strategy or improve a good one. A good strategy defines the key strategic challenge and identifies the most realistic ways of meeting it. It offers a clear pathway to higher performance. 'Bad strategy' involves setting 'blue sky objectives', and offering simple statements or re-statements of the desired state of affairs while usually skipping over altogether the annoying fact that no one has a clue how to get there.

However, there is one strategic principle which does seem to elicit broad agreement. This is called the 'Thucydidean trap', which has become a buzzword in the debate about the rise of China. In the absence of a coherent strategic narrative on which everyone can agree the United States has ended up telling itself a very old story which draws its inspiration from the ancient Greeks. The fact that we would seem (if we believe the strategists) to have fallen into the trap many times before clearly suggests that we actually learn very little from history, or that we learn the wrong lessons.

The Thucydidean trap

> The general war of 1914 overtook me expounding Thucydides to Balliol undergraduates ... and then suddenly my understanding was illuminated. The experiences we were having in our world now had been experienced in his world by Thucydides already.
>
> (Arnold Toynbee, *My View of History*, 1948)

Western military commentators have been referring to Thucydides for a long time. He was, after all, the first military historian as well as the first political scientist. As Victor Davis Hanson points out, Thucydides has always been popular with contemporary security analysts, as is reflected in the vast range of scholarly works bearing titles such as *War and Democracy: A Comparative Study of the Korean War and the Peloponnesian War* and *Hegemonic Rivalry: From Thucydides to the Nuclear Age*. After 9/11 Hanson published his own book, *A War Like No Other*, which informed the reader that the struggle between Athens and Sparta provides striking military lessons for the present—a war involving terror and dirty fighting, forcing democracy down the throats of sometimes unwilling states, domestic and cultural upheavals at home brought on by the frustrations of fighting abroad. '[C]ontemporary opponents and supporters alike of the so-called war on terror have all looked back to find their own Thucydides,' Hanson added, and we are just beginning to do so with respect to the possibility of war between the world's two greatest powers (Hanson, 2005: xvi).

Anyone who has spent a significant amount of time studying the classics will recognise that the lessons learned from the past are rarely applied in practice. However, despite the fact that the classics tend to be misread and abused to suit particular circumstances, there is a reason why modern authors keep returning to the Greeks, namely their inductive reasoning and powers of insight. Although their ideas can and have been reformulated in modern scientific language, the Greeks were the first to observe the patterns of life that remain important in terms of how we understand the world. In *The Savage Mind* the French anthropologist Levi-Strauss remarked that scientific explanation does not rest in the reduction of the complex to the simple, rather it consists in a substitution of a complexity more intelligible for one which is less. But simplicity has a pervasive clarity of its own which is why Thucydides' famous trap is often used when considering the dilemma of how a status quo power can avoid coming into conflict with a rising one.

The Thucydidean trap, also known in social science-speak as a 'security dilemma', would certainly seem to apply in the case of the United States and China. As China's capabilities and power continue to grow, the United States will be nervous about what this portends for both regional security and its own primacy in the Western Pacific. And as long as the United States remains in East Asia China will become increasingly anxious about how much the United States will invest in constraining its own military ambitions. 'This is the nature of the beast ... Both sides must manage the dilemma in ways that prevent it from degenerating into open conflict' (Tellis, 2013).

In an article on the future of power in the *Bulletin of the American Academy of Arts and Sciences* in the spring of 2011, the Harvard Professor Joe Nye expressed the hope that the United States would have time to manage the rise of China without succumbing to the second part of the trap: overreacting because of fear (Nye, 2011). In a comment in the *Financial Times*, Nye's Harvard colleague, Graham Allison, also cast China and America in the role of Athens and Sparta. What is unbalancing the system, he argued, is the speed of China's rise and America's relative decline as a result of the 2008 financial crisis, and of the two China's rise is perhaps the more destabilising (*Financial Times*, 21 Aug. 2012). Within a generation a nation whose GDP was smaller than Spain's has become the second largest economy in the world.

Thucydides' appeal is not limited to politicians and academic historians. Ever since George Marshall claimed that great power competition could only be understood by reading Thucydides, senior officers have also been encouraged to take the Greek historian seriously. He has been on the Marine Corps' reading list since 1972. So it is not surprising that General Dempsey, the chairman of the US Joint Chiefs of Staff, should have remarked in May 2012 that his principal responsibility was to ensure that the United States did not 'fall into the

Thucydidean trap' (*Financial Times*, 21 Aug. 2012). Even the military is now 'on message'.

The US military is concerned about falling into the Thucydidean trap due to the steady erosion of America's position in the Western Pacific. According to a Carnegie Foundation report, the United States will 'probably' lose its dominant position or see it severely compromised within the next twenty years (*The New York Times*, 1 May 2013). However, the report's authors expressed the belief that the economic interdependence of the two powers could prevent the trap from being sprung.

Although the authors of the report claimed that the United States and China could avoid falling into the trap due to the economic interdependence between the two powers, they also put forward three scenarios describing how events might turn out very differently. In the first China's rise continues undiminished and America goes into economic free-fall with stagnant economic growth and continually declining defence budgets. In the end it has to concede control of the Western Pacific by 2030, leaving Japan to reach a separate deal with Beijing. This would be the worst-case scenario—unlikely but not inconceivable. Instead of resisting China's rise the United States deals itself out of the game. The status quo power is unable or unwilling to defend its position; the rising power rises largely unopposed.

The second scenario offers a quite different future. China's growth falters; the technological gap with the United States is not closed. The same military deficiencies identified today remain unaddressed. The United States recovers its nerve and energy; the empire strikes back. It manages to maintain defence spending at 4 per cent of GDP. In this scenario the status quo power remains pre-eminent while the rising power fades like an athlete who peaks too soon. The report concluded that this outcome was unlikely—the United States would simply lack the financial means or technological capacity to trump the Chinese.

In the third scenario America's position continues to erode, but the country does not decline either. It is still able to compete, as can a rejuvenated Japan. Here the trap waits to be sprung, triggered by an incident in the South China Seas, or diplomatic tensions which are allowed to translate into open competition. But both powers manage to avoid war—just. The tensions between them prove to be manageable. The status quo power still retains a marginal but important advantage: the rising power is not sufficiently strong or internally cohesive to take too many risks. This is the scenario that the report considers to be the most likely, although its authors also admitted that the situation was too 'volatile' to make a definitive prediction.

Client states

Our understanding of history's lessons is constrained by the metaphors at our disposal. A metaphor is not a correspondence, but an analogy: it translates the strange into the familiar by transforming the experience into an idea. This is why metaphors do so much of our thinking for us—they communicate complex ideas and channel our thoughts along certain predetermined axes. Traps, for example, come in many forms, and falling into them can often be fatal. But a close reading of Thucydides reveals that the actual trap in question is more complex than many suppose.

Thucydides argued that neither Athens nor Sparta wanted to go to war against each other. But their respective allies persuaded them that war was inevitable, which led both powers to try to seize a decisive early advantage. They made this decision because they listened to their client states. The war began when Athens came to the aid of Corcyra (a city without allies) which was then at war with one of Sparta's allies, Corinth. The Athenians made the fatal mistake of listening to what the Corcyrans told them: namely, that they were already at war with Sparta. The Corinthians, on the other hand, warned Sparta that if it did not invade Attica then it would be attacked by the Athenians. The Corinthians were especially contemptuous of the Spartans' failure to appreciate the real dangers of their position. They accused them of failing to consider 'what sort of antagonists you will encounter in the Athenians, how widely, how absolutely different from yourselves' (Thucydides 1.3.70).

Can the United States and China avoid being pulled into conflict by their respective allies? In an article in *The New York Times* in August 2013, the historian Paul Kennedy expressed the opinion that they might be reluctant to be dragged into a confrontation with one another because of their shared fear of the unforeseen consequences of any change in the current balance of power. Can we look forward, therefore, to a great peace, similar to that which Europe enjoyed after 1815 (*International Herald Tribune*, 14 Aug. 2013)?

Kennedy acknowledges that wars might occur in the future. However, he argues that these wars are likely to be localised or quarantined (as the Great Powers were able to quarantine the protagonists in the last of the Balkan Wars in 1913). But this will require China and the United States to show great self-restraint: 'Their job is simply to hold firm the iron frame that keeps the international system secure.' Kennedy's argument is consistent with the prevailing pragmatism of the Western world in terms of international relations. Few in the West continue to hope for a new world order. Consequence-management is the abiding principle of international security. States prefer to go to war against non-state actors who threaten the system, not against other states that may want to change it.

Yet none of the Great Powers wanted war in the period leading to the First World War either. War broke out in 1914 because the Great Powers ignored Thucydides' warning with regard to maintaining control over their client states. Russia, some historians argue, allowed Serbia to provoke Austria–Hungary in 1914; others accuse Germany of issuing a blank cheque to Vienna to retaliate against what it chose to see after the assassination of the Archduke as Serbian 'aggression.' Client states are never as pliable as their patrons expect. There is a tendency for clients to pull their patrons into needless conflicts because a patron overestimates its ally's strategic importance. The relationship often creates a vicious cycle of misjudgement, as it did with Russia and Serbia, and Germany and Austria–Hungary in 1914.

This is the trap that the United States and China need to avoid. The United States is currently seeking to reinvigorate its regional alliances as part of its efforts to sustain 'global leadership'. It is in a strong position to achieve this goal. None of the major regional powers, with the exception of China and North Korea, fear the United States in the way that some fear the rise of China. The US Pivot is seen by many (though not by China) as a stabilising factor in Asian politics. But the United States should not take its allies for granted as they may have to make some difficult choices in the near future in response to China's growing power and influence. However, unlike the city-states discussed by Thucydides and the client states of the European Great Powers in 1914, none of the United States' or China's regional allies would appear at the moment to want to embroil their patrons in war.

It is certainly not in South Korea's interests and probably never has been. Seoul at present enjoys both a 'comprehensive co-operative partnership' with China and an alliance with the United States and relies on both to secure it against its northern neighbour. The United States is also trying to rebalance the relationship by redeploying its forces south of the Han River and transferring its wartime operational control to Seoul by the end of 2015.

North Korea is another matter. No one quite knows its grand designs, if it has any, and it is both unpredictable and provocative. In March 2010 the sinking of a South Korean corvette which was torpedoed by the North Koreans with the loss of forty-six sailors threw this into particularly stark relief. The Chinese declined to accept the evidence and insisted on being 'even-handed' between North and South Korea, a decision which Obama condemned at the time as based on 'willful blindness' (Sanger, 2012). They claimed that a Russian investigation had concluded the ship had been sunk by a sea mine.

The episode was indicative of the chief problem the two powers face in that they have different mental maps. The United States continues to adopt a confrontational stance in insisting that it is China's responsibility to exercise more control over Ponyang given that it has concluded a formal defence treaty with North Korea. Jonathan Fenby's book *Tiger Head, Snake Tails: China Today* is an example of a widely-held western belief that China should flex its muscles and rein in its ally. Whether it is prepared to do so will be a test of whether it is ready to become a responsible great power (Fenby, 2012). China's apparent reluctance to play the role is all the more surprising for those Americans who are well aware of the deep misgivings the Chinese have about their ally. And the North Koreans make no secret of their dislike of their larger neighbour. The 200,000 Chinese soldiers who died in the Korean War barely receive a mention in the museums celebrating the 'heroic sacrifices' made in the Korean War. Mao's son was one of the volunteers; he never made it back.

From a US perspective the Kim dynasty in North Korea is a quasi-religious personality cult based around an eternal president who has been dead for nearly twenty years, and China's alliance with North Korea is viewed as counter-productive in the same way as imperial Germany's alliance with Austria–Hungary (the joke in Berlin was that being allied to Vienna was like being shackled to a corpse). The only difference is that North Korea is far more lethal and powerful than Austria–Hungary ever was. It claims, after all, that its missiles will soon be able to hit the United States and there is mounting evidence that its *Hwaseong-13*s now under development may eventually be able to do just that (*The Times*, 6 Nov. 2013). The situation, one must conclude, is unpredictable in part because there is no one dominant interest or position or even narrative. In North Korea the pro-Chinese faction confronts the ultra-nationalists who are deeply sceptical of China's support for the regime should it come to a crisis. In China there are those in the military who see the regime as the only card they can play to prevent reunification on South Korea's terms. Others are concerned that North Korea might misjudge the situation, and provoke an American response to the detriment of regional stability.

The United States wants China to exert greater influence over North Korea because the US administration does not believe that the regime can be trusted. After all, it broke its agreement with Clinton in 1994 to abandon work on graphite nuclear reactors capable of producing weapons-grade plutonium; and a US-DPRK Agreed Framework broke down in 2002–3 over allegations that the North had a highly enriched uranium (HEU) programme. Some in Washington would now like the international community to name North Korea as a money-laundering state in the hope that even tougher sanctions will be applied and the regime weakened further, perhaps even fatally.

The Chinese position seems to be consistent on one issue. It does not want an American presence on the Yalu River any more than it did in 1950 when the Chinese 'volunteers' were first sent into battle. 'Win a quick victory if you can; if you can't, win a slow one,' Mao told the Chinese Commander Marshal Peng. The armistice between the two Korean states is now sixty years old, and there is little reason to believe that a permanent peace treaty will be concluded in the near future. China knows that North Korea would not prevail in any conflict with South Korea and the United States. However, the Chinese military believes that it is in Washington's strategic interest to undermine China–North Korean ties in the hope that a reunited Korean state could serve as a strategic front in a new cold war. All of the parties involved also seek to avoid the chaos that would inevitably result from the collapse of the North Korean regime.

The contending positions that China and the United States have adopted with regard to North Korea is largely a product of their divergent worldviews, or different ways of understanding the world. G.E.R. Lloyd, who is an expert in Chinese and Greek thought, argues that there is a fundamental difference between the Greek and Chinese traditions. Whereas the Greek tradition tended to focus on fundamental questions and was prepared to countenance extreme and radical solutions, Chinese thought tended to prioritise practicalities and the ways in which practical measures could best be put to use. Lloyd claims that this difference derived from differences in socio-political context. The Warring States period of China lacked the plurality of constitutions and political organisations that characterised the Greek city-states. Moreover, while the Greeks argued in the marketplace or the Assembly, Chinese sages argued at court, a milieu which demanded less polemical and confrontational forms of argumentation (Shankman and Durrant, 2000: 6).

The confrontational position adopted by the United States also has a socio-cultural and socio-political context. Indeed, much of US policy is partly derived from the nature of the US political system, culture and institutions: from an agonistic legal system with the jury at its heart, a bi-party system of parliamentary government and a commercial marketplace in ideas. An example of the last is religion. Chinese religious systems such as Buddhism and Daoism have usually co-existed peacefully; they have survived side by side in relative harmony for centuries. (It is communism that has proved more intolerant of Tibetan Buddhism since the occupation in 1959, and perhaps the country has always been ambivalent in its attitude to Islam in the north-west.) In the United States, by contrast, we find a highly competitive 'marketplace' of religious beliefs (the description is Jefferson's): over 300 sects and churches compete for the attention (and usually money) of the believers, each claiming to represent the 'truth'. Confrontation, in other words, is the American default mode, its unique cultural style.

If these differences in cultural reasoning are acknowledged, then it is possible to find merit in both the US and the Chinese positions with regard to North Korea. The North Korean regime is far more unstable than it was during the Cold War, when it was able to rely on Soviet subsidies. Due to the collapse of its economy and state distribution system in the 1990s North Koreans have been forced to produce their own food and to trade in an illicit black market. Hundreds of thousands of North Koreans cross and re-cross the border with China every year in search of jobs, returning home with DVD players and discs of South Korean TV shows. Many families have home computers with miniature micro-sticks that contain a library of smuggled books and films. This has steadily eroded the regime's ability to control how its citizens think. But this does not mean that the regime will collapse in the immediate future. Its refusal to reform is vital for its survival, as any reforms similar to perestroika would likely result in the regime's collapse. According to Andrei Lankov, the best way to continue to facilitate 'the slow-motion erosion of the Kim family dictatorship' is to leave sanctions in place and keep North Korea open to the influence of the outside world while preparing for its inevitable collapse (Lankov, 2013).

Yet the US position with regard to North Korea is also understandable. North Korea could unravel quickly if a calculated act of aggression was to end in a colossal miscalculation. If tension escalated the Japanese and South Korean stock markets could collapse within weeks. Foreign workers might begin leaving in droves. North Korean cyber-attacks could paralyse South Korea's public services. The Japanese and Chinese navies might shadow each other before coming into conflict. Henry Kissinger is not alone in believing that the real danger is of an accident, incident or simply miscalculation on the Korean Peninsula, and he is particularly critical of the fact that the United States and China do not appear to have a plan to deal with that situation should it arise.

The other potential regional flashpoint is of course Taiwan. There is no formal defence agreement between the United States and Taiwan, only a requirement by the United States to take 'appropriate action' in the event of a Chinese attack (*The Economist*, 22 Oct. 2009). It has always been assumed that any attack on the island would be met by a strong conventional response. The Chinese continue to see Taiwan as the main US strategic asset in the region. In the long term China aims to remove the island state from the strategic equation, first by making deterrence unviable, and secondly by imposing penalty costs on any American attempt to prevent the Chinese from muscling in.

But many Taiwanese take a less confrontational stance than the Americans. Some in Taiwan are even beginning to question the costs and benefits of the US link. The situation may even resolve itself. There is a growing osmosis between the island and the Chinese mainland, with Taiwanese investments in China now accounting for 83 per cent of Taiwan's total outward direct investment. Since 2009 the Taiwanese have opened many of their high-tech industries to investors from mainland China. A Taiwanese defence minister has even stated that China stands to gain more from 'buying' Taiwan than it does from attacking it (ibid.). The relationship between the Taiwanese military and the People's Liberation Army (PLA) has also grown increasingly close. In 2012, for example, a controversy erupted when a retired Taiwanese

Air Force general (a former deputy chief of the General Staff and president of the National Defence University) claimed that both the Taiwanese military and the PLA were the 'armed forces of China' because they both shared the same goal of unification. Remarks such as these, which are not uncommon, reflect the fact that most senior Taiwanese officers are *waishengren*, Han Chinese immigrants who came to the island after 1945 and who have retained a strong attachment to the mainland ever since.

However, the future of Taiwan, and the course that US–Chinese relations are likely to take over this disputed territory, is far from clear. One writer suggests that China's influence is likely to increase while that of the United States declines, something which is likely to prove problematic given that Taiwan is now a vital part of the US Navy's plan with regard to the maritime containment of the Chinese mainland along the first island chain (Stuart, 2012: 146). As the Chinese military position improves it is possible that it will grow more impatient.

It is entirely possible that a renewed crisis on the Korean Peninsula or over Taiwan could lead to war between the world's two greatest powers. The need to counter this possibility is increasingly urgent because the Pacific Rim has become one of the world's most dangerous strategic fault lines. We should indeed be concerned about the possibility of an accidental war but remember this book is about the logic of conflict, not the contingent events that often trigger it.Great power wars occur for a reason; they have the Aristotelian unities: preconditions, precipitants and triggers. The precondition of a Sino-American war is most likely to be the rivalry between a dominant power and one that seeks to take its place; the precipitant, China's attempts to undermine the relationship between the US and its allies/client states; but the trigger could well be naval spats, bullying that goes too far.

This again raises the question of social intelligence. The strategic environment is a complex system. We interact with complex systems very successfully most of the time, but we do so by managing them rather than claiming to understand them. People and states watch for what happens and then respond as quickly and imaginatively as they can to the rise of some powers and the decline of others, and the emergence over time of new threats, risks and qualitatively different challenges. There is an endless iterative interaction that acknowledges that we do not know what the system will do. We never know what will happen. What we have to guide us is social intelligence, and it is social intelligence which provides the basis for grand strategy. There is some evidence that the Chinese have appreciated this fact for a much longer period of time than the West.

Outmanoeuvring the United States

> [A]ccording to Chinese thought, a great power imbalance contains within itself not merely the potential, but the propensity for a great rebalancing. If one understands ... and can shape the energetic forces that are already playing out, conflict itself may be avoided, even as the desired outcome is achieved.
>
> (Zolli and Healy, 2012: 212–13)

'Mentalities' (or different cultural styles of reasoning) and their role in how states behave have rarely been discussed in the literature largely because they are an inherent and often unacknowledged part of Western and Chinese discourse. In the West, for instance, those who take risks and succeed in defiance of the odds can often receive praise for doing so. One example of this is Captain McWhirr in Joseph Conrad's novella *Typhoon* who steers his ship directly into a tropical storm, rather than sailing around it, and manages to survive. He later considers the alternative: [S]uppose I went swinging off my course and came in two days late, and they asked me: "Where have you been all that time, Captain?" What could I say to that? "Went around to dodge the bad weather," I would say. "It must've been dam' bad," they would say. "Don't know," I would have to say; "I've dodged clear of it."' Those who avoid taking risks tend to be less celebrated in the West than those that do so. In the same way, many in the West admire Alexander for taking his army as far as the Indus Valley and back (though the retreat was a disaster), and Hannibal for taking his elephants over the Alps (though he lost most of them in the process, which might not have been the case if he had taken the coastal route).

People who take such risks have traditionally been viewed very differently in China. They are an example, in Sun Tzi's words, of 'emptiness'. Sun Tzi sought to illustrate why the indirect approach is the preferred one. The economist John Kay prefers the term 'obliquity'. In general, he writes, the oblique approach recognises that complex objectives tend to be imperfectly defined and that the nature of the objectives and the means of achieving them can only be learned during a process of experiment and discovery. The oblique approach delivers the best results (Kay, 2011: 3–4). According to Kay obliquity is only a process of adaptation and discovery. Those who impose a direct solution to problems do not always approach complex relationships between objectives, goals and actions. Those who take the direct approach may be more vulnerable than those who do not. The 'victory at all costs' culture often destroys the organisations that foster it.

One of the defining features of Chinese thought is its emphasis on managing affairs by identifying the logic behind them and going with the flow. It is this, according to Francois Jullien, which is the great Chinese 'originality' (Jullien, 1995: 35). In Chinese thought the logic of strategy demands that the propensity inherent in events is exploited. Since the time of Sun Tzi Chinese strategic thought has emphasised the need to adapt to the movements of the enemy rather than to confront an enemy in a direct battle. The advice in *The Art of War* is not to meet an opposing army in a 'decisive' engagement but to exploit the propensity for conflict or cooperation so that the battle is already won before the two forces actually meet. Everything results from internal developments which require no external causalities to trigger them off.

Sun Tzi's advice with regard to seeking a confrontation with the enemy only after the war has been won is very different from the emphasis in Western strategic thought on bringing the enemy to battle early. Battle always involves risk and should never constitute the decisive moment on which the war turns. The core collision between forces should always be an outcome, not a determinant (Jullien, 1999: 37). From a Chinese perspective, human factors such as courage are merely part of a situation, rather than an independent variable. A soldier is brave not because of innate virtue, but because he is forced to be brave due to the circumstances in which he finds himself. As Sun Tzi writes, a good general 'expects victory from the potential born of disposition [propensity] not from the men placed under his command' (Jullien, 1995: 30).

The Chinese word '*shi*', which is sometimes translated as 'power' or 'potential', refers to an inherent potentiality or tendency, an unfolding of a situation which can be foreseen or managed. States that follow the flow of events will be victorious. There are many ways in which China could adopt this strategy: placing pressure on America's allies to distance themselves from Washington, attacking the US technological edge through cyber-warfare or out-manoeuvring the United States globally through economic largesse (in 2010 China become the largest capital provider in the world, outspending even the World Bank). Another limited war with India (similar to that of 1962) could even rob the United States of its great prize—a truly democratic partner in Asia.

Unlike Germany in 1914, which was seeking to escape a strategic endgame of its own making (it had effectively encircled itself), China will not necessarily seek to 'break out' of its perceived encirclement by US allies by gambling and possibly losing everything on one throw of the dice. The Chinese realise that the best strategy draws on a shrewd understanding of the possibilities inherent in the circumstances of the moment. Or as Jullien puts it, their preference is not to avoid confrontation but to dispense with it altogether.

Jullien has sought to provide a perspective that enables us 'to envisage our thought from without' (Jullien, 1995: 9). Some Sinologists have criticised Jullien's work on the grounds that he has established an 'other' (China) without having first explicitly defined and clarified his principal point of reference (the West) (Reding, 1996: 160–8). Other critics have insisted that obliqueness and indirectness are not foreign to Western thinking. Comparison, if it is to proceed at all, must first attempt to understand each intellectual tradition in its own terms. However, despite these criticisms, there is clearly a distinctive Chinese strategic logic, or at the very least a predisposition for obliquity that is far more pronounced than in Western thinking. This is likely to be the strategy that China will pursue in dealing with America's most important regional allies. China is likely to try to encourage the United States' allies to distance themselves from Washington through a combination of bullying, seduction and bribery until such time that the flow of events is in its favour. This could in turn lead to a situation where the United States finds itself increasingly isolated, in contrast to the present situation in Asia where China has a clear lack of regional allies. This could lead to a strategic endgame for the United States, and when confronted with the stark choice of war or being sidelined by history it might even choose the latter. There is no reason to think that it would follow imperial Germany's example and stake everything on one of William James's leaps of faith. Its isolationist instincts might rise to the fore. China could ultimately be victorious without firing a shot.

Japan and the United States: allies of a kind?

Is there a possibility that China and the United States could enter into a grand bargain? This idea is put forward in Hugh White's *The China*

Choice. Although China is challenging American pre-eminence in the Western Pacific, in August 2012 Hilary Clinton declared that the Pacific is 'big enough for all of us' (*The Straits Times*, 2012). But as the Chinese news agency Xin Hua immediately pointed out, it is also small enough to create conflicts that can threaten peace (*The Economist*, 8 Sept. 2012). White proposes that China and the United States should establish a new order in which China can continue to grow in power and influence and in which the United States will still be able to secure its interests. If the two powers do not reach such an accommodation, then White contends that a minor confrontation could result in great power war. He also recommends that the United States should seek to enter into an agreement with China while America's 'decline' can still be concealed and while China is still willing to engage in conciliation rather than confrontation. White maintains that it is particularly important for the United States to recognise that its allies (and possibly even Japan) might refuse to choose sides in the event of a US–China conflict breaking out (White, 2012).

White's main fear is that the United States will drift into war as a result of territorial disputes in the South China Sea, or US naval exercises in the Yellow Sea, or quarrels between China and Japan in the East China Sea. In 2012, for instance, Japan engaged in a military exercise known as 'Iron First' which led to heightened tension between Beijing and Tokyo and raised questions with regard to whether Japan is abandoning its post-war pacifism. The exercise involved recapturing a Japanese island from an imagined invader. Yet as China is the only country the Japanese believe will be able or willing to occupy their islands, it is clear that the exercise was primarily aimed at a potential Chinese threat to Japanese sovereignty. Where the exercise differed from those of the past was that Japanese soldiers were calling in American naval force and air strikes themselves, and for the first time the leaders of the elite unit helped to plan the war game, taking on a role closer to equals than junior partners. Until recently such an exercise would have been considered unthinkably provocative (Cooper, 2014).

However, while there is evidence of greater maritime competition between China and the United States, there is not yet an appetite in Beijing or Washington for a direct military confrontation. Clear rules have yet to be established with regard to how the Asian states should interact with each other. But it looks as if the Chinese are preparing for a protracted confrontation with Japan. Indeed, China may be able to 'detach' Japan from the US embrace if it remains faithful to its own understanding of strategic logic. Ultimately, however, Japanese culture and history suggest that a Sino-Japanese conflict is highly unlikely.

Japan's sun is rising again, claims David Pilling. Two lost decades notwithstanding it would be foolish to count it out just yet (Pilling, 2013). The country remains the world's third largest economy; its political system has even reinvigorated after the return to power of the Liberal Democratic party; it is developing a more proactive foreign and defence policy and it has embarked on a programme of fiscal and structural reform that would have been considered fanciful only a few years ago. But geography tells its own story: China has always loomed in the Japanese imagination, since Japan lacks strategic depth. It has confronted its political class with the reality of living with or against its giant neighbour, and often, as a result, led it to miss the larger picture.

Let me offer a telling snapshot of this. During the D-Day landings American paratroopers thought they had captured a Japanese soldier, only to find out later that he was a Korean. His name was Yang Kyoungjong. He had been forcibly conscripted by the Japanese and sent to Manchuria where he was captured by the Red Army after the battle of Khalkhin Gol (the defeat that persuaded the Japanese High Command not to go to war against Russia in 1941). He was then sent to a labour camp and drafted by the Russians. Early in 1943 he was taken prisoner by the Germans at the battle of Kharkov. A year later, now in German uniform, he was sent to Normandy where he met his destiny. He later chose to migrate to the United States where he lived until his death in 1992.

'God writes straight with crooked lines' is the old expression. What was critical for the Allied victory was not the Axis alliance between Nazi Germany and Imperial Japan but the fact that the Japanese were not fighting Russia at the time of the D-Day landings. It remains a classic example of lack of strategic foresight. Even more surprising was Tokyo's decision to declare war on the United States even after the German Army's advance had been halted before Moscow. It would have been much wiser to have waited until the following year to see whether the German attack had fatally stalled. In the end, the notion of a global Axis strategy faded in January 1942 when both powers signed a military agreement with longitude 70 degrees defining their respective operational spheres.

Geography shapes national destiny, and it is possible that Japan's failure to think globally reflects this fact. History and geography are symbiotic. We can understand spirit and intellect best when we locate them in one grid of the natural world. The fixed elements of geography do not always shape the more variable elements of human choice, but sometimes they do, and in Japan's case geography seems to have made it intractably provincial.

Japan has often relied on the prevailing great power of the day to underwrite its regional ambitions, beginning with Britain in the early twentieth century during its confrontation with Russia. It then entered into an alliance with Nazi Germany to balance the United States. In the post-war period the United States helped Japan to emerge as one of the victors of the Cold War and Japan also relies on the United States to balance against China. The US security guarantee is its only real defence. But it is always possible that the Japanese will come to the conclusion that that the United States is no longer a reliable ally. After all, while it often establishes 'red lines', Washington does not always act when others cross them.

Despite David Pilling's upbeat assessment of Japan's future, the country is in a poor economic and political situation. In 1992 Seymour Lipset posed this question: 'In the coming years, will the world be more interested in American exceptionalism or Japanese uniqueness?' (Dogan and Kazancigil, 1994: 201). At the time Lipset was writing, the Japanese economy had already entered the deflationary spiral in which it has languished for the past twenty years. There have been encouraging signs of renewal but the underlying structural problems threatening the country's economic potential have not disappeared. Japan's central dilemma is neither its debt burden nor its falling currency, but its unbalanced demographic situation. The nation is facing a serious demographic crisis with a birth rate in terminal decline, an ageing population and negligible levels of immigration (Kaku, 2011: 79). By 2050 Japan's working-age population is projected to fall by 40 per cent, while its rapidly ageing population is further driving up a debt burden that already exceeds 200 per cent of Japan's GDP.

Japan also has the smallest percentage of foreign workers among OECD countries (1.7 per cent of the workforce), and it is squandering its indigenous human resources. A report by Goldman-Sachs suggests that if the number of females employed in the Japanese economy rose to the comparable level for men then this would add 8 million employees to the workforce and increase GDP by 15 per cent. However, the current employment rate for Japanese women remains the lowest of any developed country, even though it is rising. Without deep labour market reforms and a change in cultural attitudes, many Japanese women will continue to leave work after having their first child.

Despite the fact that Japan became the world's second largest economy in the 1970s, the country has never really emerged from its provincialism. Although it is a major power, it is very much an inward-looking one. There are 100,000 Chinese students studying in the United States, yet the number of Japanese students studying in the United States has been in decline for some years. Japanese TOEFL (Test of English as a Foreign Language) scores are the second worst in Asia (after North Korea). No prominent Japanese politician has held an international position in the period since Sadako Ogata served as UN high commissioner for refugees. Japan has practically no visibility in organisations such as the WTO, and there are no foreigners in permanent positions in Japanese companies, universities, think-tanks or NGOs.

Given Japan's poor and deteriorating economic and political situation, the Chinese might seek to test the depth of the US–Japanese relationship. Although there are powerful nationalist groups in Japan who may seek a confrontation with China, or which would encourage a military response if China acts unpredictably, Japan is much more likely to try to appease rather than provoke the Chinese in the hope of reaching some form of political accommodation.

India and the normative dream

India could prove to be one of America's most attractive allies in terms of defending the norms that govern the international system. Both countries are democracies. India is the largest democracy in the world and the oldest in Asia. While English itself is only spoken by a relatively small number of Indians, it remains the language of higher education, media and commerce. Indeed, the Indians claim to be the second largest (and some say largest) English-speaking country in the world. 'Hinglish'—a mixture of English and Hindi—now rivals English itself.

The subtext to the relationship between Delhi and Washington was written in the Clinton years when the United States called for a 'concert of democracies', an alignment some commentators chose to see as a possible alternative to the UN. This later resurfaced in Senator McCain's vision of a League of Democracies (2008), a community of more than 100 nations, an idea that drew inspiration from the 'Atlantic Charter' which the United States and Britain signed at the height of the Second World War (Sloan, 2010: 272). However, nothing ultimately came of either idea as both would have been seen by China as a provocation.

While the proposals for a closer US–Indian alignment did not come to fruition, India clearly remains important for US strategy in Asia. The DoD's 2012 'Defense Strategic Guidance' holds that 'the long-term strategic partnership with India' is one of the main sources of regional stability (U.S. Department of Defense, 2012: 2). A close partnership of sorts has indeed emerged. India and the United States regularly conduct bilateral military exercises and work together on a range of defence issues. In recent years the US–India strategic relationship has become the centrepiece of the Indo-Pacific security architecture.

An additional factor in the US–Indian relationship is the concern that both powers share about the future of Pakistan, which is no longer viewed as a reliable ally in Washington. After the United States and India reached an agreement with regard to US–Indian civil nuclear cooperation in 2005, the Chinese helped Pakistan to launch its first satellite and to build a ballistic missile manufacturing plant near Rawalpindi. They also helped develop its solid-fuel *Shakeen-1* missile. The Chinese have invested millions in the seaport of Gwador, over which they may even have assumed operational control. Gwador could become an important facility for a Chinese aircraft carrier group if it decided to deploy one in the Indian Ocean (possibly around 2020).

However, the record of US–Indian relations is somewhat mixed. Obama has proclaimed that the two countries have 'a responsibility to lead' and he has also voiced his support for India to be given a permanent seat on the UN Security Council. But the strategic partnership between the two powers has also encountered some problems. India has tried hard to circumvent the sanctions regime against Iran, and like Brazil it is pushing back against the American-managed international order. It is lukewarm in its support for many American initiatives and its liberal agenda, and like all the BRICS India has a reflexive dislike of Western dominance. India and the United States also disagree over the future of Afghanistan, further casting into doubt the common values that supposedly underpin the relationship, and raising questions with regard to how much support India will receive if relations with China deteriorate.

After Japan, China is likely to place pressure on India with the aim of distancing the latter from the United States. Beyond Tibet India claims over 130,000-square kilometres of Xinjiang as part of the province of Kashmir, while China claims much of the eastern part of the Indian province of Arunachal Pradesh. According to a 2010 report in *The New York Times*, China has already absorbed the Gilgit–Baltistan region with the acquiescence of Pakistan (Lin, 2011: 17). This was a wake-up call for New Delhi, which is now challenging China's drive west into Central Asia by deepening its military ties with Tajikistan. It is possible that China and India could reach a grand bargain in which India would cede Arunachal Pradesh to China and thus fully recognise China's control over Tibet in return for Beijing's acceptance that Jammu and Kashmir are de facto Indian. But that would require China to risk its ties with Pakistan, given the latter's competing claims over Kashmir, as well as to remain neutral in any potential Indian–Pakistan conflict. Neither prospect is very likely.

India is thus likely to find itself in a dilemma. If China continues to expand its influence into Central Asia and deepen its relationship with Pakistan while projecting its naval power directly into the Indian Ocean and the Gulf, the two countries could be on a collision course. In the event of a crisis between India and China, it is more than possible that the United States would support India in what would effectively be a proxy war akin to those so often fought during the Cold War.

Yet India has shown little by way of strategic acumen in the past, and it is doubtful whether its current politicians are capable of crafting a strategic narrative that would be relevant to the present international and regional situation. Moreover, while regional rivalries are certainly important, India also has severe internal weaknesses. To a visitor from the outside world, India appears to be a thoroughly modern country. Nevertheless, a third of India's population has no electricity supply and the adult literacy rate (65 per cent) is the same as Malawi. It is a country which allows 1.7 million children under the age of five to die every year from preventable diseases. Of those that do survive, half are stunted because child malnutrition is worse than in Eritrea (*The Australian*, 2013).

According to the UN Development Programme (UNDP) 37 per cent of Indians live below the poverty line. There are more poor people in the eight poorest Indian states than all of the twenty-six poorest African countries combined. The distance between the English-speaking political class and the electorate in age, outlook and behaviour is larger in India than in any other established democracy.

India is a work in progress. It is a society, writes Amartya Sen in *An Uncertain Glory*, that is riven with contradictions. Sen quotes Ambrose Bierce who in *The Devil's Dictionary* called patience 'a minor form of despair, disguised as a virtue'. India confronts its own existential crisis and may be unwilling—or even unable—to hold the line against its neighbour if push comes to shove. Another 1962 style 'war' is one the Chinese might well win quite easily; it might be enough to rein in New Delhi's pretensions to play a big power role in the Indian Ocean and make it wary of taking further any strategic partnership with the United States.

China, grand strategy and strategic autism?

In short, it is unlikely that China and the United States will be drawn into a conflict by their respective allies. It is much more likely that they will come into conflict over the norms and rules of the international system, as has been the case with most great power wars over the past 200 years. If such a conflict were to break out, then the United States might not have the allies that it wants or needs. In any case, as will be discussed in the following chapter, such a war might not even require allies or alliances.

In 2011 a Chinese writer suggested that China lacks a grand strategy (J. Wang, 2011), and this opinion is also held by many in the West. Edward Luttwak, one of America's most thought-provoking strategic thinkers, even suggests that China is unable to think strategically. On his own Western-based understanding of the 'logic of strategy' he concludes that China is bound to provoke an inevitable reaction if it continues to maximise its power without purpose.

Luttwak discusses the logic of strategy at length in *Strategy: The Logic of War and Peace* (2002). The book argues that the growth of power evokes a reaction which eventually slows down its growth. Countries which aim to become too powerful do not remain powerful for long. He goes much further in a more recent work, arguing that China has never had to think strategically because it has been cut off from the world for so long. It suffers from 'strategic autism' and 'strategic deficiency syndrome'. It is autistic in mirror-imaging and attributing to the United States what it would do itself in America's place. It is also Sino-centric, unable to see the world other than through an exclusive Chinese lens (the Russians, he adds, suffer from the same disposition). As a result, decisions on foreign policy are made on the basis of highly simplified, schematic representations of unmanageable complex realities, while its grasp of reality too often yields to gamesmanship and opportunism (Luttwak, 2012: 14).

Yet the aspects of Chinese behaviour that Luttwak criticises are not specifically Chinese. Indeed, imperial Germany could be said to have been suffering from 'strategic autism' in the run-up to the First World War. Germany talked the language of encirclement but the problem was largely of its own making. What the Germans saw as their encirclement is more aptly described as a reactive policy of containment. In effect Germany 'circled herself out' of the great power concert (Kagan, 1995: 153).

Germany was also deficient in social intelligence—it too was suffering from 'a strategic deficiency syndrome'. Social intelligence is the first requirement of grand strategy: the ability to choose the right enemies and the right allies and so ensure, as Edward Mead Earle suggested, that if war does break out, a country is at least in a better position to prevail.

Social intelligence is a central component of strategic thinking. In order to be socially intelligent a country must be capable of primal empathy: the ability to put itself in another country's position. Empathy requires an understanding of what others feel and think. It requires what Richard Sennett calls 'emphatic listening'. In *The Theory of Moral Sentiments*, Adam Smith wrote that imagination is needed to put oneself in the position of another and to bring home to oneself every little circumstance of distress which can possibly occur to the sufferer 'in its minutest incidents', even beyond one's own personal experience (Sennett, 2003: 20). That can be challenging if one doesn't like what is reflected back.

Social intelligence also demands a high degree of social cognition, including knowledge of how another society works, as well as an understanding of its social conventions and taboos. It requires us to decode the semiotics and see the signal through the noise (Goleman, 2000: 90). It provides us with a chance to build successful partnerships and relationships and so diffuse crises before they go critical.

None of these attributes were to be found in imperial Germany's diplomacy. It went out of its way, for example, to provoke the British for no obvious reason. It intervened in the settlement of Japan's war against China in 1895 because of a groundless fear that Britain would otherwise make new gains in the region. It picked fights everywhere in the 1890s over the Congo, Sudan, Morocco and even Portugal's African colonies. In June 1894 the British foreign secretary wrote to his ambassador in Berlin: '[I]f this is to continue it may have far-reaching consequences and it is difficult to understand what advantage they expect to gain by such a policy' (Kagan, 1995: 130). The Germans angered the British even more over the Jameson Raid in South Africa (an attempt to destabilise the Boer government of the Transvaal) by congratulating the Transvaal's president for maintaining the independence of his country against external attack. It was this action that prompted the first public criticisms of Germany in the British popular press.

German policy with regard to these issues was the prelude to its most serious mistake of all: the decision to build a first-class navy, which managed to provoke both the British government and the public at the same time. The purpose of this decision continues to be the subject of debate. The German navy was probably designed to enhance Germany's status as a world power. But the naval race with Britain was exorbitantly expensive. While Germany was the second largest economy in the world, its economic position was in no way comparable to that of the contemporary United States. Britain still had the second highest income rates per capita ($244 compared with Germany's $184), and although the German economy was larger, it was only marginally so by 1914 ($1 billion difference). By comparison, even a century ago the United States not only had the highest per-capita income ($377) but an economy larger than the next four countries including Germany and the UK. In 1912 the naval race had to be abandoned. However, at the same time as abandoning the race, the German naval chiefs pressed for war, as the diary of Admiral von Muller reveals. He was present at the War Council in December of that year which was the first occasion in which a naval war with Britain was discussed in detail (ibid.).

This is a clear example of 'strategic autism'. The psychologist Simon Baron-Cohen refers to autistics as being 'mind-blind' and suggests that a better way to conceptualise people with autism is to view their sensitivity to others and their general mental skills as being diluted rather than missing altogether (Bering, 2011: 81). Autism is thus an emotional deficit and there is no reason to think that countries do not live emotional lives. Indeed, there is growing evidence that feelings along with the appetites and needs that explain them play a decisive role in social behaviour (Damasio, 2004: 140). Feelings are the mental manifestation of balance and imbalance, of contentment and disharmony. They do not necessarily reflect the real harmony or disharmony of the external world, but the disharmony of the self, the state of life deep within. There is reason to wonder, writes the neuroscientist Anthony Damasio, whether bearing witness to life within our minds is the reason feelings prevail as one of the features of the complex species we are. Feelings are not a mere decoration, an add-on to emotions. They can be and often are revelations of the state of life to be found within a person or an entire society. 'If anything in our existence can be revelatory of our simultaneous smallness and greatness, feelings are,' Damasio insists (ibid.: 7). This assertion is also important when discussing conflict. In recent years a number of writers have identified feelings and emotions as the most likely source of future wars, in place of the political beliefs that fuelled many of the wars of the last century (Moïsi, 2009).

One of the most important feelings to have been discussed in this literature is resentment, or 'ressentiment'. Though this term will always be associated with Friedrich Nietzsche, the authors who use it in the political science literature tend to make only passing reference to his work. The term was most thoroughly discussed in Richard Ira Sugarman's *Rancor Against Time: The Phenomenology of Ressentiment* (1979). The concept was used by John Rawls in describing the disappointed expectations which are one of the central impulses for the creation of justice (Rawls, 1999). The American philosopher Robert Solomon makes much of the centrality of power and the lack of it, though in his treatment of the term he prefers to use the English word 'resentment' (Solomon, 1994). The French meaning of the term, however, covers everything from 'acrimony' and 'umbrage' to 'grudge', and sometimes a combination of all three.

As it entered the twentieth century Germany sought '*Geltung*' (respect), '*Anerkennung*' (recognition) and '*Gleichberechtigung*' (equal authority)—a host of emotionally and psychologically revealing terms. All three of these aspirations reflected Germany's desire to improve its position and enhance its status at the expense of others. But these aspirations were to prove counterproductive in that they were ultimately dangerous (Coser, 1961). When a society lacks self-confidence it is unlikely to express respect for the achievements of others, and it will instead retreat into itself (Sennett, 2003: 188). Self-preoccupation tends to create an ego that is at over-inflated and overly sensitive at the same time. When a nation becomes enclosed in itself it can come to believe that the self is all that matters and that validation from outside is of almost no importance. As David Brooks writes, when nations become locked in a cycle of insecurity and self-validation, they will often squander their previous achievements in the hope of achieving more (*International Herald Tribune*, 7 Aug. 2013). This is certainly true of imperial Germany, which was always concerned that it could not compete on equal terms, that because it had come into history late in the day, it had to be self-assertive. It could command respect, but it was unable to earn it. If it failed to be assertive, German policy-makers were concerned that it might suffer what the imperial chancellor called *Selbstentmannung* (self-castration).

Yet resentment is not without its psychological rewards. It enables people to feel morally superior in a world which they believe has dealt them a dismal hand. It also serves to make people less aware of the consequences of their actions. Indeed, as Scott Atran writes, when a nation such as pre-1914 Germany is unable to become what it wants to be, the thought of the consequences (such as the destruction or devastation that might follow defeat in war) is unlikely to stop it from acting on its own impulses. As neuroscientists now claim, people process 'sacred values' such as the demand for recognition in parts of the brain devoted to rule-bound behaviour rather than utilitarian calculation (Atran, 2013: 9).

David Shambaugh argues that China is suffering from the same condition. He describes China as a 'partial power' that remains deeply insecure, confused, frustrated, angry, dissatisfied, selfish, truculent and essentially lonely. Although he does not invoke the term 'resentment', he seems to be describing the concept. He adds that it is a 'lonely power, lacking close friends and possessing no allies'. While China frequently states what it is opposed to—Western interference in Tibet, or US engagement with Taiwan—it is much more modest about saying what it wants or represents (Shambaugh, 2012). Shambaugh has also noted other historical parallels between contemporary China and imperial Germany. During the celebrations for China's National Day on 1 October 2009, for example, he watched an enormous parade with 10,000 goose-stepping soldiers and massive trucks ferrying ICBMs, a visible sign of strength, but also of anxiety. The juxtaposition of pride and patriotism on the one hand, and the Party's deep insecurities on the other, spoke of China's conflicted identity.

Luttwak's analysis of China's rise is among the most persuasive. He contends that China is unable to comprehend the world in all its complexity. It instead relies on a highly simplified and schematic representation of unmanageably complex realities. It attributes motives to others that it would hold if it was in the same position. It feels victimised and is becoming more assertive. But is this really a product of culture (or a mentality) or of its strategic DNA? Or is it also likely to be a product of history, the fact that China is only now beginning to come to terms with the nature of its power? As Zhao Ming argues, even if a different regime were in power it would still face challenges which are likely to put any society's social intelligence to the test.

The first of these challenges involves evaluating its power. Although China is the world's second-largest economy, the country's GDP per capita and its ranking on the Human Development Index (the UN ranking of a country's standard of living) are 120 and 101 respectively. Its average standard of living is somewhere between Ecuador and Jamaica. Its per-capita income is 20 per cent of the comparable figure in the United States and there is no prospect of it catching up in the near future because of its aging population. Japan reached a similar point in 1990, the year in which it plunged into a twenty-year recession (by then, however, its living standards were already 90 per cent of the comparable figure in the United States). In *Stumbling Giant* Timothy Beardson identifies demographics as the single biggest obstacle to China's hope of escaping the middle-income trap and becoming rich and powerful at the same time. China even suffered its first labour shortage in 2011. By 2030 there will be more than four older workers for every three of their younger counterparts. As Beardson adds, it may eventually decline demographically. The present Chinese to American population ratio of 4:1 could fall to 1.9 to 1 by the end of the century.

It is important to remember that there was also a general consensus that Germany would rise. In science it remained ahead of the United States until 1945. In the Second World War it was the Germans, not the Americans, who built the first jet engine, the first cruise (V1) and the first ballistic (V2) missiles and the first intercontinental bomber. It also came much nearer to building an atomic bomb then is often assumed (even with some of its best (Jewish) scientists working on the Manhattan Project) (Ball, 2013). If the First World War had never broken out Germany would have remained one of history's significant players, but the Germans were overly pessimistic about their future and chose to force the pace with disastrous results.

The second challenge China faces involves translating its power into influence. It is especially deficient in cultural power. Despite 400 or more Confucius Institutes, few people dream of becoming Chinese or of permanently relocating to China for work. Unlike the 'inner England' in imperial Germany, there is no 'inner China' in any country in the world. 'We are all Americans now', wrote the editor of *Le Monde* the day after 9/11, and nothing has really changed, despite the follies of the Bush administration. The United States speaks for all those countries that still need its protection or who continue to live behind its protective shield. 'Inasmuch as it is a world-hegemonic power,' the author J.M. Coetzee wrote, '[America] is in an important sense my country too, and everyone else's on the planet' (Franklin, 2013: 74).

The third challenge pertains to the fact that China will find it extremely difficult to share power with others as it has never had to do so before. It lacks the historical experience of working closely with allies and has only very recent experience of multilateral institution-making. It has never put together, or led, an international coalition. Moreover, its social networks of power (in international agencies and NGOs), though growing all the time, are still negligible by comparison with those of the United States (*New York Times International*, 13 July 2012). Although it is gradually seeking to create such networks, they are still 'thin' when compared with those of the United States and the 'imagined communities' of the West more generally.

Although Zhao is a research fellow at the China Centre for Contemporary World Studies at the International Department (i.e. the think-tank for the Central Committee of the CCP), his analysis is quite compelling. China has a long way to go to convince other countries of its 'sincerity'. It will have to learn how to change its behaviour, and its political stance, and curb what he calls its 'imperialistic impulses'. But the rest of the world and especially the United States will also need to display peculiar social intelligence as well—especially empathic listening, if it is to be better placed to understand Chinese anxieties about the future.

Unfortunately for China, the country is faced with a power that refuses to abandon its leadership of the international system. The United States has shown little empathy for important aspects of China's position. I have written of the US rotating only a 'modest' force of Marines through Darwin but what if the shoe was on the other foot? What if China were rotating a 'modest' force through Venezuela as well as maintaining bases around America's periphery and activating alliances in Latin America? What if it were to declare a Trans-Pacific Partnership of its own from which the United States was excluded while telling it to become a responsible stakeholder in the world system? The United States has become so used to being the principal player in East Asia and the Western Pacific since the Second World War that it has great difficulty imagining how a rising power might feel threatened, or at least boxed in. The problems stemming from this inability to empathise with its main competitor are further compounded by the United States' complacency about the possibility of a major war breaking out.

Grand strategy is an emergent property of social intelligence, and the United States—at the moment at least—has a distinct advantage: it is simply much better at navigating its way through the international political world and its constant turmoil. At times it can be crass (the 'Ugly American' syndrome) or even naïve (the 'Quiet American' syndrome); at times it can even be boorish. But it also learns quickly. This is partly because it has to cater to so many allies and manage so many alignments and alliances (in Walter Lippmann's words: 'alliances are like manacles: they stop your hands from shaking'). The social quality of alliances, like the emotional quality of personal relationships, depends on the time we spend interacting with allies and friends; social intelligence is partly an emergent property. Networking demands coordinating and synchronising behaviour with that of others; ensuring reciprocity (to counter free-riding); and all of these require manipulation, seduction and even implicit threats if a commitment is to be maintained and one is to avoid being manipulated oneself (the true Thucydidean trap). What is demanded, in short, is strategic acumen, and countries that have a history of fighting genuine coalition wars (unlike Germany or Japan in the first half of the twentieth century and the USSR in the second) are usually more intelligent in the strategies they devise.

Chinese military and The Art of War

What is striking about China's strategic discourse is the way in which in which Sun Tzi is still invoked time and again. As Henry Kissinger writes:

> In no other country is it conceivable that a modern leader would initiate a major national undertaking by invoking strategic principles from a millennium-old

event—nor that he could confidently expect his colleagues to understand the significance of his allusions. Yet China is singular. No other country can claim so long a continuous civilisation, or such an intimate link to its ancient past and classical principles of strategy and statesmanship. (Kissinger, 2011: 2)

The Art of War and *The Seven Military Classics* are central to the identity of the PLA. Its military handbooks regularly refer to battles fought 4,000 years ago as object lessons in strategic thinking, and the esteem in which the works of ancient Chinese strategic wisdom is held is central to the belief that the country's strategic culture is not only different but superior to that of the West (Mahnken, 2011: 3). However, as anyone who has tried to read *The Art of War* will know, the book does not make for easy reading. It is both epigrammatic and enigmatic. It is as difficult to understand as the aphorisms of the pre-Socratics. One of the reasons for this is the fact that the book was influenced by a prior tradition of Zhou military thought with which Sun Tzi expected his readers to be familiar. Moreover, in trying to compensate for the obscurity of the text, the translators often supplied interpretations of what the author intended which can be misleading. In their eagerness to make the concepts and arguments Sun Tzi uses more intelligible to a contemporary Western audience, the translators have often done little to help readers understand his ideas in their true historical and cultural context.

However, it should be noted that that there are two important principles in ancient Chinese military thought which the Chinese themselves may be in danger of overlooking. The first is the speed with which war tends to tap into irrational forces more quickly than expected; the second is the absolute need for war to remain political. If both continue to be ignored there is a distinct possibility that China may overplay its hand.

With regard to the first principle, Sun Tzi's thinking is not entirely dissimilar from Clausewitz's. Clausewitz invokes a trinity: irrational forces such as violent emotions (including hatred); non-rational forces such as friction 'and the fog of war'; and rationality, war's subordination to reason (its use as an instrument of policy). Two of the elements, emotion and reason, are forces internal to the human mind; chance and probability are external. Emotion and reason are both a matter of human intent. Chance and probability represent concrete reality—the non-rational real world upon which our intentions must be forcibly imposed and which often makes those intentions unrealisable. In other words, war is a complex system with a dominant human dimension. It is that dimension which has a propensity to escape political control.

Sun Tzi says much the same thing. Indeed, the Chinese military classics have a much deeper understanding of how quickly war taps into irrational forces and they are much more sceptical than Western strategic thinkers with regard to the extent to which reason can impose itself on the non-rational world. Unfortunately, there is a danger that Chinese nationalism will spiral out of political control. The ferocity of the spontaneous attacks on Japanese businesses in 2012 came as a surprise to the Chinese leadership despite the latter's use of the diplomatic row over the islands known to the Japanese as the Senkaku and the Chinese as the Diaoyu in its official propaganda. The tension was such that *The Economist* even began to speculate whether an inter-state war might be about to take place.

The second theme of Chinese thinking on war is the need for the state to control the military. The relationship between the military and the state has been far from cordial in Chinese history. Warlordism was not merely a product of the collapse of the first Chinese Republic in the 1920s. As W.J. Jenner writes, the genealogies of the Chinese military system remain as vitally important to understanding Chinese politics in the past as do the noble and royal kinship structures in mediaeval European history (Jenner, 1992: 59). The generals on the outer frontiers often became independent warlords and they were able to overthrow the Han dynasty. The Tang dynasty also suffered from the phenomenon of provincial governors becoming warlords in their own right.

In the first forty years of Communism, by contrast, the army had a history of respecting civilian control. In the early years of the Communist state the PLA ran a number of regional administrations until the Party was able to take over (the army handed power back to the civilians between 1953 and 1954). Even more remarkable, after regional army commanders had been forced to impose military control over most sectors of society in the country at the height of the Cultural Revolution to prevent the total breakdown of order, they once again withdrew to their barracks. But ever since the Party was forced to call in a (reluctant) army in Tiananmen Square, the balance of forces has begun to shift.

When the Bo Xilai scandal first erupted in February 2012, Xilai flew to Yunnan Province to visit the headquarters of the 14th Group Army (the unit had been commanded by his father, a prominent figure in the

Mao era). This alarmed the leadership in Beijing and doubtless contributed to his eventual disgrace. Like all militaries, the Chinese army has hawks and doves, and Xi has rehabilitated a group of ultra-hawkish generals and military advisers, some of whom are outspoken in their belief in an 'inevitable' showdown with the United States. More worrying still, he has embraced the ideas of Colonel Liu Mingfu whose predictions of a coming war with the United States resulted in his book being banned. It is now back on the bookshelves. The work of the Air Force Colonel Dai Xu, who uses an idiom resembling that of the turbulent 1960s, is also widely published. Xu describes some of China's neighbours as 'running dogs of the US' and advises the leadership: '[W]e only need to kill one, and it will immediately bring the others to heel' (Saunders, 2013). Chinese military figures are not coy in reminding their neighbours who is now in the ascendant. The CCP mouthpiece, *The Global Times*, has emphasised that China will not allow its neighbours, including Vietnam, to determine where the Chinese navy is able to sail. In doing so the language it used could not have been more bellicose. China would also 'play ball' if Vietnam really wanted war. It would crush any Vietnamese naval operations (Mason, 2011).

This might be unimportant but for the fact that the PLA often acts unilaterally. One example was the EP-3 spy plane crisis in which an American plane was forced down without the Chinese Foreign Ministry being informed. Another was the test launch of an anti-satellite weapon in January 2007. A third was the test flight of the J-20 stealth fighter in January 2011 during the visit of the US defence secretary, Robert Gates, to China. It is rumoured that even the president was unaware of the flight in advance. The Central Military Commission seems to hold itself unaccountable to all but the most senior party leaders, and possibly only to the party general secretary, who is also its chairman.

The problem is compounded by the fact that many in the military seem to think that the United States is in terminal decline. The civilian leadership is much more wary of second-guessing history before it happens. Some of its leaders suspect that the United States will rebound and even recover; others expect China's growth to decline and the gap between the two countries to expand, not contract. They want to manage the United States rather than confront it. But a popular belief in the military is that China will overtake the United States by 2025, and thereafter be in a better position to assume global leadership.

Chinese defence expenditure has risen, and continues to rise, by substantial amounts. In March 2013 the Chinese government announced another multi-billion dollar increase in its defence budget (a 10 per cent nominal increase over the previous year). This continues a trend of nominal double-digit spending increases since 1989. The sole exception, 2010, was probably due to a reallocation of funds in order to finance a major stimulus package in response to the global financial crisis. Although China's military development began from a relatively low base in the mid-1990s, in the past decade its defence spending has increased to such an extent that the funding stream of the PLA is now second in size only to that of the US military (although it is several hundred billion dollars smaller). Some commentators have speculated that in terms of Purchasing Power Parity Chinese defence spending is much higher than the official figure (Beldon, 2012: 38). Combined with the $500 billion reduction in the US defence budget over the next ten years, China could even overtake the United States by 2035 (*The Economist*, 7 April 2013).

The unrelenting increase in Chinese defence spending is a matter of concern for the United States because the increases are taking place at a time when the amount that the United States' allies spend on defence is in decline. In 2012 global military spending declined by 0.5 per cent, and for the first time since 1991, the US proportion of total global spending fell below 40 per cent. Most of America's European allies have reduced their own defence budgets by 10 per cent since the financial crisis. The same is also true of most Asian countries. At the end of the world war Asian countries spent an average of 3.4 per cent of their GDP on defence but this has steadily declined. By 2012 the figure had fallen to 1.75 per cent. East Asian nations are richer than ever but it seems that most choose to spend more in percentage terms on areas other than defence. The main exception is China: its military budget now accounts for 90 per cent or more of the aggregate increase in Asia as a region.

The Chinese military continues to claim that the country's history is pacific, non-expansionary and purely defensive, and that any future use of force will only be in response to American 'provocations' (Scobell, 2002: 6). One prominent Chinese military scholar argues that most of the wars that China has fought in its 4,000 years of dynastic history were either civil wars, or wars to unify the country, and that all military actions since 1949 have been waged in self-defence—a clear misreading of Chinese history (ibid.: 8). 'The Chinese are a defensive-minded people,' argues Lieutenant General Li Jijun, who speaks of the country's ancient strategic culture being rooted in the philosophical idea of 'unity between man and nature' and harmony among men (ibid.: 6–8). This is clearly similar to the euphemistic description of the invasion of Vietnam in 1979 as a 'self-defensive counter-attack', a formulation that not so subtly blurs the line between offence and defence. Not that the United States is any stranger to such euphemisms: the 1983 invasion of Grenada, for example, was described as a 'pre-dawn vertical insertion of American forces'. But all euphemisms ultimately serve to affirm what is known to be untrue. They allow those who employ them to evade confronting the truth and they actively encourage ethical blindness.

'Active defence' is one example of this. This concept is a new buzzword in the Chinese military that serves to occlude the difference between defence and attack even further (ibid.: 13). According to Scobell, the West should be alarmed by this concept due to the insistence of many military experts that China may have to fight for its own vision of permanent peace (Confucian justice). The United States is often seen as an innately aggressive power that has resorted to war throughout its history to spread the message of liberal internationalism. As a result, the country has found itself in an almost semi-permanent state of conflict.

This again raises the role that different mindsets or worldviews play in the way that states behave. As James claimed with regard to different rationalities, all strategic cultures are biographical. While the Chinese claim that the United States tends to think in terms of just war theory, the Chinese argue that there is little evidence of an ethical approach in US strategic thinking. Indeed, they claim that there is a dangerous lack of ethical restraint in US policy. But, as China's neighbours will point out, China is not quite as pacific as it likes to claim.

Some philosophers argue that beliefs determine how we 'interpret' what we see rather than our beliefs, sculpted by history or culture, determining what we see. However, what we ultimately believe on the basis of empirical observation—what we believe we observe—depends on our beliefs and assumptions about the world. We tend to impose an order on a disordered world. We are victims of cognitive dissonance and confirmation bias. We are often misled by what we expect to see. As General Li Jijun himself acknowledges:

> Culture is the root and foundation of strategy. Strategic thinking, in the process of its evolutionary history, flows into the mainstream of a country or a nation's culture. Each country or nation's strategic culture cannot but bear the imprint of cultural traditions, which in a subconscious and complex way, prescribes and defines strategy making. (ibid.: 1)

China's belief that it only fights defensive wars does not quite square with its increased defence spending and the increasingly irrational tone of much Chinese military writing. The US Naval War College claims that there is a conspicuous lack of calculations with regard to the costs or the possible reaction of other powers in challenging the US Navy in the Western Pacific in the Chinese military literature. Nationalist assertions tend to be characterised by extreme if not irrational assessments of threats to China's interests and an unwarranted expectation of the country's ability to develop its military resources to counter the American 'threat' (Terjesen and Tunsjø, 2012: 21).

Conclusion

Reference was made earlier in this chapter to Rumelt's argument that any grand strategy needs both a coherent design and an insightful reframing of a competitive situation. With regard to the first of these, the Chinese have a perfectly consistent understanding of the logic of strategy, though they have yet to craft a convincing strategic narrative. With regard to the second, it is possible that China's military and its politicians are operating separate policies.

Yet while it may indeed be the case that the Chinese military is in danger of becoming increasingly independent of political control, it is worth pointing out that the US military is not entirely under political control when it comes to war planning either. The US military has always been an 'independent variable'. This is partly a function of its size, even if it is to be downsized in the future. Indeed, there have been several times in recent history when the military seemed determined to force through a conflict that politicians did not want. Robert McNamara discovered a stubbornly intractable high command when he came to the Defense Department in 1961. The near insubordination of the chiefs of staff a year later during the Cuban Missile Crisis almost proved to be fatal. The problem today is that after a lacklustre military performance in Afghanistan and Iraq, many military leaders are intent on preparing for a war against China in the hope of slowing down if not reversing the impending defence cuts.

While the political leadership of both countries talks about peace and cooperation, their respective defence ministries seem to be pre-occupied with war. The main focus of concern is Air–Sea Battle strategy, which has failed to receive a thorough review from elected officials in the United States, either in the White House or the Congress (Saunders, 2013).

Much of the current thinking regarding a conflict between China and the United States is highly reminiscent of the beliefs held in Europe in the run-up to the First World War. The prevailing complacency regarding great power conflict has led many in China to conclude that 'China's military moment is coming' (Dobbins, 2012). The PLA *Army Daily* often carries articles calling for an end to 'romantic pacifism' and the need for a realistic discussion of the prospects and possibilities of war with the United States (*The Sunday Times*, 24 March 2013). It is consequently sensible to ask what form such a war would look like, and whether it would ultimately be the United States or China that would prevail in the event that war breaks out.

4

WAR (AND ITS PROTEAN LOGIC)

Predicting the likelihood of any war is usually a thankless task. War either breaks out or it does not break out, leaving the prophets of doom embarrassed if their predictions fail to come true. In the early nineteenth century the climate of intellectual opinion was largely optimistic. Although there were war scares in Britain over the rise of imperial Germany, these mostly found expression in works of popular fiction. In intellectual circles, especially among liberal intellectuals, the end of great power war was deemed to be as inevitable as the end of religion or superstition. *The Economist* even went as far as to conclude that the 1904 accord between Britain and France was 'the expression of tendencies which are slowly but surely making war between the civilised communities of the world an impossibility' (Emmerson, 2013b).

By the 1930s the mood had soured. Pessimism was in the air. The dangers that the Nazis posed were foreseen almost from the very beginning. In his novel *The Shape of Things to Come*, H.G. Wells not only predicted that there would be another world war, but he even came near to identifying the date (he predicted 1940; he was out by a year), and he did identify successfully the likely flashpoint: the Danzig corridor. Thirty years later the American journalist Harrison Salisbury published *The Coming War between Russia and China* (1969) in which he predicted that China and Russia were on a collision course and had probably passed the point of no return. The question was not whether, but only when, war would occur. He was not altogether mistaken.

Both countries came very near to war at this time (we now know what he did not, that the Russians were even contemplating a pre-emptive nuclear strike against their erstwhile ally). More recently, Richard Bernstein and Ross Munro envisaged a future war with China in *The Coming War with China* (1997).

Because the future has yet to happen, when writers make a prediction they are in the privileged position of not yet being proven wrong. The purpose of citing these examples is not to scoff at futurologists or futurists but to suggest that their greatest mistake is to pay too little attention to the protean nature of war itself.

At first glance H.G. Wells would seem to be an exception. In 1902 he foresaw the critical importance of dominating the sky, and imagined the fate of civilians far below the coming aerial battles: 'Everybody, everywhere, will be perpetually looking up, with a sense of loss and insecurity' (Farmelo, 2013: 17). He also envisaged the invention of the atomic bomb, as well as 'land machines' (i.e. tanks) and even submarine-launched missiles (or 'long-range air torpedoes'). However, although his predictions were impressive and largely accurate in some areas, in other respects they were quite limited. In *The Shape of Things to Come* the war in the Pacific is really the First World War at sea writ large, without the decisive application of air power (Gardner, 2010: 4). He thought of tanks as mobile artillery slugging it out shell for shell. Even the atom bombs he imagined were dropped from bi-planes rather than being delivered by long-range bombers. As he later admitted, the vision of the future to be found in his novel *War in the Air* (1908) had never been intended to be more than an entertainment, 'a preposterous extravaganza' (Stearn, 1983: 9).

The same shortcomings are found in a book by George Friedman and his wife, Meredith Lebard, *The Coming War with Japan*, which was published in 1990. The authors predicted that the two countries would find themselves in conflict within twenty years. The same geopolitical dynamic that had led to war in 1941 would soon be at work (Friedman, 1990). This prediction now seems rather dated. It was of course a reflection of the general paranoia over Japanese economic growth which was manifest in a number of contemporary works, including Michael Crichton's fictional thriller, *Rising Sun*. Ironically, Japan had already gone into recession by the time the book appeared. The book sold well because it caught the mood of the times and was framed in yet another national debate about America's decline. Once again the authors had their readers believe that the war at sea would be a re-run of the war in the Pacific with great fleet actions mimicking those between the United States and the imperial Japanese navies.

The idea that great power war is now obsolete is an example of the complacency which makes the West ill-equipped to face future challenges. Even if the thesis is believed to be true then it should still be open to challenge. As Kenneth Waltz once remarked, it is impossible to perpetuate peace without solving the problem of war. War is problematic because it is not fixed. It has changed in the past and is continuing to change. As I have argued elsewhere, we will never see the end of war until it has exhausted its evolutionary possibilities (Coker, 2014).

The changing character of war

> Is China a military threat to the US and to the West more generally? The answer is probably not, but perhaps only if we think of war in conventional terms.
>
> (Watson and Freeman, 2013: 267)

Everyone believes that they know what a 'war' looks like. The term invites us to see something concrete. But all reality can only be spoken of through metaphors. Clausewitz outlined three such metaphors: war as a clash of wills, a duel and a wrestling match. Yet duelling does not always lead to the spilling of blood (as long as honour is vindicated, and more importantly, is seen to be vindicated); and wrestling does not usually involve the shedding of blood at all. Even a clash of wills can take a non-violent form. However, as far as Clausewitz and his devotees are concerned, blood-letting is a central part of war.

We define as 'true' or 'false' not the things themselves but our definitions of them. One pertinent example of this is the Spanish insurrection which plagued Napoleon after 1808. The two outstanding military thinkers of the day, Henri Jomini and Clausewitz, disagreed with regard to whether or not the Spanish insurrection could be classed as a war. Whereas Jomini thought that the insurrectionists, history's first 'guerrilla' fighters (the word derives from the struggle), were engaged in war, Clausewitz disagreed. Yet the city of Saragossa saw the worst urban fighting before the Second World War. The difference of opinion was only in part dictated by the tactics of the insurrectionists. It was also a difference of opinion about whether religion could play any part in war. In the course of this terrible conflict the Enlightenment encountered the spiritual values of an earlier age. Napoleon had once boasted that 'nations with lots of friars are easy to subjugate', but historians today tend to look back upon the campaign in Spain as the first religious war since 1648 (Bell, 2007). The historian William Napier attributed the reluctance of the Spanish to surrender to the fact that their priests persuaded them that 'the aggressive stranger' was 'accursed of God; processions, miracles, prophecies, distribution of relics and the appointment of saints to the command of armies, fanaticised the mass of patriots' (Haythornwaite, 1996: 100). It is religion that currently provides so many of the foot soldiers for urban terrorism, whether they are Sunni, Shia, Hindu, Buddhist, Christian or Jewish. It is from the ranks of the faithful that suicide bombers are recruited.

In other words, people tend to understand different phenomena by reference to a definition they have come to take for granted. But all definitions are contestable. To say that the sum of the angles of a triangle is 180° is true only in the context of the Euclidean system (it is not true for non-Euclidean mathematics). To say that an apple is an angiosperm is true only on the basis of certain rules of botanical classification. To argue that war must be violent (or kinetic) is a prevailing Western idea that is no truer for being asserted so often.

The American pragmatist Charles Peirce claimed that a definition is only true if it proves to be useful and that it shows its usefulness when it is true (true for us—the only real definition of the truth). War is a cultural phenomenon which is informed by a particular historical experience, and this is why Clausewitz and Jomini differed over their interpretation of the Spanish insurrection. Differences of opinion often arise within a culture, yet they are amplified even more in the dialogue between cultures. This is why Western readers often find Sun Tzi so baffling. His is not a Western understanding of war, but instead represents a Daoist reading of the world. It is hard for a Western audience to understand the Chinese preference for fighting wars before they are declared and winning victories before the two sides even come into conflict, but it is perfectly consistent with the Chinese understanding of *shi*—going with the propensity of things rather than trying to force one's own will on reality. If Western and Chinese understandings of war are incommensurable, like the Ptolemaic and Copernican systems (only in the first do notions of epicycle and deferent assume a precise meaning), the fact that they are incommensurable does not mean that they are not comparable. Indeed, it is through comparison that we have been able to understand the celestial phenomena in cosmology that Ptolemy explained with notions of the epicycle and deferent. It is through comparison that we are able to grasp the fact that they are the same phenomena that Copernicus wanted to explain using a different set of concepts (Eco, 2013: 34). That is why people still read Sun Tzi 2,000 years after his work first appeared and why his ideas still resonate today (especially, ironically enough, in the US military). What makes them likely to resonate even more in future is that we are moving into a new phase of warfare—an era of 'cool wars' and 'code wars', and other non-kinetic means of using coercion, of imposing one's will on another at minimum cost to oneself.

The coming war with China at sea?

History is messy: continuities exist side by side with deep discontinuities. Although war is protean, it constantly draws inspiration from the past. The old realities are not always replaced by new ones. In 1944 George Orwell questioned whether the world was really shrinking. He criticised the progressive books that had appeared before 1914 for their careless use of stock phrases, including the 'abolition of distance' and 'disappearance of frontiers' (Ridley, 2011: 235). The world is in danger of making the same mistake today. For all the talk of globalisation, geography is still vitally important. One way to illustrate this is through reference to the work of a major but neglected geopolitical thinker, Nicholas Spykman.

Spykman is not as widely read as he should be. His work fell out of favour after the 1950s. Spykman is usually only read today because others did so in the past (some historians claim that he inspired the policy of containment). Spykman was writing during the Second World War and he was anxious, once the war was won, that the United States should not return to the disastrous policy of isolationism that it had pursued in the inter-war years. He was prescient in forecasting that China would eventually become the dominant power in Asia and that the United States might have to take responsibility for Japan's defence.

Spykman claimed that the geography of a country is material for its policy rather than the cause of a particular policy. He was arguing that geography frames behaviour rather than determining it. It provides opportunities and constraints that have profound implications for policy and strategy. This point has often been reiterated by a contemporary geopolitical thinker, Colin Gray, who claims that geography defines the players and the stakes for which they contend, and will always define the terms on which they measure their own security relative to that of others (Gray, 1996: 248). Geography defines the political discourse as well. It even mediates identity. It could hardly be otherwise. A nation's size and natural resources have a huge impact on its political cohesion. In the case of China this has been one of the determining factors in its long history.

Spykman's ideas remain relevant for understanding the principal strategic reality confronting the United States and China. The former is a sea power, the latter a land power. Where they differ most is in their understandings of space:

> A sea power conquers a large space by leaping lightly from point to point, adjusting itself to existing political relationships wherever possible, and often not establishing its legal control until its factual domination has long been tacitly recognised. An expanding land power moves slowly and methodically forward, forced by the nature of its terrain to establish its control step by step and so preserve the mobility of its forces. Thus a land power thinks in terms of continuous surfaces surrounding a central point of control, while a sea power thinks in terms of points and connecting lines dominating an immense territory. (Spykman, 1938: 224)

The current strategic reality in the Asia-Pacific region is much the same as it was in Spykman's day. The Chinese dominate the region on land. They are now as powerful as they were in the mid-eighteenth century when they occupied Tibet and secured their borders against the nomadic tribes from the Central Asian Steppes. On the border with Russia they are stronger than ever before and will continue to remain so until—or if—Russia can modernise its armed forces. Even if Russia were to succeed in this task, its presence in the Far East is likely to prove tenuous. Vladivostok is already a bilingual city in which knowledge of Chinese is as essential as knowledge of Russian, and the Chinese penetration of Siberia also continues apace. China now dominates the mainland of East Asia with the single exception of South Korea, which still has an alliance with the United States and hosts a number of American bases.

It is possible that China will decide to extend its strategic depth inland rather than confront the United States at sea. Geopolitics is not just a Western science, any more than grand strategy is a Western preoccupation. China is developing its own geopolitical discourses. In response to the US Pivot, Wang Jisi (a former foreign policy adviser to both Jiang Zemin and Hu Jintao) advocates a 'march west'—enhancing and deepening China's presence in Central Asia and the Middle East. He urges China to remain true to its roots as a continental power, and argues that China should try to outflank the United States by turning westward (Yun Sun, 2013). Not only would marching west accelerate the Grand Western Development, a national strategy launched to promote the growth of China's western provinces, but it would also 'rebalance' its historical, singular emphasis on East Asia, which is largely a product of the Qing era (ibid.). This would involve nothing less than a new geopolitical reality—transforming Central Asia from being landlocked to land-linked, thereby providing the region (and China) market access and seaports to the Indian Ocean and the Persian Gulf.

Wang argues that naval power would be of little use in defending strategic lines of communication in bottlenecks like the Straits of Malacca, which are too narrow and shallow for use and can easily be blocked by mines and anti-ship weapons. His preferred option is to exploit China's own strategic depth—its interior lines of communication—the overland routes to central and south-east Asia. A century ago Halford Mackinder argued that Eurasia was inaccessible to sea power, but lay open to railways which would extend state power. He saw in the latter the conditions of a 'mobility of military and economic power of a far-reaching and yet limited character'. For him this is what made Eurasia 'the geographical Pivot of history' (Mackinder, 1904: 434).

Some American experts would broadly agree with this assertion. In 2013 Barry Posen argued that the United States could no longer afford the open-ended nature of engagement that George Kennan feared and others accused him of fostering during the Cold War when the United States chose to confront communism everywhere from the Korean Peninsula to Central America (Posen, 2013). Posen wants the United States to replace an 'unnecessary', ineffective and expansive hegemonic agenda with a more focused strategy of preventing China from upending the global balance of power. The best way to do this is by establishing itself in Eurasia, which Mackinder viewed as the world's geopolitical axis, for any power that dominates the area would control two out of three of the world's most advanced and economically productive regions. As Brzezinski notes, Mackinder even foresaw that China would eventually displace the only other contender, Russia, from the global chessboard (Brzezinski, 1997: 48).

Strategic depth is a material reality. But even a cursory glance at Mackinder's writings reveals that he felt that Eurasia's strategic importance was defined not only by geography but the 'vitality' of the powers that might exploit it and the technological advances of the time. From Mackinder's perspective railways were one of the most important advances, and railways seem to be of growing strategic importance in the modern era. China has invested a great deal of effort in building new rail networks and expanding old ones across Central and South East Asia. Strategic depth is also—most importantly of all—an idea, and our ideas to a certain extent create material realities (the extension of rail networks and energy pipelines), which in turn have a feedback effect on the choices we make. Strategic depth therefore constitutes a social reality of its own. We are only what we think ourselves to be—it is one of the immutable factors of great power politics. If competition (like war, to invoke Clausewitz's famous analogy) is a clash of wills, what is of primary strategic importance is that the opponent is forced to negotiate on one's own terms. This is what George Kennan grasped when urging the United States to forge an alliance with post-war Japan, so that Washington could negotiate with the Soviet Union from a position of strength. The emphasis in the Cold War was not to exploit the advantage in actual conflict but to ensure that it posed an implicit threat.

From the vantage point of China the Eurasia card offers the chance to outflank the United States through Central and North West Asia in terms of overland access to the Persian Gulf and the Indian Ocean, negating or severely reducing America's own advantage in being the dominant power at sea, able to control the world's main maritime trade routes and to play the hegemonic role in policing the seas or 'the global commons'. Some bipolar rivalries, writes Robert Ross, can be more stable than others thanks to the logic of geography (Ross, 1999: 97). The US Navy effectively dominates the critical shipping lanes connecting East Asia with the Middle East due, in part, to naval access agreements with most countries in the region.

In the words of another classic geopolitical thinker, Alfred Mahan:

> [A] ... most obvious light in which the sea presents itself from the political and social point of view is that of a great highway; or better, perhaps, of a wide common, over which men may pass in all directions, but on which some well-worn paths show that controlling reasons have led them to choose certain lines of travel rather than others. (Gray, 2013: 35)

The United States still 'controls' the choke points of world trade (and in the event of war is best placed to close them off). It is also—for the moment—best placed to police the 'established rules of the road'. Freedom of navigation has always been a key mandate of the US Navy in the same way that it once was for the British. American strategists sometimes invoke Sir Eyre Crowe's famous 1907 memorandum which explained why third parties (even Britain's rivals) had come to reconcile themselves, however grudgingly, to British naval supremacy. They might not like the *Pax Britannica*, Crowe ventured, but Britain was the least objectionable of any potential naval hegemon. The Royal Navy policed the sea lanes as the globocop (Seton-Watson, 1939: 153–4). That is America's strongest suit: demand- rather than supply-side politics.

Will that demand be challenged? When the Chinese Navy harassed the surveillance ship USNS *Impeccable* in 2009 it raised the question as to whether freedom of navigation is one of the 'normative rules' of the system that the Chinese are seeking to challenge. Another concern is Chinese naval activity in the region's Exclusive Economic Zones (EEZs). The activities of the Maritime Police agencies' vessels are of particular concern because they tend to operate by less restrictive rules of engagement than naval ships, and the numbers of these vessels are increasing. China believes it has a right to regulate foreign military activity in its own EEZ, as it does in its own territorial waters even though these are recognised in international law as the 'high seas' in which no country has exclusive economic rights. Despite asserting this right with regard to its own EEZ, China has breached the EEZs of Vietnam and the Philippines.

There is also an increased perception that China is engaging in 'bullying' tactics. The vessels of the China Maritime Surveillance, the Fisheries Law Enforcement and Maritime Safety Administration, though lightly armed, have intimidated local vessels such as fishing boats and survey ships. This has led to a shift in regional alignments, with an increasingly warm relationship between the Philippines and Japan, who are planning to strengthen their coastguards in response to China's behaviour. The Japanese claim that since 2003 Beijing has repeatedly broken its commitment to inform Tokyo in advance whenever Chinese survey vessels enter waters claimed by the Japanese, while Filipino officials have accused China of reneging on a 2012 deal to withdraw patrol vessels from the Scarborough Shoal. These actions inevitably raise doubts about the extent to which China is prepared to respect international maritime agreements in the South China Seas.

China is the rising power, and rising powers often seek to challenge the prevailing order. The Chinese are building up their naval profile.

In the first decade of the twenty-first century they led the world in submarine construction, building almost three submarines a year. Although this growth is impressive, it should be seen in the larger context of moving from a platform-centric navy almost wholly dependent on individual ships and aircraft operations with only rudimentary radio and data link coordination, to a coherent naval force able to project power beyond its shores (Terjesen and Tunsjø, 2012). China may even entertain a much greater if longer-term ambition, however: not only to make life hard for the US Navy in the Western Pacific but eventually to force it back to Pearl Harbor from where the United States embarked on the road to becoming the power that it is today.

Air–Sea Battle

What form would a protracted confrontation between the United States and China take? The US Navy has an operational concept called Air–Sea Battle. While Air–Sea Battle used to be referred to as a strategy the military is now very careful to avoid using the term. It is clearly more than just an operational concept. Whereas some experts view it as a tactical battle plan, others claim that it is simply designed to deter China from confronting the United States.

A jargon-laden Pentagon briefing in November 2011 which announced the creation, three months after the fact, of the Air–Sea Battle Office (ASBO) did not help throw much light on the concept itself. However, enough is known about the concept to arrive at certain conclusions. In the event that China challenges the United States in the Western Pacific (the Americans are insistent that they will never be the first to initiate hostilities), the US Navy would endeavour to withstand the initial attack before striking against Chinese battle networks, suppressing the enemy's long-range strike systems and regaining the initiative. The US Navy would subsequently be able to restore strategic supremacy in a non-permissive environment.

The United States would then enlist the help of the Japanese Navy—America's largest aircraft carrier in the Pacific—with the aim of dominating the routes which the Chinese North and East Sea Fleets would have to use to access the Western Pacific. The success of the United States in such a confrontation would depend in large part on whether or not it will have been able to maintain its technological lead, especially in stealth technology, and whether Chinese cyberwar capabilities will continue to grow to the point where they could play havoc with America's command-and-control systems.

In 1999 the authors of *Unrestricted Warfare* argued that it would be unwise for China to confront the United States directly (as imperial Japan tried to do in the 1930s). It would be preferable to neutralise US advantages: to prevent the United States from deploying its aircraft carriers in the Taiwan Straits and to blind the United States by compromising its satellite capabilities. This more indirect approach appears to be part of China's current strategy. The Chinese have invested heavily in anti-access denial (A2/AD), using submarines and land-based missiles, including the DF-21 (a missile that at present has a range of only 800 nautical miles, but which could be upgraded to 1,500). For its part, the United States is investing in counter capabilities in the hope that its naval ships will be able to shoot down incoming missiles, or better still prevent them from locating their targets. It would also aim to use its superior submarines to neutralise Chinese submarines near home waters and thus protect its surface fleet. The Chinese would face problems of their own as many of the surveillance and weapons platforms needed for the A2/AD are deployed by the Air Force and the Second Artillery rather than by the navy (Mahadevan, 2013). All three services may have different organisational perspectives and this could prove to be either an asset or a hindrance depending on the degree of inter-service coordination.

One Pentagon official has claimed that the importance of the Air–Sea Battle concept resides in the fact that 'it focuses the services on what the problems are' (LaGrone and Majumdar, 2013). The main problem the United States confronts is the increasing vulnerability of its aircraft carriers, the main target for the DF-21 (and a highly tempting one as 60 per cent of US Navy manpower is assigned to the carrier force). Intermediate-range ballistic missiles, though less technologically advanced than anti-submarine ballistic missiles, could also target US naval facilities in Guam. Missile technology is cheap (compared with the cost of ship-building), and it is also well within China's technological capabilities. It would also be difficult for the United States to destroy land-based missile sites. Yet it is also difficult to hit a moving target at sea, and long-range surveillance systems depend on over the horizon radar systems which rely, in turn, on an array of low-earth orbit surveillance satellites and China only has a small number of these. The United States, writes Robert Ross, would probably hope to 'degrade' China's surveillance capacity without attacking its land-based systems through cyber-warfare and other non-kinetic means. To reduce the target signature of its own ships, it is likely that the United States will build smaller platforms and try to offset the threat that Chinese submarines pose by deploying submersible drones or Unmanned Underwater Vehicles (UUVs) (Terjesen and Tunsjø, 2012).

Much like the Royal Navy in the nineteenth century, the US Navy has always assumed that it faces no clear competitors at sea. But this has now changed. The Chinese Navy is not anywhere near as powerful as the US Navy, but China itself has the critical advantage of strategic depth. To counter this, the US Navy is deploying new littoral combat ships for the same purpose—to press home a local advantage in territorial waters.

However, when the mechanics of the Air–Sea Battle concept are placed under greater scrutiny, it would appear that there is a danger that the United States would have to strike at China's radar stations and land-based missile sites and thus risk escalating the war. Long-range stealth bomber and fifth-generation fighters along with cruise missiles would have to be targeted against command-and-control nodes, surface-to-air missile batteries and Anti-Ship Ballistic Missile (ASBM) launch sites. Cyber-attacks would probably extend to other land-based systems as well. Indeed, the ever-increasing interconnectedness of cyberspace with the tangible material (as opposed to virtual) environment—often referred to by terms such as 'the Internet of things' or 'cyber physical infrastructure'—means that the distinction between military operations in these two domains is quickly eroding (Applegate, 2013: 164). Moreover, as all Chinese land-based ballistic missiles are controlled by the Second Artillery, any attack on DF-21 launchers must strike the Second Artillery infrastructure which also supports China's nuclear deterrent. It would thus be indistinguishable from a pre-emptive strike and would almost inevitably be interpreted as such.

Many military experts outside the ASBO are concerned that US logistic vulnerability would necessitate considering a first-strike option, and if the United States waits to be attacked first, sooner or later the conflict would escalate beyond political control. Air–Sea Battle could involve a protracted war of attrition and prove to be deeply unpopular at home. From the US perspective it is less an ideal strategy than what Max Weber called an 'ideal type'. It is a scenario that looks good when played out on computers but not when the practical political realities are taken into account. America's allies might only want to take part if they found themselves in the front line. In the event that North Korea was to launch a Chinese-backed attack on South Korea, or if China invaded Taiwan or the Chinese attacked Japanese command-and-control centres it is questionable whether the other allies would seek to become involved.

Even Australia, America's oldest regional ally, might be reluctant to find itself boxed-in. States crave room for manoeuvre (as Thucydides argued, allies embroil great powers in war and allies sometimes shift their allegiances). Some leading Australian defence experts are highly sceptical with regard to the wisdom of taking part in a strategy that is unlikely to result in a decisive victory. If the United States were to launch air strikes from bases in Australia, and still more if the Australian Navy were to take part in a blockade at choke points such as Malacca, Lombok or the Sundra Straits, then the country could find itself deeply embroiled in a conflict that could end in a nuclear exchange (such as a tactical nuclear strike on Guam). It is because of the island's perceived vulnerability that Saipan is being transformed into an alternative military base. The United States Air Force (USAF) is also planning to deploy aircraft on a regular basis not only to Darwin and Tindal in Australia, but to Changi East airbase in Singapore, Korat in Thailand and Thiruvananthapuram in India. If the allies feel threatened by the strategy, will these facilities still be available in ten years' time?

Air–Sea Battle is an operational concept. All operational concepts can be disastrous in the absence of a clear strategy, as the German army found with the *Blitzkrieg*, which was highly effective against France in 1940 but proved totally ineffective against Russia the following year where all it was able to deliver were a series of 'lost victories' (tactical successes which yielded no decisive strategic outcome). One alternative option to Air–Sea Battle would be Offshore Control, a classic blockade strategy proposed by T.X. Hammes, which would involve a combination of ground, naval and air, and rented commercial platforms which would allow the US Navy and its allies to intercept and divert the super tankers and post-PANAMAX container ships that are essential to China's economy. A maritime exclusion zone would be policed inside the first island chain. The US Navy could intercept and subject inspected ships to seizure and sale.

As one might expect of the author, Hammes makes a persuasive case for Offshore Control. It would require no attacks on the mainland of

China, or action at sea outside the first island chain. China would still be able to function economically, but its economy would quickly become non-competitive globally when its chief trading partners began to look elsewhere (Hammes, 2013). The United States would ask much less of its allies than it would in the case of Air–Sea Battle since the strategy would not require allied basing rights except in Australia, even though some allied navies might be involved in the blockade. China would also be unable to intimidate them. Any Chinese attack on US bases (e.g. in Japan or South Korea) would risk bringing those countries into the conflict on the US side. China could of course extend the war by counter-blockading Japan and attacking convoys bound for the country, but this would lead to an escalation that China would be unable to deal with. This would also apply for unconventional attacks via cyberspace (a domain needed for the strategy to be applied effectively).

It could also have a further advantage, one which does not appear to have been mentioned by Hammes. In the event of substantial damage to the global economy, the United States would remain the major outlet for global trade. If the United States was prepared to buy the goods, and was able to produce substitute goods for those supplied by China, its share of (admittedly reduced) global trade would increase and is likely to be sustained provided hostilities could be concluded on terms tolerable to both sides. However, while the proposal arguably has more benefits than Air–Sea Battle, this could change in the future if the naval balance tilts further against the United States. It requires a rational actor approach, favoured in US military academies: a utilitarian calculus of the costs, benefits and consequences of escalation. It is an example—to return to my discussion of the First World War—that shows how a strategy can be entirely rational while being entirely unreasonable at the same time.

Hammes assumes that a blockade could last for months without doing grave damage to the international economy or America's legal and moral authority. He concludes that a blockade (the traditional Western preference after 300 years of naval supremacy) would provoke fewer passions in Beijing than a direct attack on the mainland or against the country's critical infrastructure. Unfortunately, the longer a conflict lasts the more difficult it would be for the politicians to concede ground. Although the strategy is ingenious it clearly has many shortcomings as well. The US Navy is likely to discuss similar strategies and operational concepts in the years to come. Of all the services, the US Navy is critically placed to resist the coming defence cuts by being able to craft a story, and stories are what make sense of the future. But they will come up against China's main asset: its strategic depth. However, there is no strategic depth in the two other domains, space and cyberspace, in which a Sino-American war is most likely to be played out.

From cool war to code war: the prospects of a great power cyberwar

Richard Clarke's *Cyber War* depicts a scenario in which the Chinese launch a cyber-attack on the US homeland, activating 'logic bombs' already pre-installed in America's electricity grid. Financial systems crash; planes in American airspace cannot land; trains are derailed; cities are plunged into darkness; chemical plants void poison gas; nuclear power plants are at critical risk of meltdown (Clarke, 2010: 3). In a no less apocalyptic vision of the future the author of *Dark Market* writes of a potential Chinese attack that might trigger huge refinery explosions in Philadelphia and Houston, release clouds of lethal chloride gas from chemical plants in New York and Delaware and precipitate the total collapse of the air traffic system in Virginia (Glenny, 2012). It is easy to conjure up such fears because of the world's reliance on cyberspace. These fears are apocalyptic because the effects of such an attack would be felt not only in the economy, but would quickly cross 'infrastructure boundaries'. They could even threaten to undermine structures of government and lead to social collapse.

Scenarios such as these throw into stark relief both the shape of the time and the play of our fears. Those fears go back to the end of the Cold War. In 1991 the security specialist Winn Schwartau published *Terminal Compromise* (1991), a novel which predicted an electronic Pearl Harbor, a veritable existential catastrophe:

> [T]he target is one of the most crucial segments of our way of life: Information ... the key building block upon which modern society functions ... the lifeblood of the United States and the world ... a global and national strategic asset that is currently under attack ... Without information, without the machinery that allows the information to remain available, a veritable electronic library, the United States steps back thirty years.

The novel tapped into a much wider concern that the United States was about to be overtaken by the world's second largest economy, Japan. The villain of the piece is a Japanese citizen who seeks to attack the United States in order to avenge his parents who were killed at Hiroshima, as well as to assuage his own shame for being stigmatised a *hibakusha* (a survivor of the nuclear blast): 'We may have lost after Pearl Harbour,' he remarks, 'but we won with the transistor radios and VCRs. The war is not over' (Schwartau, 1993). In the author's post-9/11 reissue of the novel *Pearl Harbor Dot Com* (2002) the attack represents 'the ultimate cyberwar ... against the United States' (Schwartau, 2002). Both books reminded Americans that the most devastating attack they have ever suffered emanated not from the Middle East but from East Asia, and that a similar attack may one day emerge from there again. The only factor to have changed in the interim is that the most likely suspect is no longer Japan, but China.

In 1997 the prospect of a cyberwar was simulated in one of the first US cyber-security exercises, known as 'Eligible Receiver'. In the exercise the enemy was not China but its ally, North Korea, which—encouraged or not by Beijing—hacks into US military operations in the Pacific theatre. Over a two-week period the National Security Agency (NSA) 'red team' not only successfully attacked US command-and-control systems in-theatre but was also about to attack power grids in the United States itself. Official sources described the outcome of the exercise as 'frightening' (*Washington Times*, 16 April 1998). According to the then deputy secretary of defence it took three days before anyone at the Pentagon became aware that the computer systems were under attack. Although the exercise was deemed to be a much-needed wake-up call, critics complained that because of its classified nature there was no public debate about whether the North Koreans—or anyone else—had such capabilities or would even be able to acquire them. It did not take long to find out that someone had: in an attack only a year later, which the US government called 'Moonlight Maze', classified information at the Pentagon, the National Space Agency (NASA) and other facilities was hacked. Officials only discovered this by accident in 2000—it had gone unnoticed for two years (Strickland, 2008).

A similar scenario was discussed in a report authored by Michael Bronk. The report envisages a future in which a powerful China seeks to bring the city-state of Singapore into its influence, having already achieved this goal with regard to Hong Kong, Macau and Taipei. Prior to launching an attack on a Singaporean guided-missile frigate in the South China Sea, China had launched a massive cyber-campaign designed to degrade and disrupt America's communication capabilities as well as those of its allies. Members of its 60,000 strong cyber-warfare group had penetrated America's military, government and corporate networks. When the conventional attack against Singapore takes place, the US Armed Forces discover that their communications capabilities have been severely compromised. Key military networks and servers come under crushing denial-of-service attacks, hampering its efforts to mobilise its conventional forces. The conflict ends fifty-five days later in a stand-off between the Chinese and US navies. War is averted at the eleventh hour. Singapore manages to retain its independence, though only just (Bronk, 2011). The whole episode confirms the city-state in what my former colleague Michael Leifer called its own 'exceptionalism'—not its economic achievements (impressive though these are) but its unique 'sense of vulnerability' (Leifer, 2000: 9).

In this engagement, of course, no one 'wins' and the war fails to escalate. Both sides back down and continue their competition by other means. But there are several worrying features in Bronk's scenario that suggest war itself may be evolving. War could begin in the future long before one of the parties knows it has already broken out. A hacker who has managed to penetrate a system can sabotage it in a way that avoids detection. By tweaking lines of code in subtle ways they would be able to make the systems less accurate and less reliable or even entirely unresponsive. This method falls short of a pre-emptive strike (like Pearl Harbor) but it might be far more effective because it is more difficult to detect and prevent or repair. The United States might try to scramble their planes on their own aircraft carriers due to a fear of Chinese air attacks. But with the loss of electronic tools, clearing each fighter for take-off would become a drawn-out, manual process reminiscent of the Second World War.

In Bronk's scenario China's secret weapon is a computer code that has the capability to disappear and reappear and not only adapt but to use its host code against the host in new and unlimited ways. In other words, the cyberwar begins long before the United States knows it. Personal computers, radio networks, satellite receivers, control systems and battlefield communications hardware would fail, leaving the Americans reliant on only a few dedicated high-end satellite-based communication channels to connect field commanders in Japan and Hawaii. Even these would be interrupted when the war finally goes 'kinetic' and the Chinese destroy some US satellites, which would cause damage to US telecom satellite coverage over the Pacific. The Chinese would be able to stay on the right side of the escalation trap. Instead of using electromagnetic pulse (EMP) weapons to target the communications grid, the scenario envisages the use of botnets to attack the global fibre network (Byrne, 2011).

'Most likely, a cyber-conflict will be an "always on" engagement, even if international policy is enacted to forbid it,' Bronk writes. 'The only certainty in cyber-conflict is that conflict there will not unfold in the ways we may expect.' However, Bronk is guardedly optimistic that if a cyber war does break out then it is unlikely to involve power grids being knocked offline and planes falling out of the sky (Bronk, 2011). In other words, he identifies with the school of thought that believes that the threat has been exaggerated. Cyber-attacks occur every day and cause enormous damage. Cyber-espionage is something of a Chinese specialism (with the United States following close behind). Cyber-sabotage has already been inflicted by other states in the case of Estonia, and in Iran where a US virus (Stuxnet) reportedly caused considerable damage to an Iranian nuclear facility. Cyber-subversion is likely to be the tactic of choice for terrorist movements in the future.

Many have claimed that cyber war between states is unlikely to break out in the immediate future, yet the nature of cyberspace itself brings this assertion into question. As Philip Ball argues, cyberspace is problematic because it is difficult to grasp and understand. It does not correspond to any physical structure that can be examined from the outside. We may have built it but we cannot tell exactly what we have built, so it is hardly surprising that we are unable to grasp what future it may deliver (Ball, 2005: 478–9). We are operating largely in the dark. But our speculations make up for our lack of knowledge. The first academic paper to argue that cyberwar was possible, which was published by the RAND Corporation nearly twenty years ago, was confident that an attack on an enemy's computer systems could have a 'strategic effect' (Langø, 2013: 10). Since then the exponents of cyberwar have gone on to coin a series of cyber-neologisms, including 'cyber-security', 'cyber-power' and 'cyber-strategy'. Most misleading of all, perhaps, is the concept of a cyber-Pearl Harbor which offers a profoundly misleading analogy as the Japanese attack on 7 December 1941 had no decisive strategic outcome.

Many technophiles have an imperfect grasp not only of strategy but of military history. In Clive James's words, strategy requires a 'considerable appreciation for the mundane', or the do-able:

> A poetic flair has an impatient mind of its own: it likes to make an effect, and it has a propensity for two qualities that can easily be inimical to a broad strategic aim ... [Japan's] plan for deciding the war on the first day was not only the equivalent of a roulette player's betting his whole bundle on a single number, it was also the equivalent of trying to cram the whole of the *Tale of Genji* into a single *haiku*. There was bound to be material that didn't fit. Even if the American aircraft carriers had been in harbour they would not have sunk far enough in the shallow water to be beyond salvage. One way or another, the American fleet was bound to come back. (James, 2007: 817)

In many ways the current discussion around cyber-warfare resembles that which emerged at the dawn of air power (the third dimension), when experts argued that the third dimension could and would deliver strategic results independent of the other services and dimensions. In other words, air power alone could deliver victory. Yet however much Allied bombers rained death and destruction on German and Japanese cities, even after the firebombing of Hamburg and Tokyo, the Second World War was not won by air power alone. At some point a cyberwar will also become a conventional war.

This is not, however, to dismiss the dangers inherent in cyberwar. While the Obama administration has never publicly discussed Chinese cyber-espionage activities, a secret State Department cable, written the day before Obama was elected president in November 2008, described American concerns about its attacks on government sites. The cable complained that the Chinese had stolen technological blueprints, manufacturing processes, clinical trial results, pricing documents, negotiating strategies and other proprietary information from more than 100 companies in the United States. It identified attacks on twenty industries from military contractors to chemical plants and satellite and telecommunications corporations.

China probably has the most effective and certainly the most robust cyber-espionage system in the world. In February 2013 over 140 attacks were traced to a single PLA unit in Shanghai. China has more than 60,000 cyber experts working in the military field, and its universities, such as the Shanghai Jiatong, collaborate with the PLA on cyber-espionage capabilities, even though only some of this hacking activity has been linked directly to Chinese agencies or the PLA. One of the most egregious examples occurred in August 2006 when a USAF general revealed what he believed to be a Chinese attack against the country's defence establishment. The perpetrator had downloaded 10–20 terabytes of data from non-classified IP router networks. This is a huge amount of information. If the same amount had been printed on paper the physical transportation of documents would have required a line of moving vans stretching bumper to bumper from the Pentagon to the harbour of Baltimore 50 miles away (Rid, 2013: 86). Although the information was not classified it allowed the Chinese to trace and identify every single person working for the Defense Department, and will thus (in theory) enable the Chinese to access the Pentagon's classified network using false identities at some point in the future. The cyber-attack was so extensive that it prompted one expert to describe it as 'the first act of World War 3' (Rosenbaum, 2011: 23).

The haemorrhaging of information from a defence establishment is one way of waging war without fighting directly, and it was in light of this threat that the Pentagon recruited 4,000 new cyber specialists in March 2013. Moreover, such an attack would deny the United States a competitive advantage, the 'technological edge' that the Department of Defense claims it still retains. It would threaten the United States' technological lead. Unlike the arms races on land and sea that preceded the First World War, today's arms races are taking place in the digital world and are rarely reported. The weapons that the Pentagon believes have been targetted so far (possibly by China) include the F35 Joint Strike Fighter, America's most expensive military project. The potential 'compromising' of more than two dozen other weapon systems has already forced the Pentagon to take counter-measures to ensure that they remain operationally viable. A report by the Defence Science Board warns that the sheer scale of the hacking could have 'severe consequences' for US forces engaged in combat (*The Times*, 29 May 2013).

In early 2013 the Obama administration publicly stated that the extent of Chinese cyber-attacks against the United States was jeopardising the relationship between Beijing and Washington. While the United States has cyber-warriors of its own, it claims that these operate under different rules to the Chinese with restrictions against using offensive weapons for non-military purposes or stealing corporate data. In other words, the United States finds itself fighting an asymmetrical digital war.

The use of cyber-attacks is entirely consistent with Chinese strategic thinking. 'Force' (or '*Li*') only appears nine times in *The Art of War*'s thirteen chapters. As far as Sun Tzi was concerned victory and defeat are essentially psychological. The object is to inflict pain psychologically rather than physically—to put the enemy on the back foot and keep him there. In 2012 the US Secretary of Defence Leon Panetta warned that a series of cyber-attacks aimed at critical US infrastructure could paralyse the nation by creating a profound sense of vulnerability (Langø, 2013: 16).

Cyber-espionage, in short, offers an example of a Sun-Tzian approach to war: indirect, non-violent and devastating in the long term. The Chinese have written about war more extensively than any other civilisation and have developed a very different understanding of its character and nature. The principal difference between Chinese and Western strategic thought is that Western philosophers and military thinkers begin with Aristotle's instrumental distinction between ends and means. War is an instrument for attaining an end—it is a continuation of policy by other means. Whereas Western strategic thought emphasises the use of maximum force in order to impose one's will on an enemy, the Chinese emphasise the use of minimum force to prevent an enemy from imposing his will.

A cyberwar is not only possible but could even prove as dangerous as the Cold War. According to Craig Mundie, Microsoft's chief strategy officer, the fact that it is extremely difficult to attribute a cyber-attack to a single individual or state means that such a conflict would be more clandestine and surreptitious than would be the case in the classical definition of war (Schmidt and Cohen, 2013: 105). The problem of attribution could permit states to do things to each other online that they would consider far too provocative offline. It could encourage a high degree of recklessness. It could lead to what Google calls a 'Code War', rather than a cold war or 'cool war', a virtual contest carried on in parallel with trade and diplomatic exchanges in the 'real' world. Yet a code war would still share certain features of a cold war. One of these would be the central role of espionage, with worms, key-logging software and location-based tracking replacing the embedded moles and dead-letter drops of the 1950s. Another feature that would resemble a cold war would be the use of proxy conflicts, in which attacks could be redirected through non-state actors or third parties (e.g. North Korea). Such attacks would be extremely difficult to attribute to a single party, given that, unlike missiles, cyber-attacks do not leave a vapour trail behind them (ibid.: 16).

The critics of the concept of cyber-warfare take issue with the claim that the use of non-violent digital attacks to achieve political objectives can be understood as part of a new form of warfare. For them the concept of cyber-warfare represents an attack on the idea of violence itself. Violence mediated through cyberspace is less physical, less emotional and ultimately less symbolic than the conventional use of violence. Thomas Rid argues, like Clausewitz, that violence is the central element in defining a war. So too is taking full responsibility for one's actions: 'History does not know of acts of war without eventual attribution' (Rid, 2013: 2).

Rid is not alone in expressing this kind of scepticism. Erik Gartzke argues that the introduction of cyber-attacks entails a broadening of the dimensions of warfare (Langø, 2013: 21). Dorothy Denning insists that cyber-attacks will never be able to achieve the same effects as the use of armed forces, such as overthrowing a government, seizing land or maximising human casualties (ibid.: 22). But in the event that two thermonuclear powers were to engage in war, it is unlikely that these objectives would be attainable in any case. Neither power could realistically aim to overthrow the government of the other power (though the defeated government might well implode afterwards). The number of casualties would also have to be limited. As an American general stated on the eve of the 1991 Iraq War, 'We can't do Dresden any longer'. If this applies to Saddam Hussein's Iraq, then it will surely apply to any future conflict with a great power.

Our understanding of military history may need to be updated in order to accommodate the threat posed by cyberwar. The critics are overly reliant on the role that violence plays in Clausewitz's thinking with regard to war. War is not always violent. For much of history, successful commanders tried to avoid battle. Even Napoleon, whom Clausewitz admired for his success on the battlefield, managed to outmanoeuvre General Mack at Ulm (1805) and forced him to surrender his army without firing a shot. The duke of Marlborough—the greatest English commander of all—was able to turn the *Ne Plus Ultra* Lines (the last line of defence before Paris) by outflanking and outfoxing the French, not outfighting them. After reviewing a host of cyber-attacks a NATO-sponsored panel of experts concluded that 'an act need not have immediate physical consequences to comprise a use of force' (Schmitt, 2012: 20). One example of this would be a virus or computer code that shuts down the catapult system on an aircraft carrier. It may not involve the destruction of a single aircraft or the carrier but it would still make a $15 billion platform redundant.

Naval blockades, as Phillip Meilinger argues, are a clear example of war being waged with minimum violence:

> The nature of war is mutable. Warfare in the modern world remained deadly and destructive, but it need not be violent or bloody. The fundamental aspect of war in centuries past may have taken the form of sanguinary battles between infantrymen, but that is no longer necessarily the case. Traditional sea warfare, as well as present-day cyber operations, can become enormously deadly and destructive—but neither violent nor bloody. (Meilinger, 2010: 28)

And the same may apply in space—satellites can be destroyed without any immediate loss of life, yet such an attack would blind the enemy and nullify their greatest asset: information dominance.

War in outer space

Space has been militarised ever since the United States successfully deployed its first photo-reconnaissance satellite *Constellation* in 1961 to support the new Polaris strategic force two years later. Weapons have yet to be deployed in space. However, the age in which they are is likely to arrive almost as quickly as the age of air power after Orville Wright first took to air. After all, it took states only fourteen years from *Kitty Hawk*'s first flight before they began to bomb cities.

Space power is in an analogous position to that of airpower early in the twentieth century. It serves a supportive role by providing navigation (GPS), communications and intelligence in much the same way as air power was initially used to identify the fall of shot for artillery and as an alternative to the cavalry in reconnaissance. The idea of an actual war in space first emerged in the 1950s, when US Air Force General Bernard Shriver called for 'space superiority'. Remarks such as these were suppressed during this period in order to avoid entering an arms race in space with the Soviet Union. However, the United States is likely to find itself in this kind of arms race with China in the near future. The introduction of warfare to space will require new organisations, new operational conditions, new ways of war and, above all, new ways of thinking about war.

At the close of the twentieth century Colin Gray concluded that space power suffered from a dearth of strategic theory, and this situation has not changed a great deal in the intervening period (Gray, 1999: 255). Space power still awaits its Clausewitz. In seeking to fill this void, Gray, one of the world's leading Clausewitzian scholars, tried to apply Clausewitz's ideas to space in his seminal work *Modern Strategy*.

Gray argues that space is a modern equivalent of the 'high ground' that commanders aim to seize in a conventional war. Space offers the ultimate high ground both for the purposes of reconnaissance and communication between forces at sea and on land through the use of satellites. During the First Gulf War in 1991 the use of satellites served as a 'force multiplier', leading Arthur C. Clarke to describe 'Desert Storm' as the first ever satellite war (Dolman, 2002: 152). Rather than being applied to nuclear deterrence, satellite technology thus played a vital part in a conventional military campaign. It heralded a new age, one which Xavier Pasco calls 'a first adaptation to the post-Cold War era' (Pasco, 2012). The Chinese military learned a great deal from that campaign as it confirmed their fears that the United States had forged ahead in terms of the use of new military technologies.

Pasco argues that space, which was initially a tactical force multiplier in the mid-1990s, has now become a security enabler, allowing what came to be known as network-centric warfare. Military earth-observation satellites offer increased resolution (geometric and spectral) and enlarged fields of view, networked to genuine space architecture. Space power has given the United States a decisive advantage in terms of combat timing, operational tempo, synchronising its forces, manoeuvre and the integrated application of firepower (Gray, 1999: 263). In 1991 it provided the United States with an edge over Saddam's forces, while in the Second Gulf War (2003) it provided the United States with 'full spectrum dominance'. At the time of the latter conflict it had become increasingly clear that any country which sought to defend itself against a competitor would have to deny the enemy the ability to use space. It was for this reason, according to one Chinese commentator, that China tested its first anti-satellite system in 2007 (Baohui Zhang, 2011).

The militarisation of space is probably inevitable. In 2009 the Chinese Air Force Chief of Staff General Xu Qiliang claimed that China had entered the space age 'to expand its national interests' (*PLA Daily*, 1 Nov. 2009). China's interests in space can of course be interpreted as being purely defensive in nature, and as long as the United States enjoys primacy in space it will still be able to think of conducting a strategy such as Air–Sea Battle with some hope of success. However, it is unlikely that China will settle for anything less than parity with the United States in terms of any arms race in space. It may already be too late for that. A survey published in *Space Review* found that the point of departure in many recent PLA publications is the strong belief that the militarisation of space is unavoidable. Three internal Chinese sources are often cited—*Space War*, by Colonel Li Daguang; *On Space Operations*, by Colonel Jia Junming, and *Joint Space War Campaigns* by Colonel Yuan Zelu (Pillsbury, 2007: 10). Kevin Pollpeter has provided a candid assessment of these works: the Chinese argue that not only is the militarisation of space inevitable, but so too is an eventual confrontation with the United States. 'As the struggle over air and space control is becoming the new focal point of war, space will become the main battlefield of future wars' (Pollpeter, 2005: 338).

As the Chinese continue to make progress in their space programme, the Outer Space Treaty is likely to wither away. China will have its own international space station by 2020 and it is also developing a heavy thrust space rocket. Thirty-five Chinese satellites will soon be orbiting the earth as part of China's second-generation *beidou* navigation satellite system which will offer the same geo-location services as GPS (including a military function). The United States was sufficiently concerned about China's progress in these areas to warn that it reserved the right to respond in self-defence in its 2011 National Space Security Strategy. Diplomatic cables leaked by WikiLeaks have revealed that the United States is growing increasingly concerned about precisely this issue, with Condoleezza Rice specifically warning China about the prospects of escalating tensions (in effect an arms race in space) (*io9*, 2011).

It is impossible to understand what a space war would look like without recognising that it is impossible to use all of space for military purposes. The low-earth orbit (LEO) from 60 to 300 miles above the atmosphere is ideal for intelligence satellites, which provide obvious advantages in terms of imaging because they are relatively close to earth and can take high-resolution pictures. The medium-earth orbit (MEO) from 300 to 22,000 miles above the atmosphere houses GPS satellites. The geostationary orbit (GEO) is the most important of all because its satellites are the least vulnerable to attack, and it is this orbit where communications and missile early warning systems are based.

The United States has satellites in all three orbits. Its warships rely on LEO satellites for enemy ship surveillance, while its unmanned aerial vehicle (UAV) pilots rely on LEO satellites for intelligence. The military relies on NAVSTAR, a satellite system that currently consists of thirty-two navigation satellites which are needed to guide precision-guided munitions and pilot drones. The United States also has significant deep space assets including six early warning satellites that are needed to detect a nuclear strike. All of these orbits would feature in a Sino-American war, regardless of whether or not such a conflict would be constricted to space or would take the form of a conventional conflict using space assets.

The former UN weapons inspector Geoffrey Forden has published a compelling scenario:

> High above Asia, as the bars and clubs of Beijing begin to fill up at the end of another work day, a US early warning satellite spots the tell-tale plume of a missile streaking out of the wastes of Western China. Warning bells sound all through the Pentagon. Tensions have been running high between China and the United States, as the two countries struggle to resolve the latest installment of the Taiwanese crisis. And China has had a run of unprecedented activity in space: the past two days have seen China launch four large missions into deep space, three within the last 6 hours. Fortunately, a high resolution American spy satellite will be over that second launch site within minutes, giving the US a unique ability to determine what is going on. But even though tasking orders are given to photograph the suspected launch site, none are returned. The satellite, code-named Crystal 3, no longer responds to commands. Within minutes, US Space Command reports that four NAVSTAR/GPS satellites—used to guide American drones and precision bombs—have stopped broadcasting. China's space war against the United States has started. (Forden, 2008)

In Forden's scenario a Chinese–US space war would not seriously damage the capabilities of the United States. He argues that even if every Chinese anti-satellite attack missile (ASAT) were to hit its targets and the Americans did not respond despite evidence of an attack well ahead of time, an attack is unlikely to cripple the United States as it would still have enough space assets to mount a conventional counter-attack.

The capabilities needed for such a scenario to unfold in reality will not be available for some years to come. China's only ASAT test in 2007 was aimed against an obsolete weather satellite. The missile is likely to have tracked its target through the use of an on-board telescope using visible light, which, unlike US missile defence interceptors (which focus on the infra-red light that the heat of a target emits), requires that a satellite is attacked in bright sunlight. Indeed, even though the site from which the interceptor was launched was cloaked in darkness, the target satellite was high enough to be illuminated by the sun.

In Forden's future scenario the Chinese would destroy nine US satellites on the first day of the conflict. But they would have difficulty maintaining secrecy in the period prior to an attack. A total of thirty-six mobile launchers (with two or more missiles assigned to each target) would be required and they would have to be positioned around the country weeks beforehand. The United States would be able to observe their deployment. Even missiles assembled inside buildings would need to be moved to the launch pad one at a time. Four days prior to any attack, China's *Long March* rockets, carrying deep space attack ASATs, would have to be parked in space in an orbit of 200 miles altitude, awaiting others—a tell-tale sign of an impending strike. Further missiles would have to be fired six hours before the main attack began.

This would prove to be a formidable undertaking, even if the United States chose not to pre-empt such a strike. It would be impossible to destroy all US military communication satellites, the early warning satellites that observe missile launches and its surveillance satellites in geostrategic orbit. The United States also has commercial back-ups—satellites owned or operated by commercial operators, as well as civilian and military communication satellites in low-earth orbit. 'The United States may be the country most dependent on space for its military activities. But it is also the least vulnerable, because of the tremendous redundancy of its space assets' (Forden, 2008: 3).

Forden also considers the other options available to China in such a scenario. China could choose, for example, to attack navigation satellites, denying the United States the GPS system it needs for its precision-guided munitions and UAVs. If these were destroyed, the US Air Force would be forced to fly missions during daylight hours and to conduct some of the dangerous missions now flown by UAVs. But the Chinese would only be able to do this in phases. They would not be able to launch enough missiles to degrade US capabilities in the first few days of such a conflict. They could opt to attack communication satellites, of course, which would significantly reduce the bandwidth the US military would need. But this would still leave a great deal of bandwidth, not to mention the civilian satellites which were used extensively in the 2003 invasion of Iraq. China could try to destroy America's early warning satellites, but that too would be a risk as the United States relies on these satellites to detect a nuclear attack and it could thus provoke a nuclear exchange. The Chinese could alternatively elect to attack the low-altitude satellites which orbit the earth in closely spaced groups of two or three, and triangulate on the radio signals emitted by US warships. This would be the most attractive option from a Chinese perspective as it could also take the United States by surprise. However, the United States could respond by changing the orbital speeds of its remaining satellites which would make them almost impossible to target. Much like the attack on Pearl Habor, Forden concludes that while a pre-emptive Chinese strike in space would be a major tactical setback for the United States, it would not constitute a strategic endgame. The United States would still be able to continue the war.

However, it is possible that Forden is overly sanguine about the future. China's micro-satellite programme has already sparked major concern. Micro-satellites have many potential offensive uses, such as latching on to American satellites, disrupting their proper functioning or exploding within range and destroying them altogether. China's *kaituozhe* launch vehicles may already give it that option. In the future, other weapons systems such as high-powered microwave and particle beam weapons (already under development) as well as ground laser ASATs (already tested, according to one source) may change the balance of power still further. In 2012 the Pentagon's annual report to Congress on China's military made particular reference to its 'jamming, lasert, microwave and cyber weapons', and the continuing close proximity operations between satellites which were conducted with little in the way of transparency or explanation (Klotz, 2012).

Nevertheless, as Forden acknowledges, a space conflict between China and the United States would still have disastrous consequences. The destruction of just nine satellites during the first hour of an attack would put nearly 20,000 pieces of debris over 4 inches in diameter into the most populated belt in the low-earth orbit. Over time this debris would 'clump' together before fanning out and causing a run-away chain of collisions that would render space unusable. It would shut down many of the systems on which the world relies, from commercial air flight to everyday credit card transactions.

All of this may be entirely academic of course. Space weapons are costly and may be unnecessary. Satellites can be destroyed from earth by attacking ground stations or using high-altitude nuclear explosions. Satellite uplinks and downlinks can be jammed. Conventional attacks on laser sites would be more effective (DeBois et al., 2004: 58–59). In the case of an attack by space mines the United States could rely on the sheer number of its satellite systems given that many perform the same function, so the loss of one would not necessarily be disastrous.

But the status quo in space, based on US space supremacy, might not last much longer. It was this prospect that led Everett Dolman to suggest that the United States should withdraw from the space treaty, put weapons in space and seize control of low-earth orbit. Through the use of space-based laser or other kinetic energy weapons the United States should then seek to prevent other states from putting weapons in space with the aim of guaranteeing the free commercial use of space just as the Royal Navy guaranteed free navigation at sea by eliminating piracy. Dolman consequently argues that the United States should use its military power to guarantee a safe space environment (including protection from space debris) (Dolman, 2005: 157).

Dolman claims that this would not necessarily lead to war, and that it might actually decrease the likelihood of any such conflict breaking out in the future. The reasoning behind this is the idea that no other state would be able to engage in a space conflict with the United States if the latter seized control of LEO. The United States could prevent any other nation from deploying weapons by simply shooting them down. It would also be able to destroy any terrestrial ASAT facilities if a crisis deteriorated (Dolman, 2002: 158). If the United States chose to adopt this course of action then it would undoubtedly be perceived as nothing other than a form of 'military blackmail' in China (to quote an official military publication) that would lead to further conflict and distrust between the two powers (*Chinascope*, 2011). However, as Dolman argues, this is likely to be preferable to a US–Chinese arms race in space, which would almost inevitably spiral out of control (Dolman, 2012: 94).

Given the potential consequences of this kind of arms race, it is important that both powers stop short of confronting each other directly in space. In 1962 the United States detonated a nuclear bomb 250 miles above Johnson Island in the Pacific, a 1.4 megaton explosion that created an electromagnetic pulse much larger than expected, and worse still, generated an artificial radiation belt that crippled a third of all satellites in low-earth orbit. Even a limited war in space would have devastating consequences and they would last for much longer. Forden suggests that the United States should seek to create and act as a guarantor for a code of conduct in space that will establish new 'rules of the road' while simultaneously trying to persuade all space-faring nations from Australia to Japan to agree to a ban on the so-called 'kinetic kill interceptors' that would inflict the most damage.

What would victory in a Sino-American war look like?

The foregoing might appear to suggest that both China and the United States have a highly limited range of military options, all of which are extremely unattractive and particularly so in the case of a limited nuclear war (which is certainly possible with regard to the Air–Sea Battle concept or an anti-satellite strike in space). The nuclear dimension is of course central to the belief that a war between the two powers is decidedly 'improbable'. Both China and the United States believe that their nuclear weapons will serve to prevent a US–Chinese war from ever being fought. Based on public pronouncements from Chinese military figures, China has enough nuclear warheads to decimate the west coast of the United States. In the words of one Chinese general, China has the capability to leave Los Angeles 'a smoking ruin' (Rosenbaum, 2011: 23).

However, while the military options available to China and the United States are far from attractive, it should be noted that the military options available in 1914 were not particularly attractive either. From a political perspective the most likely scenario would be a Chinese–US conflict at sea, but this would quickly escalate. A conflict in outer space would have catastrophic consequences for all concerned. This leaves the final scenario, a cyberwar between the two powers, but as both are armed with nuclear weapons this would clearly take the United States and China into uncharted territory. Both might expect the other to blink first in much the same way as the diplomats in the First World War who gambled and lost so much on the idea that a pre-emptive blow would decisively change the balance of forces in favour of the side that struck first,

This book has eschewed making predictions and has instead sought to craft stories which the reader can explore. In the words of one prominent futurologist, learning from the future involves 're-perception' (Watson and Freeman, 2013: 20). By exploring the wilder shores of war we are better placed to see the present in a new light, which enables us to engage with the world in new ways (ibid). This is what Stephen Rosen tries to achieve in *Winning the Next War* (1994), which claims that one of the challenges with the evolving state of war involves identifying the new metrics (or measurements) of effectiveness. In the absence of a clear set of metrics for achieving victory 'war seems unlikely to fulfil its post-war pay-offs' (Martel, 2007: 308–9). What, asks Frank Hofmann, if cyber-power—the ability to control and manipulate the cyber domain which is increasingly merging with the physical—is not only a force-multiplier, but a new form of power and influence? (Hoffman, 2013).

The nature of victory is beginning to change, and the rise of unorthodox forms of conflict is not only redefining the nature of war but forcing us 'to think through the relationships between force, violence and lethality more systematically than has hitherto been done'. 'Force does not necessarily imply violence particularly if violence implies lethality' (Stone, 2012: 103). If this is true, then it also follows that we may have to re-assess what we mean by 'victory'.

It is the elusive nature of victory in recent conflicts that is necessitating that the very term itself is redefined. One writer identifies the need to distinguish between victory and the outcome of the employment of force through strategy; another makes a distinction between decisive military victory and a possible, often elusive, overall achievement on a political level. 'Decisive [military] victory ... is hard to translate into desired political effect' (Heuser, 2013). William Martel is mostly concerned with the wars the United States has fought in the twenty-first century, where despite being victorious on the battlefield it has lost its way in the post-war period. 'When the battle's lost and won', the witches tell Macbeth. It is important to note that the two are not alternatives. Shakespeare used the crucial word 'and' rather than lost 'or' won. The victor becomes the vanquished, as is the case with Macbeth. His victory in battle is the beginning of his unravelling as a man. His whole career, as he recognises at the end of the play, has been 'a tale told by an idiot'. How often has this also been said of victors who have gone on to lose the peace?

With the exception of the exponents of the Air–Sea Battle concept, most in the US military know this to be true. War is so varied in register, style and content that it subverts any single attempt to define it, and the same applies to its political outcomes. Victory is no longer marked by surrender ceremonies or victory parades, let alone by war crime tribunals like those held in Tokyo in 1946. Even local successes in the war on terror, maintained Donald Rumsfeld, would never be known to the public. The big battles would not be caught on screen. There would be no iconic snapshots of the Marines storming on to the beaches as they did at Iwo Jima and Okinawa. The real stories would be off-stage, as the security services intercepted terrorist communications traffic with the aim of preventing any future outrages on the scale of 9/11. The same is likely to be true of a future inter-state war too.

The key to understanding how force can achieve direct political outcomes lies in the communicative nature of political violence. In Emile Simpson's words, war provides an analytical framework for armed force to reach a decision and 'force is simply another way to communicate meaning' (Simpson, 2012: 27). One of Simpson's most important insights is that in contemporary conflicts political actors increasingly circumvent tactical military confrontations—or battles—and choose to deploy force in a diverse spectrum from terrorism to insurgency and drone strikes over the skies of Waziristan—all for directly political effects. In the words of another author, the aim is to draw on a 'range of symbolic resources' to win a war on one's own terms (Chong, 2013: 3).

A cyber strike that briefly crippled the United States would communicate a purpose and it would also pose a challenge with regard to whether or not it would choose to escalate the situation. In Hugh White's book a tactical nuclear strike against Guam serves the same purpose—the US president blinks first and declines to escalate the war any further. Yet a strike will always invite a counter-attack with or without nuclear weapons. The Pentagon found White's scenario so provocative that it removed the author from the guest list of the US embassy in Canberra when Robert Gates visited. Imagine a similar first strike in space which compromises America's ability to scan the planet for—among other things—nuclear missiles. The essence of any war is to destroy not the capability but the will of the opponent and thus make a military engagement unnecessary, or short-lived. Yet as Martin van Creveld argues, all technological innovations, however impressive, do not change the nature of conflict. War is always 'an affair of the heart' (Van Creveld, 1991: 314).

The Chinese have always known that chance and contingency are central to war. *The Art of War* never assumes that there is such a thing as absolute victory. Decisiveness is a sheer impossibility. The truth about war lies beyond victory and defeat. Clausewitz is fighting against the impossibility of war; Sun Tzi actually celebrates it. But in the end, of course, one side usually prevails.

5

CONCLUSION

'[W]ar is a dangerous place.'
(George W Bush)

No more great power wars?

In his much-acclaimed book *The Better Angels of our Nature*, Steven Pinker offers several explanations for the absence of a war between any of the great powers in the period since 1945. The book concludes that war has simply become increasingly unthinkable (Pinker, 2013: 303). Although Pinker concedes that the long peace between the great powers is not a perpetual one, he claims that the probability of war between them is now more remote than ever.

A similar claim was put forward in an article in *The Washington Quarterly*, 'The Demise of Ares: The End of War As We Know It?'. The article argues that inter-state conflict has now become an exception. 'Classic international conflict has practically *disappeared* from the modern world.' The number of wars between the great powers has been in steady decline ever since the Westphalian system was established in 1648. While there were between nine and eleven great power wars between 1700 and 1815, between two and six took place in the period from 1815 to 1930 and only between two and three such wars have broken out in the period since (Tertrais, 2012: 9).

However comforting these figures might appear, it is important to avoid being drawn into a sense of complacency given the vast destruction that the two great power wars of the twentieth century caused throughout the world. Great power wars may have become more infrequent, but the impact of such conflicts has clearly increased: after forty-three years of peace, the First World War resulted in the deaths of 37 million people, while the number of fatalities in the Second World War was around twice that figure. At the time of the Cuban Missile Crisis the United States estimated that a Third World War would cost 150 million lives, and possibly many more. While the latter event was avoided, it is not inconceivable that two or more states will miscalculate in the future. In 1998, for example, India and Pakistan came extremely close to nuclear war, and the two countries seem to have learned very little from the near-miss. In the 2008 Mumbai killings the Indian navy wanted to blockade the port of Karachi. It was only dissuaded from doing so after the United States brought pressure on New Delhi to avoid yet another state-to-state confrontation (just as it had done in 1998) (Rossbaum, 2011).

A Sino-American war could prove to be the most ruinous war that the world has ever witnessed, if not in terms of loss of life then certainly in terms of the disruption it would cause to the world economy, particularly if the conflict was at least partly conducted in space. Every great power conflict has been worse than the last. The British often describe the First World War as the 'Great War', but this term was previously reserved for the Napoleonic Wars (in which 2 million soldiers died, including 800,000 alone in one campaign, the invasion of Russia in 1812). It is unlikely that the Second World War will be the worst and last great power war. If the past (1914–18) did not resemble the past that preceded it, why should the future not yield even more surprises?

None of this is to deny the declining appeal of war despite the fact that great powers still compete with each other. Over time trade has become a far more profitable vector for wealth creation. War has been pricing itself out of the market for some time and its declining incidence can be attributed to many factors. Nevertheless, before interstate war is declared 'obsolete', two inconvenient truths need to be brought into play.

The first is that the statistics do not tell the whole story. It would be foolish to jump from statistical correlations to causal conclusions. The fact that the great powers only fought a small number of wars between themselves in the twentieth century does not mean that this figure will continue to decline in the future.

As Karl Popper wrote in *A World of Propensities* (1990):

> The tendency of statistical averages to remain stable if the conditions remain stable is one of the most remarkable characteristics of our universe. It can be explained, I hold, only by propensity theory: by the theory that there exists weighted possibilities that are more than mere possibilities, but tendencies or propensities to become real: tendencies or propensities to realise themselves that are inherent in all possibilities in varying degrees, and which are something like forces that keep the statistics stable.

In other words, it is possible to discover 'weighted possibilities' that may be at work in the international system. The world is no longer what we once thought, a 'causal machine'. It is instead a world of unfolding outcomes. We may never know for sure where those propensities will lead but we can still work with what Popper called an 'objective theory of probability' (Popper, 1990: 148). Some outcomes are more likely than others. In the end, those propensities restrict the number of things that can happen, determine some of the things that will happen and make it possible to assign greater or lesser probabilities to the rest. It is in that limited but still vital respect that it is worth discussing them.

On that basis it is perfectly plausible to deduce that another great power war is improbable. But the world also believed this to be true in 1913, and there were good grounds for holding to such a belief—some of the conflicts which should have broken out had failed to do so. But as historians would contend, each non-event such as a war between Russia and Britain in the 1890s has to be explained on its own terms. It is clearly the case that great power wars have become increasingly rare, and one reason for this could be the ever growing complexity of the contemporary world. The costs of war have risen while the pay-offs have decreased. But complexity does not negate the logic of great power conflict, it merely complicates it.

This leads to a second inconvenient truth: although great powers clearly seem to derive more from cooperation than ever before and much less from conflict, competition is still the name of the game—'neither friend nor enemy' is a common Chinese formulation for China's relationship with the United States. Cooperation simply offers greater efficiencies and in the end yields greater rewards. Indeed, it is quite extraordinary how much the great powers have been able to increase their wealth and general quality of life by avoiding war altogether. But the absence is not, alas, based on a 'power law'.

A power law refers to a functional relationship between two entities. Power laws are especially popular in science. Phase transitions in thermodynamic systems are associated with the emergence of a power law distribution of certain qualities such as the critical exponents of a system. It is believed that power laws are universal (i.e. they do not depend on the details of a physical system but only on its dimension). The ubiquity of power law relations in physics is partly due to dimensional constraints, while in a complex system power laws are thought to be signatures of particular stochastic processes (random fields being a case in point). In the market a power law occurs when three conditions are met: variety (many different products are on sale); inequality (some are better quality than others); and networked effects (such as reputation or fashion which tends to amplify differences and promote better quality products). Success, in short, breeds success (Anderson, 2007: 126).

In the case of great power conflict a power law (towards peace) would occur when social and economic complexity reduces the payoffs of war. Great powers would be deterred from going to war because of the costs and the longer this situation obtains the more difficult it is to 'imagine' conflict being useful. Once the utility of war is thrown into doubt then its morality must also be questioned. In the words of the novelist Milan Kundera, Germany and France are now 'anthropologically' incapable of going to war against each other.

But power laws are complex too. One of the features of power laws is that they are fractal (however far you zoom in, they still look like power laws). Mathematicians describe this as 'self-similarity at multiple scales'. The long tale of a decline in great power war is made up of many smaller tales, each of which is its own little world. Markets become ever more complex (an example is Angell's bond markets) and societies becomes less homogenous (nations become less essentialist: Europe, some would argue, is becoming increasingly diasporic; one day there may be no nations left to go to war against each other). But the real outlier in this picture is war itself; it is remarkably resilient. War, wrote John Keegan, is like a disease in that it exhibits a capacity to mutate and it mutates fastest in the face of efforts to control or eliminate it. Keegan's BBC Reith lectures *War and our World* (1998) ended on an admonitory note. War will never disappear from politics unless we address its causes. The principal 'cause' of great power conflict, unfortunately, is what it always has been: competition.

We are an innately competitive species and great powers, with much more to lose, are more competitive than most. However, Hobbes claimed that it was important to draw a distinction between competitiveness and competition. Competition is hard-wired into the species: the very qualities that enable us to live together are the source of competition. In primitive societies, security is purchased through 'dense sociality' such as families, kinship groups or a tribe, all of which separate 'insiders' from 'outsiders'. The same propensity to be communal and socially cohesive makes us aggressive to and excessively fearful of others.

Competitiveness is very different. As Hobbes claimed, it is a form of quarrel. Competitiveness leads humans to quarrel even over a 'trifle'. War is often about status—great powers seek to maintain it; lesser powers enter into alliances with great powers to secure it. In the anarchic order which constitutes the international system it is still dangerous to be dishonoured. Richard Lebow has challenged the neo-realist emphasis on material factors, stressing instead the old realist belief in the need for reputation, status and standing. Indeed, contrary to realist expectations he argues that the search for security was responsible for only nineteen of the ninety-four wars he investigated. Standing, by contrast, was responsible for sixty-two wars as a primary or at least a secondary motive. Revenge, also a manifestation of status (especially when one's credibility is on the line as it was for the United States after 9/11) is implicated in another eleven. In short, 'spirit' has been the principal cause of war across the centuries (Lebow, 2010).

Competitiveness has its own logic and no set of statistics will ever reveal the whole story, or tell it very well. It is important that this is acknowledged because the world is about to enter the most dangerous phase of great power competition since the end of the Cold War. It is possible that the resilience of the international system will be tested as severely as it was in 1914.

Back to 1914

Historians often claim that the events of the past influence the future. Yet an alternative approach would involve thinking about how our expectations of the future influence our present actions. Bueno De Mesquita provides a rather prosaic example of this when he points out that the cutting down of Christmas trees does not 'cause' Christmas.

Anticipations of Christmas 'cause' the trees to be chopped down. What we do today is not only caused by what happened yesterday but what we believe will be the consequence of our own actions tomorrow. In that sense the future influences the present as much as the past.

But it is the past to which we return again and again. Analogies open our minds to ways of seeing our own time as fragile, precarious and ephemeral. At its best, analogising allows us to think about present trends and where they may be leading us. It challenges us, in other words, to think about how things might be different.

The American academic Martin Kramer calls historical analogy 'a glib man's substitute for analysis'. However, in the words of another historian, the ability to grasp the way in which events unfolding in the present may have also occurred in the past is what separates 'glib analogies' from informed analysis. To dismiss historical analogy as a default response is to misunderstand how we understand the world, or at least how we try to (Rapport, 2012).

Some years ago Ernest May and Richard Neustadt produced a template that would enable history to be used by decision-makers. When looking at a crisis like 1914 they suggested that we should identify what we know, what is unclear and what is presumed (May and Neustadt, 1988). What, then, do we know about the present international situation? We know that policy-makers in China and the United States are aware of how war broke out in 1914 and are keen to avoid making the same mistakes. The First World War is still the Urtext of modern great power conflict. No one wanted war but not everyone went out of their way to avoid it. War broke out, many historians now believe, because so many statesmen thought it so improbable.

But what we also know is that the rise of China is taking place in a different context from that of imperial Germany. Unlike Germany, China may be seeking only a gradual modification of the international system, and it is certainly not a revisionist power. Unlike Russia, which is dissatisfied with the present order but powerless to challenge it, China is powerful enough to demand changes but satisfied enough (for the moment at least) to accommodate itself to American leadership. And while the United States may be in relative decline, it is operating from a much greater position of strength than Edwardian Britain. Even with the $500 billion defence cuts to come, the United States is immensely more powerful militarily than the United Kingdom was in 1913. The 'Pivot' towards Asia may be similar to Britain's pivot towards Europe (when it recalled its warships from the Caribbean and the Far East after striking deals with the United States and Japan). Yet it is unclear whether China is quite as resentful as Germany, still less as pessimistic about its future (the Germans were obsessed with the idea that the future belonged to the 'continental landmass powers', the United States and Russia). It is also doubtful whether the Chinese military will become quite as independent of political control as the German army in the period leading to 1914. Similarly, in the absence of a Social Darwinist mindset, it is highly unlikely that anyone will actually preach the life-affirming virtues of war, or think it historically 'inevitable'. The extreme nationalists in China may be vocal, but they are still in a minority.

In 1909 Angell popularised an economic argument according to which interdependence and the complexity of international politics had made great power war obsolete, and similar arguments are often heard today. According to those who hold this belief, the incentives to engage in a great power conflict have been reduced by the highly globalised nature of the international economy. One study finds that war between great powers is correlated with a decrease in trade relative to pre- and post-war periods, and given today's interdependent trading networks, war is simply not 'on' (Anderton and Carter, 2001). Stephen Brooks similarly argues that war is highly unlikely due to the qualitative differences in the nature of global production when compared with the international economy in 1913. Given the dominance of multinational corporations in global production and the increasing prominence of inter-firm trade and international sub-contracting (Brooks, 2007), a single good is likely to be produced in several countries, not one, thereby reducing the attractiveness of war. However, it should be noted that the level of intra-firm trade between the United States and China is not particularly high. A 2011 OECD paper found that 28.7 per cent of total exports from the United States to China and 13.7 per cent of total imports from China into the United States were intra-firm, and both figures are markedly lower than the global average of 47.8 per cent and 27.9 per cent respectively (Lanz and Miroudot, 2011). Moreover, the volume of trade before the First World War was higher than it is today (Obstfeld and Taylor, 2003: 123).

If we are fated to always speculate about the future we are also fated to recall the past, and the historical analogy that would seem most pertinent as we try to understand how Chinese–US relations might evolve remains that of the First World War. One of the reasons why Western strategic thinkers are fascinated by the First World War is that they like to think of the parties being locked into historically inevitable struggles. Political scientists would dispute this by pointing out that countries go to war because they misunderstand each other's intentions, or they stumble into war by mistake. An aspiring power might seek to achieve more than an established power is willing to share, or a former hegemonic power might prove unable to police the rules while the rising power has neither the will nor the wish to assume responsibility.

The main lesson to be learned from the First World War is the fact that different societies have different worldviews as well as different rationalities which often encourage different ways of thinking about war and peace. If the Darwinists are right, then our basic cognitive capacities have been shaped by natural selection to yield information immediately relevant to survival. Cognitive dissonance and confirmation bias may well be maladaptations of our survival toolkit, but we seem to be stuck with them, certainly for the foreseeable future.

If we are to preach the virtues of peace, we must also comprehend the attractions of war. Belief-systems like those of Norman Angell (now shared by many more people than in his day) do not form and flow on the basis of their inherent properties like blobs in a lava-lamp. Wrong ideas that should sink can rise again, propelled by the sword. Right ideas can fall victim to their exponents' complacency.

Owning the future

There is a vast range of divergent views with regard to whether a Sino–US war will ever break out. For writers like Zheng Bijian (2005), China will not only avoid the path taken by imperial Germany and by the United States and the Soviet Union after 1945, but will transcend the logic of great power conflict altogether because that logic is grounded in Western thinking, not Chinese. Similarly, the Chinese historian Wang Gungwu claims that his country is 'one of the strongest supporters of the [current] world order' and wants to shore it up by replacing an American-dominated world with a multipolar one (Wang, 2008: 7), while Dai Bingguo assures us that China will never pursue a Monroe Doctrine in East Asia, in effect retro-engineering the Sinosphere (Dai, 2010). Yet Xi Jinping constantly exhorts China's military to 'get ready to fight and to win wars' and 'to win regional warfare under I.T.-orientated conditions' (*International Herald Tribune*, 5 June 2013), and in the words of one author war may prove to be 'the midwife of the Chinese Century' (Sawyer, 1994: xiv). Likewise the inveterate realist thinker John Mearsheimer claims that China is simply unable to rise peacefully—war, after all, is 'the tragedy of Great Power politics' (Mearsheimer, 2001).

This book has argued that war is not inevitable, but nor is it as improbable as many experts suggest. The advice of experts or anyone with an interest in predicting a future conflict (particularly those in the military when faced with budget cuts) should also be treated with caution.

War can be avoided if the world follows the logic outlined in this book. One of the lessons that China and the United States should seek to learn from the First World War is to avoid placing too much faith in the ability of each to make rational decisions consistently, or to know what is in their best interests. Both powers should seek to enter into a constructive cultural dialogue about their respective values while holding each other accountable for how they interpret them. They should aim to avoid a naval arms race and take measures to prevent the militarisation of space and recognise that a cyberwar is not only possible, but the most likely form a conflict would take, at least in its initial stages. None of these steps would require them to reframe their competitive relationship in non-zero sum terms.

However, it is of vital importance that the possibility of a conflict between China and the United States continues to be discussed because the slippage, flux and confusion of the tide of history can lead to many different outcomes, and it is important to remember that the prevailing complacency regarding the obsolescence of great power war contributed to the outbreak of war in 1914. If the United States and China continue to convince themselves that war is too 'improbable' to take seriously, it is not only they but the rest of the world that may ultimately pay the price.

BIBLIOGRAPHY

Acheson, Dean (1966), 'The Lawyer's Path to Peace', *Virginia Quarterly Review*, 42, 3.

——— (1973), *This Vast Eternal Realm*, New York: Norton.

Adair, Gilbert (1997), *Surfing the Zeitgeist*, London: Faber & Faber.

Afflerbach, Holger (2007), 'The Topos of Improbable War in Europe before 1914', in Holger Afflerbach and David Stevenson (eds), *An Improbable War? The Outbreak of World War I and European Political Culture Before 1914*, New York: Berghahn.

Allen, R. (2011), 'The Unreal Enemy of America's Army', *Games & Culture*, 6, 1.

Allison, G. and R. Blackwell (2013), 'Interview: Lee Kuan Yew on the Future of U.S.-China Relations', *The Atlantic*, 5 Mar.

Ames, Roger and David Hall (1995), *Anticipating China: Thinking Through the Narratives of Chinese and Western Culture*, Albany: State University of New York.

Anderson, Chris (2007), *The Long Tale*, London: Business Books.

Anderton, C. and J. Carter (2001), 'The Impact of War on Trade: An Interrupted Time-Series Study', *Journal of Peace Research*, 38, 4.

Angell, Norman (2010), *The Great Illusion*, New York: Cosimo Classics.

Applegate, Scott (2013), 'The Dawn of Kinetic Cyber', in Karlis Podins, Jan Stinissen and Markus Maybaum (eds), *5th International Conference on Cyber Conflict*, Tallinn: NATO CCD COE Publications.

Atran, Scott (2013), 'The Power of Absurdity', in Brockman, John (ed.), *This Explains Everything: Deep, Beautiful, and Elegant Theories of How the World Works*, New York: Harper Collins.

Auden, W.H. and Christopher Isherwood (1973), *Journey to a War*, London: Faber and Faber.

The Australian, (2013), 'The world must learn from India's two nations', 20July.Availableonlineat:www.theaustralian.com.au/news/world/the-world-must-learn-from-indias-two-nations/story-fnb64oi6-1226682137704?nk=ab44c6960f98f50b91f2a346cfd0123c

Bacevich, Andrew (2008), 'Illusions of Managing History: The Enduring Relevance of Reinhold Niebuhr', *Historically Speaking*, 9, 3 (Jan.–Feb.).

——— (2009), *The Limits of Power: The End of American Exceptionalism*, New York: Henry Holt and Co.

Ball, Hugo (1996), *Flight Out of Time: A Dada Diary*, Oakland, CA: University of California Press.

Ball, Philip (2005), *Critical Mass: How One Thing Leads to Another*, New York: Arrow Books.

——— (2013), *Serving the Reich: The Struggle for the Soul of Physics under Hitler*, London: Bodley Head.

Banaji, Mahzarin (2013), 'Our Bounded Rationality', in John Brockman (ed.), *This Explains Everything: Deep, Beautiful, and Elegant Theories of How the World Works*, London: Harper.

Barraclough, Geoffrey (1967), *An Introduction to Contemporary History*, London: Penguin.

Barrow, John (2011), *The Artful Universe Expanded*, Oxford: Oxford University Press.

Basrur, Rajesh (2012), 'India's Agni V Missile: Game Changer?' RSIS Commentaries, 26 Apr., Singapore: National Technological University.

Bauman, Zygmunt (2006), *Post-modern Ethics*, Oxford: Blackwell.

——— (2010), *44 Letters from the Liquid Modern World*, Cambridge: Polity.

Beardson, Timothy (2013), *Stumbling Giant: The Threats to China's Future*, New Haven: Yale University Press.

Beatty, Jack (2012), *The Lost History of 1914: Why the Great War was not Inevitable*, London: Bloomsbury.

Beldon, James (2012), 'The Chinese threat to US interests in the Asia-Pacific Region and implications for US defence arrangements with Southeast Asia and Japan', *Air Power Review*, 15, 3 (Autumn/Winter).

Bell, David (2007), *The First Total War: Napoleon's Europe and the Birth of Modern Warfare*, London: Bloomsbury.

Bering, Jesse (2011), *The God Instinct*, London: Nicholas Brealey.

Berman, Marshall (1982), *All That is Solid Melts into Air: The Experience of Modernity*, London: Verso.

Bernstein, Richard and Ross Munro (1997), 'The Coming Conflict with America', *Foreign Policy*, 76, 2, March–April.

Bijian, Zheng (2005), 'China's "Peaceful Rise" to Great-Power Status', *Foreign Affairs*, September/October. Available online at: www.foreignaffairs.com/articles/61015/zheng-bijian/chinas-peaceful-rise-to-great-power-status

Blackburn, Simon (2013), 'Taliban and Plato', *Times Literary Supplement*, 19 July.

Bradbury, Malcolm and James McFarlane (eds) (1976), *Modernism: A Guide to European Literature 1890–1930*, London: Penguin.

Brandon, Donald (1966), *American Foreign Policy: Beyond Utopianism and Realism*, New York: Appleton and Century Croft.

Brands, Hal (2012), *The Promise and Pitfalls of Grand Strategy*, Carlisle, PA: US Army War College, Strategic Studies Institute.

Bronk, Christopher (2011), 'Blown to Bits: China's War in Cyberspace, August–September 2020', *Strategic Studies Quarterly*, 5, 1.

Brooks, David (2011), *The Social Animal: The Hidden Sources of Love, Character, and Achievement*, New York: Random House.

Brooks, Stephen (2007), *Producing Security: Multinational Corporations, Globalization, and the Changing Calculus of Conflict*, Princeton, NJ: Princeton University Press.

Brooks, Stephen, Jay Ikenberry and Jay Wohlforth (2013), 'Lean Forward', *Foreign Affairs*, 92, 1.

Brzezinski, Zbigniew (1997), *The Grand Chess board: American Primacy and its Geostrategic Imperatives*, New York: Basic Books.

——— (2013a), *Strategic Vision: America and the Crisis of Global Power*, New York: Basic Books.

——— (2013b), 'Interview with *Renmin Ribao*', *Center for Strategic & International Studies*, 20 Mar. Available online at: http://csis.org/publication/dr-zbigniew-brzezinski-interview-renmin-ribao

Byrne, Michael (2011), 'Never Forget the Great U.S.–China Cyberwar of 2020', *Motherboard*, 27 Mar.

Cai, F. (2012), 'The Coming Demographic Impact on China's Growth: The Age Factor in the Middle-Income Trap', *Asian Economic Papers*, 11, 1.

Callahan, William (2008), 'Chinese Visions of World Order: Post-hegemonic or a New Hegemony?', *International Studies Review*, 10, 4.

Cantril, Hadley (ed.) (1951), *Public Opinion 1935–46*, Princeton, NJ: Princeton University Press.

Canadine, David (2013), *The Undivided Past*, London: Allan Lane.

Chen, Shang Sheng (ed.) (2008), *Confucian Civilisation and Traditional Chinese Foreign Relations*, Jinan: Shandong University Press.

Chesterton, G.K. (1922), *What I Saw in America*, New York: Dodd Mead.

Chinascope (2011), 'How China Deals with the US Strategy to Contain China', 17 Feb. Available online at: http://chinascope.org/main/content/view/3291/76/

Chong, Alan (2013), 'Information Warfare? The Case for an Asian Perspective on Information Operations', *Armed Forces & Society*, 9 May.

Clark, Christopher (2013), *The Sleepwalkers: How Europe Went to War in 1914*, London: Penguin.

Clarke, Richard (2010), *Cyber War: The Next Threat to National Security and What to Do About It*, New York: Ecco.

Coker, Christopher (2014), *Can War Be Eliminated?* Cambridge: Polity.

Cohen, Warren (2000), *East Asia at the Center: Four Thousand Years of Engagement with the World*, New York: Columbia University Press.

Condon, Stephanie (2011), 'Obama: "We Welcome China's Rise"', CBS News, 20 Jan. Available online at: http://www.cbsnews.com/news/obama-we-welcome-chinas-rise/.

Conrad, Joseph (2006), *The Rescue: A Romance of the Shallows*, Project Gutenberg EBook. Available online at: www.gutenberg.org/files/1712/1712-h/1712-h.htm

Cook, Theodore (2001), 'The Chinese Discovery of the New World, 15th Century', in Robert Cowley (ed.), *More What If?: Eminent Historians Imagine What Might Have Been*, London: Macmillan.

Cooper, Helene (2014), 'In Japan's Drill With the U.S., a Message for Beijing', *The New York Times*, 22 Feb. Available online at: www.nytimes.com/2014/02/23/world/asia/in-japans-drill-with-the-us-a-message-for-beijing.html?_r=0

Cooper, Robert (2000), *The Breaking of Nations: Order and Chaos in the Twenty-First Century*, London: Atlantic.

Crook, Paul (1994), *Darwinism, War and History: The Debate over the Biology of War from the 'Origin of Species' to the First World War*, Cambridge: Cambridge University Press.

Cronin, P.M. and Robert Kaplan (2012), *Co-operation from Strength: The United States, China and the South China Sea*, Washington, DC: Center for a New American Security.

Dai, Bingguo (2010), 'Stick to the path of peaceful development', *China Daily*, 6 Dec. Available online at: www.chinadaily.com.cn/opinion/2010-12/13/content_11690133.htm

Damasio, Antonio (2004), *Looking for Spinoza: Joy, Sorrow and the Feeling Brain*, London: Vintage.

Darwin, John (2012), *Unfinished Empire: The Global Expansion of Britain*, London: Penguin.

DeBlois, Bruce et al. (2004), 'Space Weapons: Crossing the U.S. Rubicon', *International Security*, 29, 2 (Fall).

Dehio, Ludwig (1959), *Germany and World Politics in the Twentieth Century*, London: Chatto & Windus.

Dennett, Daniel (2003), *Freedom Evolves*, London: Penguin.

Dewey, John (1982), *Reconstruction in Philosophy*, in *The Middle Works, 1899–1924*, vol. 12, J. Boydston (ed.), Carbondale, IL: Southern Illinois University Press.

Dogan, Mattei and Ali Kazancigil (eds) (1994), *Comparing Nations: Concepts, Strategies, Substance*, Oxford: Basil Blackwell.

Dolman, Everett (2002), *Astropolitik: Classical Geopolitics in the Space Age*, London: Frank Cass.

——— (2005), *Pure Strategy: Power and Policy in the Space and Information Age*, London: Frank Cass.

——— (2012), 'New Frontiers, Old Realities', *Strategic Studies Quarterly*, 6, 1.

Drolet, Jean-Francois (2011), *American Neo-conservatism: The Politics and Culture of a Reactionary Idealism*, London: Hurst.

Dobbins, James (2012), 'War with China', *Survival: Global Politics and Strategy*, 54, 4.

Dumont, Louis (1994), *German Ideology: From France to Germany and Back*, Chicago: University of Chicago Press.

Earle, Edward Mead (ed.) (1943), *Makers of Modern Strategy: Military Thought from Machiavelli to Hitler*, Princeton, NJ: Princeton University Press.

Echevarria, Autulio (2011), 'Beyond Generations: Breaking the Cycle', in Karl Haug and Ole Maao (eds), *Conceptualising Modern War*, London: Hurst.

Eco, Umberto (2013), *Inventing the Enemy*, London: Vintage.

The Economist (2013a), Special Report: 'Time to cheer up', 23 Nov. Available online at: http://www.economist.com/news/special-report/21590100-after-dreadful-decade-abroad-americans-are-unduly-pessimistic-about-their-place

——— (2013b), 'The power of a party', 3 Aug. Available online at: www.economist.com/news/united-states/21582530-teenagers-san-antonio-give-foretaste-americas-hispanic-future-power

——— (2013c), 'When giants slow down', 27 July. Available online at: http://www.economist.com/news/briefing/21582257-most-dramatic-and-disruptive-period-emerging-market-growth-world-has-ever-seen

Eichengreen, B., D. Park and K. Shin (2012), 'When Fast-Growing Economies Slow Down: International Evidence and Implications for China', *Asian Economic Papers*, 11, 1.

Elias, Norbert (1996), *The Germans*, Oxford: Blackwell.

Emmerson, Charles (2013a), 'Eve of Disaster', *Foreign Policy*, 4 Jan. Available online at: www.foreignpolicy.com/articles/2013/01/04/why_2013_looks_a_lot_like_1913

——— (2013b), *1913: The World Before the Great War*, New York: Random House.

Emmott, Bill (2003), *20:21 Vision: Twentieth-Century Lessons for the Twenty-First Century*, London: Allen Lane.

Farmelo, Graham (2013), *Churchill's Bomb: A Hidden History of Science, War and Politics*, London: Faber and Faber.

Feldman, Noah (2013), *Cool War: The Future of Global Competition*, New York: Random House.

Fenby, Jonathan (2012), *Tiger Head, Snake Tails: China today, how it got there and where it is heading*, New York: Simon and Schuster.

Ferguson, Niall (1998), *The Pity of War*, London: Allan Lane.

Ford, Dennis (2007), *The Search for Meaning: A Short History*, Berkeley: University of California Press.

Forden, Geoffrey (2008), 'How China Loses the Coming Space War', *Wired*, 1 October. Available online at: www.wired.com/2008/01/inside.the.chin/

Franklin, Ruth (2013), 'He always slips away', *Prospect*, Apr.

Friedberg, Aaron (2011), *A Contest for Supremacy: China, America and the Struggle for Mastery in Asia*, New York: Norton.

Friedman, George and Meredith Lebard (1990), *The Coming War with Japan*, London: St Martin's Press.

Furedi, Frank (2013), *First World War: Still No End in Sight*, London: Bloomsbury.

Gamble, Andrew (2009), 'The Western Ideology', *Government and Opposition*, 44, 1 (Jan.).

Gardner, Dan (2010), *Future Babble: Why Expert Predictions Fail—and Why We Believe Them Anyway*, London: Virgin.

Gasset, Ortega y (1962), *History as a System, and Other Essays Toward a Philosophy of History*, London: Norton.

Gat, Azar (1992), *The Development of Military Thought: The Nineteenth Century*, Oxford: Clarendon.

Gay, Peter (1993), *The Bourgeois Experience: Victoria to Freud*, vol. 3: *The Cultivation of Hatred*, New York: Norton.

Gellner, Ernest (1988), *Plough, Sword and Book: The Structure of Human History*, London: Harvill Collins.

Gerrie, David (2011), 'War on the "Red Empire": How America Planned for an Attack on BRITAIN in 1930 with bombing raids and chemical weapons', *The Daily Mail*, 21 Sep. Available online at: www.dailymail.co.uk/news/article-2039453/How-America-planned-destroy-BRITAIN-1930-bombing-raids-chemical-weapons.html

Geuss, Raymond (2010), *Politics and the Imagination*, Princeton, NJ: Princeton University Press.

Gilder, George (1981), *Wealth and Poverty*, New York: Basic Books.

Gilpin, Robert (1981), *War and Change in World Politics*, Cambridge: Cambridge University Press.

Glenny, Misha (2012), *Dark Market: How Hackers Became the New Mafia*, London: Vintage.

Goldstein, Avery (2005), *Rising to the Challenge: China's Grand Strategy and International Security*, Stanford, CA: Stanford University Press.

Goldstein, Laurence, Andrew Brennan, Max Deutsch and Joe Lau (2010), *Logic: Key Concepts in Philosophy*, London: Continuum.

Goleman, Daniel (2000), *Social Intelligence: The Revolutionary New Science of Human Relationships*, New York: Bantam.

Gong, Gerit (1984), 'China's Entry into International Society', in Hedley Bull and Adam Watson (eds), *The Expansion of International Society*, Oxford: Clarendon.

Gray, Colin (1996), *Explorations in Strategy*, Westport, CT: Greenwood Press.

——— (1999), *Modern Strategy*, Oxford: Oxford University Press.

——— (2005), *Another Bloody Century: Future Warfare*, London: Weidenfeld & Nicholson.

——— (2007), *Fighting Talk: Forty Maxims on War, Peace, and Strategy*, Westport, CT: Praeger

——— (2013), *Perspectives on Strategy*, Oxford: Oxford University Press.

Gray, John (2013), *The Silence of Animals: On Progress and Other Modern Myths*, London: Allan Lane.

Green, Michael and Andrew Shearer (2012), 'Defining U.S. Indian Ocean Strategy', *The Washington Quarterly*, 35, 2.

Haboush, Ja-hyun Kim (1991), 'The Confucianization of Korean Society', in Gilbert Rozman (ed.), *The East Asian Region: Confucian Heritage and Its Modern Adaptation*, Princeton, NJ: Princeton University Press.

Hacker, Andrew (1970), *The End of the American Era*, New York: Atheneum.

Hall, Peter and Rosemary Taylor (1996), 'Political Science and the Three Institutionalisms', Max Plank Institute Discussion Paper, June.

Hamburger, Michael (1983), *A Proliferation of Prophets: Essays on German Writers from Nietzsche to Brecht*, Manchester: Carcenet Press.

Handberg, Roger and Zhen Li (2007), *Chinese Space Policy: A Study in Domestic and International Politics*, New York: Routledge.

Hanson, Victor Davis (2005), *A War Like No How the Athenians and Spartans Fought the Peloponnesian War*, London: Methuen.

Hammes, T.X. (2012), 'Offshore Control: A Proposed Strategy for an Unlikely Conflict', *Strategic Forum*, Washington, DC: National Defense University, June.

——— (2013), 'Sorry, AirSea Battle Is No Strategy', *The National Interest*, 7 Aug.

Hart, Gary (2004), *The Fourth Power: A Grand Strategy for the United States in the Twenty-First Century*, Oxford: Oxford University Press.

Hastings, David and Mark McClelland (2013), 'Shale Gas and the Revival of American Power', *International Affairs*, 89, 6 (Nov.).

Hastings, Max (2013), *Catastrophe: Europe Goes to War 1914*, London: William Collins.

Haythornwaite, Philip (1996), *Die Hard!: Famous Napoleonic Battles*, London: Cassell.

Hearst, Marti (2013), 'Why Programs Have Bugs', in John Brockman (ed.), *This Explains Everything: Deep, Beautiful, and Elegant Theories of How the World Works*, New York: Harper Collins, pp. 225–7.

Held, David and Andrew McGrew (1998), 'The End of the Old Order? Globalization and the Prospects for World Order', *Review of International Studies*, 24, 5.

Hersey, John (1985), *The Call: An American Missionary in China*, London: Weidenfeld & Nicolson.

Heuser, Beatrice (2013), 'Victory, Peace and Justice: The Neglected Trinity', *Joint Forces Quarterly*, 69, 2.

Hill, Steve (2011), 'China Tiptoes Toward Democracy', *China-US Focus*, 23 March. Available online at: www.chinausfocus.com/political-social-development/china-tiptoes-toward-democracy/

Hoffman, Frank (2013), 'You May Not be Interested in Cyber War, But it is Interested in You', *War on the Rocks*, 7 Aug. Available online at: http://warontherocks.com/2013/08/you-may-not-be-interested-in-cyber-war-but-its-interested-in-you/

Hood, Bruce (2011), *The Self Illusion: Who Do You Think You Are?*, London: Constable.

Holt, Jim (2012), *Why Does the World Exist?: One Man's Quest for the Big Answer*, London: Profile.

Hopkirk, Peter (2006), *On Secret Service East of Constantinople: The Plot to Bring Down the British Empire*, London: John Murray.

Howland, D.R. (1996), *Borders of Chinese Civilisation: Geography and History at Empire's End*, Durham, NC: Duke University Press.

Hughes, Christopher (2011), 'Reclassifying Chinese Nationalism: the *geopolitik* turn', *Journal of Contemporary China*, 20, 71.

Hurd, Douglas (1967), *The Arrow War: An Anglo-Chinese Confusion 1856–60*, London: Collins.

Huntington, Samuel P. (1996), *The Clash of Civilisations and the Remaking of World Order*, New York: Touchstone.

Ikenberry, G. John (2011), *Liberal Leviathan: The Origins, Crisis, and Transformation of the American World Order*, Princeton, NJ: Princeton University Press.

Ikenberry, G. John and Daniel Duedney (2009/10), 'The Unravelling of the Cold War Settlement', *Survival: Global Politics and Strategy*, 51, 6.

io9 (2011), 'The coming space war between the U.S. and China', 4 Feb. Available online at: http://io9.com/5752073/the-coming-space-war-between-the-us-and-china

James, Clive (2007), *Cultural Amnesia: Notes in the Margin of My Time*, London: Picador.

James, William (1956), *The Will to Believe and Other Essays in Popular Philosophy*, New York: Dover.

——— (2013), 'The Moral Equivalent of War'. Available online at: http://www.constitution.org/wj/meow.htm

Jenner, W.J.F. (1992), *The Tyranny of History: The Roots of China's Crisis*, London: Allan Lane.

Jiechi, Yang (2013), 'Innovations in China's diplomatic theory and practice under new conditions', *China Daily*, 16 Aug. Available online at: www.chinadaily.com.cn/china/2013-08/16/content_16899892.htm

Joas, Hans and Wolfgang Knöbl (2013), *War in Social Thought: Hobbes to the Present*, Princeton, NJ: Princeton University Press.

Johnson, Dominic (2004), *Overconfidence and War: The Havoc and Glory of Positive Illusions*, Cambridge, MA: Harvard University Press.

Johnson-Freese, Joan (2003), 'China's Manned Space Program: Sun Tzu or Apollo Redux?' *Naval War College Review*, 53 (Summer).

Johnstone, Alastair (1996), 'Cultural Realism and Strategy in Maoist China', in Peter Katzenstein (ed.), *The Culture of National Security: Norms and Identity in World Politics*, New York: Columbia University Press.

Josipovici, Gabriel (2013), *What Ever Happened to Modernism?* New Haven: Yale University Press.

Jullien, François (1995), *The Propensity of Things: Toward a History of Efficiency in China*, New York: Zone Books.

——— (1999), *Le Détour et l'accès : Stratégies du sens en Chine, en Grèce*, Paris: Bernard Grasset.

Kafka, Franz (1999), *Letters to Milena*, New York: Vintage

Kagan, Donald (1995), *On the Origins of War: And the Preservation of Peace*, London: Hutchinson.

Kagan, Robert (2003), *Paradise and Power: America and Europe in the New World Order*, New York: Atlantic.

Kahneman, Daniel (2012), *Thinking, Fast and Slow*, London: Penguin.

Kaku, Michio (2011), *Physics of the Future: The Inventions That Will Transform Our Lives*, New York: Doubleday.

Kang, David C. (2007), *China Rising: Peace, Power, and Order in East Asia*, New York: Columbia University Press.

——— (2010), *East Asia Before the West: Five Centuries of Trade and Tribute*, New York: Columbia University Press.

Kato, Yoichi (2013), 'Interview/Kurt Campbell: China should accept U.S. enduring leadership role in Asia', *The Asahi Shimbun*, 9 Feb.

Katzenstein, Peter (ed.) (2012), *Sinicization and the Rise of China: Civilizational processes beyond East and West*, London: Routledge.

Kay, John (2011), *Obliquity: Why our Goals are Best Achieved Indirectly*, London: Profile.

Keegan, John (1998), *The First World War*, London: Hutchinson.

Kermode, Frank (1967), *The Sense of an Ending: Studies in the Theory of Fiction*, Oxford: Oxford University Press.

Kharas, H. and H. Kohli (2011), 'What Is the Middle Income Trap, Why do Countries Fall into It, and How Can It Be Avoided?', *Global Journal of Emerging Market Economies*, 3, 3.

Khong, Yuen Foong (1992), *Analogies at War: Korea, Munich, Dien Bien Phu, and the Vietnam Decisions of 1965*, Princeton, NJ: Princeton University Press.

Kim, Key-Hiuk (1980), *The Last Phase of the East Asian World Order: Korea, Japan and the Chinese Empire, 1860–1882*, Berkeley: University of California Press.

Kissinger, Henry (1982), *Years of Upheaval*, Boston: Little and Brown.

——— (2011), *On China*, New York: Penguin.

Klotz, Frank (2012), 'China's Growing Space Power', *The National Interest*, 26 July. Available online at: http://nationalinterest.org/commentary/chinas-growing-space-power-7244

Kohn, Hans (1953), *Pan-Slavism: Its History and Ideology*, Chicago: University of Notre Dame Press.

——— (1964), 'Political Theory and the History of Ideas', *Journal of the History of Ideas*, 25, 2.

Kolakowski, Leszek (1989), *The Presence of Myth*, trans. Adam Czerniawski, Chicago: Chicago University Press.

Kotkin, Joel (2010), *The Next Hundred Million: America in 2050*, New York: Penguin.

Kraus, Lawrence M. (2012), *A Universe from Nothing: Why there is something rather than nothing*, London: Simon & Schuster.

Kupchan, Charles A. (2011), 'Grand Strategy and Power Transitions: What We Can Learn from Great Britain', *New America Foundation*, July.

——— (2012), *No One's World: The West, the Rising, Rest and the Coming Global Turn*, Oxford: Oxford University Press.

LaGrone, Sam and Dave Majumdar (2013), 'The Future of Air Sea Battle', *USNI News*, 30 October. Available online at: http://news.usni.org/2013/10/30/future-air-sea-battle

Langø, Hans-Inge (2013), 'Slaying Cyber Dragons: Competing Academic Approaches to Cyber Security', Norwegian Institute of International Affairs (NUPI) Working Paper 820.

Lankov, Andrei (2013), *The Real North Korea: Life and Politics in the Failed Stalinist Utopia*, Oxford: Oxford University Press.

Lanz, R. and S. Miroudot (2011), 'Intra-Firm Trade: Patterns, Determinants and Policy Implications', *OECD Trade Policy Papers*, No. 114.

Lebow, Richard Ned (2008), *A Cultural Theory of International Relations*, Cambridge: Cambridge University Press.

——— (2010), *Why Nations Fight*, Cambridge: Cambridge University Press.

Leifer, Michael (2000), *Singapore's Foreign Policy: Coping with Vulnerability*, London: Routledge.

Lemos, George (2013), *The End of the Chinese Dream: Why Chinese People Fear the Future*, New Haven: Yale University Press.

Leonard, Mark (2008), *What Does China Think?* London: Fourth Estate.

——— (2012), 'As Chimerica dissolves, distrust deepens between China and US', *The New Statesman*, 29 Aug.

Levi-Strauss, Claude (2013), *The Other Face of the Moon*, trans. Jean-Marie Todd, Cambridge: Bell Knapp Press.

Léwis-Stempel, John (2014), *The War Behind the Wire: The Life, Death and Glory of British Prisoners of War, 1914–18*, London: Weidenfeld and Nicolson.

Liang, Qiao and Wang Xiangsui (1999), *Unrestricted Warfare*, Beijing: People's Liberation Army Literature and Arts Publishing House.

Lieven, Anatol and John Hulsman (2006), *Ethical Realism: A Vision for America's Role in the World*, New York: Pantheon.

Lin, Christina (2011), 'China's New Silk Road to the Mediterranean: The Eurasian Land Bridge and Return of Admiral Zheng He', *ISPSW Strategy Series*, 165, Oct.

Liska, George (1963), 'Continuity and Change in International Systems', *World Politics*, 16, 1 (Oct.).

Litwak, Robert S. (2002), 'The Imperial Republic after 9/11', *Wilson Quarterly*, 26, 3.

Lloyd, G.E.R., (2012), *Being, Humanity, and Understanding*, Oxford: Oxford University Press

Loewenberg, Peter (1996), 'Germany, the Home Front (1): The Physical and Psychological Consequences of Home Front Hardship', in Hugh Cecil and Peter Liddle (eds), *Facing Armageddon: The First World War Experienced*, London: Leo Cooper.

Luce, Edward (2012), *Time to Start Thinking: America in the Age of Descent*, New York: Atlantic Monthly Press.

Lukacs, John (1998), *A Thread of Years*, New Haven: Yale University Press.

Lutes, Charles D. and Peter L. Hays (eds) (2011), *Toward a Theory of Spacepower: Selected Essays*, Washington, DC: National Defense University Press.

Luttwak, Edward N. (2000), 'The peace-bringing powers of war', in Gwyn Prins and Hylke Tromp (eds), *The Future of War*, The Hague: KWER Law Press.

——— (2002), *Strategy: The Logic of War and Peace*, Cambridge: Harvard University Press.

——— (2012), *The Rise of China vs. the Logic of Strategy*, Cambridge, MA: Harvard University Press.

McMeekin, Sean (2013), *July 1914: Countdown to War*, New York: Basic Books.

MacMillan, Margaret (2013), *The War that Ended Peace: How Europe Abandoned Peace for the First World War*, London: Profile.

Mackinder, Halford (1904), 'The Geographical Pivot of History', *The Geographical Journal*, 23, 4 (Apr.).

McLynn, Frank (2012), *The Road Not Taken: How Britain Narrowly Missed a Revolution*, London: Bodley Head.

Mahadevan, Prem (2013), 'Maritime Insecurity in East Asia', *Strategic Trends*, Zurich: Centre for Security Studies.

Mahbubani, Kishore (2008), *The New Asian Hemisphere: The Irresistible Shift of Global Power to the East*, New York: Public Affairs.

Mahnken, Thomas (2011), *Secrecy and Stratagem: Understanding Chinese Strategic Culture*, Sydney: Lowy Institute.

Mannheim, Karl (1943), *Diagnosis of Our Time: Wartime Essays of a Sociologist*, London: Routledge & Kegan Paul.

Mao, Haijian (2005), *The Collapse of the Celestial Empire*, Beijing: Sanlian.

Margalit, Avishai (2004), *The Ethics of Memory*, Cambridge, MA: Harvard University Press.

Martel, William C. (2007), *Victory in War: Foundations of Modern Military Policy*, Cambridge: Cambridge University Press.

Mason, Margie (2011), 'Vietnam, China hold joint naval patrol amid spat', *CNS News*, 21 June. Available online at: http://cnsnews.com/news/article/vietnam-china-hold-joint-naval-patrol-amid-spat

May, Ernest R. and Richard E. Neustadt (1988), *Thinking in Time: The Uses of History for Decision Makers*, New York: Free Press.

Mead, Walter Russell (2008), *God and Gold: Britain, America and the Making of the Modern World*, New York: Atlantic Books.

Mearsheimer, John, (2001) *The Tragedy of Great Power Politics*, New York: Norton.

Meilinger, Philip (2010), 'The Mutable Nature of War', *Air and Space Power Journal*, 24, 4.

Midgley, Mary (1985), *Evolution as a Religion*, London: Routledge.

Mill, John Stuart, *Utilitarianism*, London: Longmans.

Millar, Moorhouse (1928), *Unpopular Essays in the Philosophy of History*, New York: Fordham University Press.

Mitter, Rana (2003), 'An Uneasy Engagement: Chinese Ideas of Global Order and Justice in Historical Perspective', in Rosemary Foot, John Lewis Gaddis and Andrew Hurrell (eds), *Order and Justice in International Relations*, Oxford: Oxford University Press.

——— (2013), *China's War with Japan, 1937–45: The Struggle for Survival*, London: Allen Lane.

Moïsi, Dominique (2009), *The Geopolitics of Emotion: How Cultures of Fear, Humiliation, and Hope are Reshaping the World*, London: Bodley Head.

Morozov, Evgeny (2013), *To Save Everything, Click Here: Technology, Solutionism, and the Urge to Fix Problems that Don't Exist*, London: Allen Lane.

Morris, Ian (2014), *War: What Is It Good For? The Role of Conflict in Civilisation, from Primates to Robots*, London: Profile.

Mueller, John (2011), *War and Ideas: Selected Essays*, London: Routledge.

Murray, Charles A. (2013), *American Exceptionalism: An Experiment in History*, Washington, DC: AEI Press.

Murray, William (2012), 'Underwater TELS: PLAN a Submarine Transformation', in Andrew Erikson (ed.), *China's Strategy for the Near Seas*, Annapolis: Naval Institute Press.

Nasir, Vali (2013), *The Dispensable Nation: American Foreign Policy in Retreat*, New York: Doubleday.

Nathan, Andrew J. and Andrew Scobell (2014), *China's Search for Security*, New York: Columbia University Press.

New York Times, (2013), 'Xi Jinping's Chinese Dream', 4 June. Available online at: http://www.nytimes.com/2013/06/05/opinion/global/xi-jinpings-chinese-dream.html?pagewanted=all&_r=0

Nisbett, Richard E. (2003), *The Geography of Thought: How Asians and Westerners Think Differently—and Why*, London: Nicholas Brearly.

Northrop, F.S.C. (1947), *The Logic of the Sciences and the Humanities*, New York: Meridian Books.

Nye, Joe (2011), 'The Future of Power', *Bulletin of the American Academy of Arts and Sciences*, 64, 3 (Spring).

Obstfeld, M. and A.M. Taylor (2003), 'Globalisation and Capital Markets', in M.D. Bordo and A.M. Taylor (eds), *Globalisation in Historical Perspective*, Chicago: Chicago University Press.

Owen, Geoffrey (2013), 'The Moneybags and the Brains', *Standpoint*, April. Availableonlineat:http://standpointmag.co.uk/books-april-13-the-moneybags-and-the-brains-geoffrey-owen-the-battle-of-bretton-woods-benn-steil

Packer, George (2013), *The Unwinding: An Inner History of the New America*, London: Faber & Faber.

Paine, S.C.M. (2003), *The Sino-Japanese War of 1894–1895: Perceptions, Power, and Primacy*, Cambridge: Cambridge University Press.

Pasco, Xavier (2012), 'Space: A New Theatre of War', in Julian Lindley-French and Yves Boyer (eds), *The Oxford Handbook of War*, Oxford: Oxford University Press.

Patocka, Jan (2002), *Plato and Europe*, trans. Petr Lom, Palo Alto: Stanford University Press.

Paz, Octavio (1990), *Convergences: Essays on Art and Literature*, London: Bloomsbury.

Pei, Minxin (2012), 'The Loneliest Superpower', *Foreign Policy*, 20 Mar.

Petroski, Henry (2013), *To Forgive Design: Understanding Failure*, Cambridge, MA: Bell Knap Press.

Pfaff, William (2010), *The Irony of Manifest Destiny: The Tragedy of America's Foreign Policy*, New York: Walker & Co.

Phillips, Andrew (2011), *War, Religion and Empire: The Transformation of International Orders*, Cambridge: Cambridge University Press.

Phillips, Michael (2009), *The Undercover Philosopher: A Guide to Detecting Shams, Lies, and Delusions*, Oxford: One World.

Pilling, David (2013), *Bending Adversity: Japan and the Art of Survival*, London: Allen Lane.

Pillsbury, Michael P. (2007), 'An Assessment of China's Anti-Satellite and Space Warfare Programs, Policies and Doctrines', Washington, DC, U.S.–China Economic and Security Review Commission.

Pinker, Steven (2013), *Better Angels of our Nature: A History of Violence and Humanity*, London: Penguin.

Polachek, James M. (1992), *The Inner Opium War*, Cambridge, MA: Harvard University Press.

Pollpeter, Kevin (2005), 'The Chinese Vision of Space Military Operations', in James Mulvenon and David Finkelstein (eds), *China's Revolution in Doctrinal Affairs: Emerging Trends in the Operational Art of the Chinese People's Liberation Army*, Alexandria, VA: CNA Corporation.

——— (2008), *Building for the Future: China's Progress in Space Technology during the Tenth 5-Year Plan and the U.S. Response*, Carlisle, PA: US Army War College, Strategic Studies Institute.

Popper, Karl, (1990), *A World of Propensities*, Bristol: Thoemmes.

Posen, Barry R. (2013), 'Pull Back: The Case for a Less Activist Foreign Policy', *Foreign Affairs*, 92, 1.

Prasad, Eswar S. (2014), *The Dollar Trap: How the U.S. Dollar Tightened Its Grip on Global Finance*, Princeton, NJ: Princeton University Press.

Quiggin, John (2010), *Zombie Economics: How Dead Ideas Still Walk Among Us*, Princeton, NJ: Princeton University Press.

Randall, Bobbie L. (2001), 'Sun Tzu: The Art of Network Centric Warfare', PhD thesis, U.S. Army War College, Carlisle, PA.

Rapport, Aaron (2012), 'Making the Case for History: Using Historical Analogies in Policy Analysis', Miller Center, University of Virginia, Blog, 22 Feb. Available online at: http://millercenter.org/blog/making-the-case

Rattray, Gregory J. (2001), *Strategic Warfare in Cyberspace*, Cambridge, MA: Massachusetts Institute of Technology Press.

Rawls, John (1999), *A Theory of Justice*, Cambridge, MA: Bell Knap Press.

Reding, Jean-Paul (1996), Review of François Jullien, *Le détour et l'accès: Stratégies du sens en Chine, en Grèce*, *China Review International*, 3, 1 (Spring).

Rid, Thomas (2013), *Cyber War Will Not Take Place*, London: Hurst.

Ridley, Matt (2011), *The Rational Optimist: How Prosperity Evolves*, London: Fourth Estate.

Roberts, Andrew (2003), 'The Whale against the Wolf: The Anglo-American War of 1896', in Robert Cowley (ed.), *What Ifs? of American History: Eminent Historians Imagine What Might Have Been*, London: Macmillan.

Rorty, Richard (1999), *Philosophy and Social Hope*, London: Penguin.

Rosenbaum, Ron (2011), *How the End Begins: The Road to a Nuclear World War III*, New York: Simon and Schuster.

Ross, Robert S. (1999), 'The Geography of the Peace: East Asia in the Twenty-first Century', *International Security*, 23, 4 (Spring).

Ross, Robert S. and Zhu Feng (2008), *China's Ascent: Power, Security, and the Future of International Politics*, Ithaca, NY: Cornell University Press.

The Royal Society (2011), 'New countries Emerge as major players in scientific world', 28 Mar. Available online at: https://royalsociety.org/news/2011/new-science-countries/

Ruggie, John Gerard (2005), 'American Exceptionalism, Exemptionalism, and Global Governance', in Michael Ignatieff (ed.), *American Exceptionalism and Human Rights*, Princeton, NJ: Princeton University Press.

Rumelt, Richard (2012), *Good Strategy/Bad Strategy: The Difference and Why It Matters*, London: Profile.

Russell, Bertrand (2010), *Why Men Fight*, London: Routledge.

Salisbury, Harrison E. (1969), *The Coming War between Russia and China*, London: Martin Secker & Warburg.

Samuels, David (2011), 'Q&A: Edward Luttwak', *Tablet*, 6 Sep. Available onlineat:http://www.tabletmag.com/jewish-news-and-politics/76739/qa-edward-luttwak

Sanger, David E. (2012), *Confront and Conceal: Obama's Secret Wars and Surprising Use of American Power*, New York: Crown Publishers.

Saunders, Doug (2013), 'Why are the U.S. and China preparing for war with one another?' The Globe and Mail, 12 July. Available online at: http://www.theglobeandmail.com/globe-debate/us-and-china-smile-for-cameras-prepare-for-war/article13196146/

Sawyer, Ralph D. (ed.) (1994), *Sun Tzu: The Art of War*, Boulder, CO: Westview Press.

Schaller, Michael (2002), *The United States and China: Into the Twenty-First Century*, Oxford: Oxford University Press.

Scheler, Max (1961), *Ressentiment*, translated by William Holdheim, New York, NY: Schocken Books.

Schmidt, Eric and Jared Cohen (2013), *The New Digital Age: Reshaping the Future of People, Nations and Business*, London: John Murray.

Schmitt, Michael N. (2012), 'International Law in Cyberspace: The Koh Speech and Tallinn Manual Juxtaposed', *Harvard International Law Journal*, 54 (Dec.).

Schwartau, Winn (1993), *Terminal Compromise: Computer Terrorism in a Networked Society*, Seminole, FL: Interpact Press, online version.

——— (2002), *Pearl Harbor Dot Com*, Seminole, FL: Interpact Press, online version.

Schweller, Randall L. and Xiaoyu Pu (2011), 'After Unipolarity: China's Visions of International Order in an Era of U.S. Decline', *International Security*, 36, 1.

Scobell, Andrew (2002), *China and Strategic Culture*, Carlisle, PA: US Army War College, Strategic Studies Institute.

Scott, David (2008), *China and the International System, 1840–1949: Power, Presence, and Perceptions in a Century of Humiliation*, Albany, NY: State University of New York Press.

Seedhouse, Erik (2010), *The New Space Race: China vs. the United States*, Chichester: Praxis Publishing.

Sennett, Richard (2003), *Respect: The Formation of Character in an Age of Inequality*, London: Penguin.

Seton-Watson, Robert William (1939), *Munich and the Dictators*, London: Methuen.

Shambaugh, David (ed.) (2012), *Charting China's Future: Domestic and International Challenges*, London: Routledge.

——— (2013), *China Goes Global: The Partial Power*, Oxford: Oxford University Press.

Shankman, Steven and Steven Durrant (2000), *The Siren and the Sage: Knowledge and Wisdom in Ancient Greece and China*, London: Cassell.

Shapiro, Ian (2007), *The Flight from Reality in the Human Sciences*, Princeton, NJ: Princeton University Press.

Shirk, Susan L. (2007), *China: Fragile Superpower*, New York: Oxford University Press.

Simpson, Emile (2012), *War From the Ground Up: Twenty-First Century Combat as Politics*, London: Hurst.

Sirkin, Harold L., Michael Zinser and Douglas Hohner (2011), 'Made in America, Again: Why Manufacturing Will Return to the U.S.', The Boston Consulting Group. Available online at: https://www.bcgperspectives.com/content/articles/manufacturing_supply_chain_management_made_in_america/again/

Sloan, Stanley R. (2010), *Permanent Alliance? NATO and the Transatlantic Bargain from Truman to Obama*, New York: Continuum.

Solomon, Robert C. (1994), 'One Hundred Years of Ressentiment: *Nietzsche's*

Genealogy of Morals', in Richard Schlacht (ed.), *Nietzsche, Genealogy, Morality: Essays on Nietzsche's 'On the Genealogy of Morals'*, Berkeley: University of California Press.

Solomone, Stacey (2006), 'China's Space Program: the great leap upward', *Journal of Contemporary China*, 15, 47.

The Spectator (2013), 'Why does Max Hastings have such a hatred for the British military?', 14 Sept. Available online at: www.spectator.co.uk/books/books-feature/9016751/catastrophe-by-max-hastings-review/

Spykman, Nicholas J. (1938), 'Geography and Foreign Policy', *The American Political Science Review*, 32:2, April.

——— (1944), *The Geography of the Peace*, New York: Harcourt Brace.

Stanford, Michael (1996), *A Companion to the Study of History*, Oxford: Blackwell.

Stearn, R.T., (1983) 'Wells and War,' *Wellsian*, No 6.

Steinfeld, Edward S., (2012), *Playing Our Game: Why China's Rise Doesn't Threaten the West*, Oxford: Oxford University Press.

Stenholm, Stig (2013), *The Quest for Reality: Bohr and Wittgenstein, Two Complementary Views*, Oxford: Oxford University Press.

Steel, Ronald (1967), *Pax Americana*, New York: Viking.

Steil, Benn (2013), *The Battle of Breton Woods: John Maynard Keynes, Harry Dexter White and the Making of a New World Order*, Princeton, NJ: Princeton University Press.

Stevenson, David (2004), *1914–1918: The History of the First World War*, London: Penguin.

Stone, John (2012), 'Cyber War *Will* Take Place!', *Journal of Strategic Studies*, 36, 1.

Stone, Norman (2007), *World War One: A Short History*, London: Allen Lane.

Strachan, Hew (2011), 'Strategy and contingency', *International Affairs*, 87, 6.

Straits Times (2012), 'Clinton says Pacific "big enough for all of us"', 15 Nov. Available online at: www.straitstimes.com/the-big-story/us-election-2012/election-news/story/clinton-says-pacific-big-enough-all-us-2012 1115

Strathern, Oona (2008), *A Brief History of the Future: How Visionary Thinkers Changed the World and Tomorrow's Trends are "Made" and Marketed*, London: Robinson.

Strickland, Jonathan (2008), 'Is cyberwar coming?', HowStuffWorks.com, 13 Oct. Available online at: http://computer.howstuffworks.com/cyberwar.htm

Stuart, Douglas (2012), '"Leading from Behind": Toward a New U.S. Strategy for the Asia-Pacific', *Korean Journal of Defence Analysis*, 24, 2 (June).

Sugarman, Richard (1979), *Rancor Against Time: The Phenomenology of 'Ressentiment'*, New York: Humanities Press.

Sumida, Jon Tetsuro (2008), *Decoding Clausewitz: A New Approach to 'On War'*, Laurence, KA: University of Kansas Press.

Sun, Yun (2013), 'March West: China's Response to the U.S. Rebalancing', Brookings Institution blog, 31 Jan. Available online at: http://www.brookings.edu/blogs/up-front/posts/2013/01/31-china-us-sun

Supina, Philip D. (1972), 'The Norman Angell Peace Campaign in Germany', *Journal of Peace Research*, 9, 2.

Swaine, Michael D. and Ashley J. Tellis (2000), *Interpreting China's Grand Strategy: Past, Present, and Future*, Santa Monica: RAND Corporation.

Taleb, Nassim Nicholas (2001), *Fooled by Randomness: The Hidden Role of Chance in Life and in the Markets*, London: Penguin.

The Telegraph, (2013), 'The sun is setting on dollar supremacy, and with it, American power', 14 Oct. Available online at: http://www.telegraph.co.uk/finance/comment/jeremy-warner/10378666/The-sun-is-setting-on-dollar-supremacy-and-with-it-American-power.html

Tellis, Ashley (2013), 'China's Military Challenge: An Interview with Ashley J. Tellis', The National Bureau of Asian Research, 22 Jan. Available online at: http://www.nbr.org/research/activity.aspx?id=291

Terjesen, Bjørn and Øystein Tunsjø (eds) (2012), *The rise of naval powers in Asia and Europe's decline*, Oslo: Norwegian Institute for Defence Studies.

Tertrais, Bruno (2004), *War Without End: The View from Abroad*, London: New Press.

—— (2012), 'The Demise of Ares: The End of War as We Know It?' *The Washington Quarterly*, 35, 3.

Thorne, Christopher (1988), *Border Crossings: Studies in International History*, London: Hamish Hamilton.

Thucydides, *History of the Peloponnesian War*. Available online at: http://www.thelatinlibrary.com/imperialism/readings/thucydides1.html

The Times (2013), 'China sends a message', 30 Nov. Available online at: www.thetimes.co.uk/tto/news/world/asia/article3936783.ece

Todorov, Tzvetan (2010), *The Fear of Barbarians: Beyond the Clash of Civilizations*, Chicago: University of Chicago Press.

Tow, William T. (2001), *Asia-Pacific Strategic Relations: Seeking Convergent Security*, Cambridge: Cambridge University Press.

Trouillot, Michel-Rolph (2003), *Global Transformations: Anthropology and the Modern World*, London: Palgrave.

Tunsjø, Øystein (2008), *US Taiwan Policy: Constructing the Triangle*, London: Routledge.

——— (2012), 'China's Naval Build-Up: Drivers and Ambitions', in Saira Basit and Øystein Tunsjø (eds), *Emerging naval powers in Asia: China's and India's quest for sea power*, Oslo: Norwegian Institute for Defence Studies.

Updike, John (1997), *Toward the End of Time*, New York: Random House.

U.S. Department of Defense (2012), 'Sustaining U.S. Global Leadership: Priorities for 21st Century Defense', Jan., Washington, DC.

——— (2011) 'The National Military Strategy of the United States of America', 8 Feb., Washington, DC.

——— (2012), 'Annual Report to Congress: Military and Security Developments Involving the People's Republic of China 2012', May, Washington, DC.

U.S.–China Economic and Security Review Commission (2011), 'China's Active Defence Strategy and its Regional Impact', Hearing, 27 Jan. Available online at: origin.www.uscc.gov/sites/default/files/transcripts/1.27.11HearingTranscript.pdf

Van Creveld, Martin (1991), *Technology and War: From 2000 B.C. to the Present*, Oxford: Brasseys.

Van Tol, Jan et al. (2010), *AirSea Battle: A Point-of-Departure Operational Concept*, Washington, DC: Center for Strategic and Budgetary Assessments.

Vattimo, Gianni (2005), *The Transparent Society*, trans. D. Webb, Cambridge: Polity.

Walker, Martin (2002), 'What Kind of Empire?' *Wilson Quarterly*, 26, 3.

Wang, Fei-Ling (2011), 'Between *Tianxia* and Westphalia: China Searches for its Position in the World', American Political Science Association 2011 Annual Meeting Paper, Sept. Available online at: http://papers.ssrn.com/sol3/papers.cfm?abstract_id=1902722

Wang, Gungwu (2008), 'China in the international order: some historical perspectives', in Wang Gungwu and Zheng Yongnian (eds), *China and the New International Order*, London: Routledge.

Wang, Helen H. (2010), *The Chinese Dream: The Rise of the World's Largest Middle Class and What It Means to You*, New York: Best Seller Press.

Wang, Jisi (2011), 'China's Search for a Grand Strategy: A Rising Great Power Finds Its Way', *Foreign Affairs*, 90, 2, Apr.

Wang, Zheng (2012), *Never Forget National Humiliation: Historical Memory in Chinese Politics and Foreign Relations*, New York: Columbia University Press.

Watson, David (1992), *Arendt*, London: Fontana.

Watson, Richard and Oliver Freeman (2013), *Futurevision: scenarios for the World in 2040*, London: Scribe.

Webb, Justin (2013), 'America's future is Latin, Asian and liberal', *The Times*, 4 June.

Welch, David A. (2003), 'Why International Relations theorists should stop reading Thucydides', *Review of International Studies*, 29, 3.

White, Hugh (2012), *The China Choice: Why We Should Share Power*, Oxford: Oxford University Press.

Wilcoxon, Gregory L. (2010), 'Sun Tzu: Theorist for the Twenty-First Century', PhD thesis, US Army War College, Carlisle, PA: Strategy Research Project.

Wilson, A.N. (2012), *Hitler: A Short Biography*, London: Harper Collins.

Wolfowitz, Paul (2001), 'Building a Military for the 21st Century', Prepared Testimony, Senate Armed Services Committee, 4 Oct.

World Bank (2013), 'GDP Growth (Annual %)', available online at: http://data.worldbank.org/indicator/NY.GDP.MKTP.KD.ZG

Wright, Robert (2001), *Nonzero: The Logic of Human Destiny*, London: Vintage.

Ye, Zicheng (2011), *Inside China's Grand Strategy: The Perspective from the People's Republic*, Lexington: University of Kentucky Press.

Zakaria, Fareed (2011), *The Post-American World*, New York: Norton.

Zhai, Yuzong (2010), *China Saves the World: Chinese Culture Deals with the Crisis of Humanity*, Beijing: Central Bianyi Press.

Zhang, Baohui (2011), 'The Security Dilemma in the U.S.–China Military Space Relationship', *Asian Survey*, 51, 2 (Mar.–Apr.).

Zhang, Feng (2011), 'The Rise of Chinese Exceptionalism in International Relations', *European Journal of International Relations* (Oct.).

Zhang, Weiwei (2012), 'The China Model: a Civilizational-State Perspective', *The World Financial Review*, Mar–Apr.

Zhang, Wenmu (2006), 'Sea Power and China's Strategic Choices', *China Security* (Summer).

Zhao, Suisheng (2012), 'Shaping the Regional Context of China's Rise: how the Obama administration brought back hedge in its engagement with China', *Journal of Contemporary China*, 21, 75.

Zolli, Andrew and Ann Marie Healy (2012), *Resilience: Why Things Bounce Back*, London: Headline.

INDEX